Muslims Making British Media

Islam of the Global West

Series editors: Kambiz GhaneaBassiri and Frank Peter

Islam of the Global West is a pioneering series that examines Islamic beliefs, practices, discourses, communities and institutions that have emerged from 'the Global West'. The geographical and intellectual framing of the Global West reflects both the role played by the interactions between people from diverse religions and cultures in the development of Western ideals and institutions in the modern era and the globalization of these very ideals and institutions.

In creating an intellectual space where works of scholarship on European and North American Muslims enter into conversation with one another, the series promotes the publication of theoretically informed and empirically grounded research in these areas. By bringing the rapidly growing research on Muslims in European and North American societies, ranging from the United States and France to Portugal and Albania, into conversation with the conceptual framing of the Global West, this ambitious series aims to reimagine the modern world and develop new analytical categories and historical narratives that highlight the complex relationships and rivalries that have shaped the multicultural, polyreligious character of Europe and North America, as evidenced, by way of example, in such economically and culturally dynamic urban centres as Los Angeles, New York, Paris, Madrid, Toronto, Sarajevo, London, Berlin, and Amsterdam where there is a significant Muslim presence.

American and Muslim Worlds before 1900
Edited by John Ghazvinian and Arthur Mitchell Fraas

Anarchist, Artist, Sufi
Mark Sedgwick

Amplifying Islam in the European Soundscape:
Religious Pluralism and Secularism in the Netherlands
Pooyan Tamimi Arab

The British Muslim Convert Lord Headley, 1855-1935
Jamie Gilham

Interrogating Muslims
Schirin Amir-Moazami

Islam and Nationhood in Bosnia-Herzegovina: Surviving Empires
Xavier Bougarel

Islam and the Governing of Muslims in France
Frank Peter

Islam as Critique: Sayyid Ahmad Khan and the Challenge of Modernity
Khurram Hussain

Sacred Spaces and Transnational Networks in American Sufism
Merin Shobhana Xavier

Muslims Making British Media

Popular Culture, Performance and Public Religion

Carl Morris

BLOOMSBURY ACADEMIC
LONDON • NEW YORK • OXFORD • NEW DELHI • SYDNEY

BLOOMSBURY ACADEMIC
Bloomsbury Publishing Plc
50 Bedford Square, London, WC1B 3DP, UK
1385 Broadway, New York, NY 10018, USA
29 Earlsfort Terrace, Dublin 2, Ireland

BLOOMSBURY, BLOOMSBURY ACADEMIC and the Diana logo are trademarks of
Bloomsbury Publishing Plc

First published in Great Britain 2023
This paperback edition published 2024

Copyright © Carl Morris, 2023

Carl Morris has asserted his right under the Copyright, Designs and Patents Act, 1988, to
be identified as Author of this work.

Series design by Dani Leigh
Cover image © Brian Stablyk / gettyimages.co.uk

All rights reserved. No part of this publication may be reproduced or transmitted
in any form or by any means, electronic or mechanical, including photocopying,
recording, or any information storage or retrieval system, without prior permission in
writing from the publishers.

Bloomsbury Publishing Plc does not have any control over, or responsibility for,
any third-party websites referred to or in this book. All internet addresses given in this
book were correct at the time of going to press. The author and publisher regret any
inconvenience caused if addresses have changed or sites have ceased to exist,
but can accept no responsibility for any such changes.

A catalogue record for this book is available from the British Library.

Library of Congress Control Number: 2022940117

ISBN: HB: 978-1-3502-6535-6
PB: 978-1-3502-6539-4
ePDF: 978-1-3502-6536-3
eBook: 978-1-3502-6537-0

Series: Islam of the Global West

Typeset by Deanta Global Publishing Services, Chennai, India

To find out more about our authors and books visit www.bloomsbury.com and sign up for
our newsletters

Contents

List of tables	vi
Introduction: Muslims, media and popular culture	1

Part One Contextualizing Muslim cultural production

1	A cultural history of Muslims in Britain: From colonial newsreels to post-9/11 broadcasting	31
2	Sound and vision: From reciters and rappers to the Muslim Netflix	51
3	Understanding Muslim popular culture: Islam in the media age	79

Part Two Muslim creatives in contemporary Britain

4	Voices of authority: The changing landscape of Islamic knowledge	103
5	Ordinary Muslimness: Everyday experience, commodification and spirituality	128
6	Escaping the 'Muslim trap': Typecasting and the search for creative freedom	156
7	Transnational nomads: The Muslim Atlantic and 'global Muslim culture'	179

Conclusion: Muslim creatives, future narratives	207
References	213
Index	230

Tables

1 A Summary of English-language Television Channels in the UK   67
2 Question Topics on *Ask the Alim* and *Islam Q and A*   116

Introduction

Muslims, media and popular culture

It is a tale of our times: ten Muslims, confined in a small space, scrutinized, analysed, criticized and lauded in equal measure, shadowed in public debate by the spectres of so-called extremism and radicalism. This is not, however, an extension of the state security and policing apparatus. Rather, it is the reality television programme, *Muslims Like Us*, broadcast in December 2016, on BBC Two in the UK. Bringing together ten Muslim participants to be filmed in a house over two days, some celebrated the programme for highlighting the diversity of Muslims in Britain – differences that ranged through belief, religious practice, ethnicity, culture and sexuality – while others criticized it for 'othering' Muslims and for focusing at times on the fringe political and religious views of one participant. These debates were played out across the entire spectrum of the public sphere, from broadsheet and tabloid newspapers to politics, broadcasters and social media. More than just an ephemeral flash of entertainment, this was reality television providing intimate yet also hyperreal access to Muslims for a wider British audience. The public reaction largely dwelled on composition and format, considering for the most part whether the programme 'authentically' represented Muslims in Britain. Yet often overlooked in these debates was the centrality of Muslim involvement in conceptualizing and producing the programme: from the commissioning editor at the BBC, Fatima Salaria, to the series producer, Mobeen Azhar, the narrator, Adeel Akhtar, and the researcher, Ahmed Peerbux, not to mention the ten Muslim participants who were the central feature of the production. This was the moment, then, that British Muslims stepped forward to briefly dominate the cultural *zeitgeist* of the country, not as subjects of representation but rather through the sophisticated collaboration of Muslim professionals to produce prime-time television for a national broadcaster.

While this is one of the most high-profile examples of Muslim cultural production, it is not an isolated phenomenon but rather a bellwether for the growing cultural assertiveness, technical proficiency and artistic scope of

Muslims in Britain. The range of activity taking place across a broadly defined British Muslim cultural arena is often breathtaking: from novelists and poets, to musicians and comedians, to artists, photographers, fashion designers, film-makers and television producers. Consider the musician Sami Yusuf, from London, who draws on Western and Middle Eastern musical traditions to perform gentle pop music, infused with spirituality and humanitarian concerns. Described by *Time* magazine as 'Islam's biggest rock star' (Wise, 2006), Yusuf has released seven albums, with worldwide sales of over 34 million and live crowds numbering in the hundreds of thousands. Or Muslim film-makers, such as Conor Ibrahiem in Bradford, who in 2017 released *Freesia*, the first of a planned trilogy of films dealing with complex issues, such as Islamophobia and the Far Right, from the perspective of Muslims in Britain. *Freesia* was nominated for several new film-maker awards, including 'Best Director' and 'Best Original Screenplay', and in 2018 was picked up for distribution on the streaming service Amazon Prime. Or consider Blackburn-born comedian, Tez Ilyas, who weaves together a self-mocking yet gentle reflection on being Muslim in Britain, with a wry take on wider social anxieties, from Brexit through to a maligned 'benefits' culture. With his warm and inclusive humour, Ilyas has broken through into a cultural mainstream, with productions on BBC television and radio, Channel 4, as well as across the British comedy circuit, from comedy clubs to summer music festivals.

The rise of Muslim cultural production extends beyond individual artists. It includes Muslim institutions, networks, broadcasters and businesses – from television channels and music labels to performance venues and publication platforms – that have emerged to support these growing phenomena. Witness the implicit rivalry between the Islam Channel and British Muslim TV, two television stations with subtly different audiences and divergent approaches to the envisioning of Islam in Britain. Or the opportunities provided by new technology, such as the streaming services Alchemiya, with documentaries aimed at an intellectual Muslim audience, and Muslim Kids TV, described as the 'Disney for Muslim kids' (Cochrane, 2021). The Islamic music label, Awakening Music, founded and based in Britain, continues to grow and become a corporate behemoth, with a list of high-profile Muslim musicians who cater for an expanding middle-class Muslim consumer and cultural market, both in Britain and internationally. Meanwhile, Arakan Creative, a theatre group based in Keighley, on the outskirts of Bradford, is described as 'the first British Muslim production company', with projects that span across theatre, film and comic books.

In this book, then, I examine Muslim cultural production in Britain, with a specific focus on Muslim involvement in the performance-based entertainment industry: music, comedy, film, television and (to a lesser extent) theatre. I have chosen these forms of culture for three reasons. First, they are emergent, are often successfully distributed through forms of mass media and yet are largely unresearched, which means their impact and trajectory is not well understood. This is in contrast with other forms of Muslim cultural activity, several of which have been subject of excellent publications, such as Muslim fashion (Lewis, 2015) and Muslim fiction writing (Chambers, 2011). Second, there is significant overlap between many of these areas, with Muslim producers, writers and performers moving between these related forms – such as from music to theatre or film to television. Third, music, film, television, theatre and comedy can all often be understood as types of popular culture (I also make reference throughout this book to 'media' but in doing so I usually intend a consideration of performance-based entertainment media rather than news or print media). While definitions of popular culture, à la Raymond Williams (1983), are almost as problematic as definitions of culture itself, I draw from Stuart Hall in recognizing that popular culture is a place where 'collective social understandings are created' through a 'politics of signification' (Hall, 2009: 122–3). Given the recent surge of involvement by British Muslims in these forms of popular culture, a new and rich space has been created for the nurturing and exploration of ideas, politics, beliefs and understandings that are associated with contemporary Muslim life in the UK. Popular culture is therefore not just a normal part of everyday life for Muslims in Britain – something which can be overlooked in the rush to exceptionalize 'Muslimness' – but it is also a lens through which to better understand Muslim social, cultural and religious change in Britain.

I use the term 'British Muslim popular culture' a little cautiously, for there are inherent dangers in carving out distinctive realms of culture as if they seemingly belong to this rather than that essentialized tradition. This overly expositional approach – the naming and locating of culture (Bhabha, 1994) – is something that has been widely criticized in reappraisals of the anthropological tradition (e.g. Abu-Lughod, 1993; Clifford, 1994). Yet culture can be a powerful and welcome vehicle for group identity (Davis, 1994; Castells, 1997), whether in developing political consciousness, challenging stereotypes or enabling mobilization around specific activities, rituals or events. To take one example, the Black Arts Movement, emerging in the Civil Rights context of the 1960s, did not confine African Americans to a frozen cultural ghetto, but rather it helped to project dynamic and complex Black identities into broader cultural conversations, not just in the United States but indeed globally (Smethurst, 2006). Similarly, then, as with Nasar Meer's idea of Muslim consciousness (2010), with its Du Boisian focus on transcendent identities, shaped by the friction of minority-majority relations, there is a need to move beyond political theory and to consider the role of culture in forming, shaping and projecting these everyday identities. Or, put another way, given the often-beleaguered experience of Muslims within British society – and more widely across minority contexts in the West – it is timely to consider the way in which cultural production might be an avenue for Muslims to project authentic experiences and identities into a social and cultural mainstream.

While the term 'Muslim popular culture' (and cognate concepts) is problematic and potentially restricting, as I will explain shortly, it also acknowledges the degree to which there exists a field of Muslim cultural production, through which religious subjectivities are deliberately and self-consciously made manifest. Some Muslim cultural producers reject these terms; others embrace them. One of the aims that I pursue in this book is to explore that tension and to look at the different ways in which cultural producers can bring their religious identities – and/or other aspects of their lived experience – to bear through expressions of popular culture.

Muslim cultural representation: From cliché to contestation

Muslims are not unfamiliar with the power of popular culture to shape 'collective social understandings' (see Hall, 2009) – on the contrary, they have often been subject to distorted and dangerous stereotyping through repeated portrayals in the media and wider culture. As the comedian Tez Ilyas remarks, with deadly humour, about the dangerous mixing of fact and fiction: 'If you don't know that much about us, you will recognise us from that hit TV show *The News*.' While these myths have a long provenance that is seeped through with encounters between colonial European powers and Muslim-majority societies – a history that has been well documented and theorized by Edward Said – the post-9/11 world has of course seen Muslims thrust into the spotlight of popular culture. Such representations usually take the form of caricatures or stereotypes, which serve to reinforce the position of Muslims as the 'new folk devils' of the Western imagination (Archer, 2009: 74). Analysing the misrepresentation of Muslims, Morey and Yaqin argue that a pervasive framing – with themes that relate to alterity, violence, fundamentalism and gendered oppression – often cast Muslims as the civilizational 'other' and as incompatible with global modernity:

> The body of the Muslim, as it appears in these representations, veiled, bearded, or praying, is made to carry connotations far beyond the intrinsic significance of such externals and rituals. Time and again, behaviour, the body, and dress are treated not as cultural markers but as a kind of moral index, confirming non-Muslim viewers of these images in their sense of superiority and cementing the threatening strangeness of the Muslim other. (Morey and Yaqin, 2011: 3)

Morey and Yaqin suggest that these images are not politically innocuous, but rather that they directly flow into contemporary social debates concerning 'muscular liberalism', 'integration', 'community cohesion', 'preventing terrorism' and an endless churn of pathological discourses about Muslim minorities.

This failure of representation is perhaps partly explained by the historic absence of involvement by British Muslims in the actual production of popular culture. While there are notable exceptions – such as the literature and screenwriting of Hanif Kureishi and the music of Yusuf Islam – Muslims in Britain have not until recently played a significant role in the production of popular culture. Until the late 1990s, for the most part, there were no visibly Muslim comedians, film-makers, television producers, actors or musicians in the public eye in Britain, so there were no authentic counterweights to these otherwise distorted representations. While the tide has started to turn, there is still an institutional imbalance, whereby Muslims are disproportionately missing from cultural production, just as they are excluded from other spheres of civic and public life (Citizens UK, 2017). The reproduction of social inequality through popular culture is not surprising, nor is it confined to religion, with similar issues found across a spectrum that includes class, gender, ethnicity and disability (Oakley and O'Brien, 2015). However, it should be noted that religious identity can often be overlooked as a dimension of cultural inequality. The BBC's *Diversity and Inclusion Strategy 2016-20* (BBC, 2016), for example, makes only a single, passing mention to religion, despite featuring the hijab-wearing *Great British Bake Off* winner Nadiya Hussain on its front cover. This is indicative perhaps of long-standing institutional confusion over whether to prioritize racial, ethnic or religious identities (Meer and Modood, 2009), often leading to a situation whereby intersectionality and self-identification can be overlooked in broadcasting and cultural circles (Saha, 2015).

Yet we must be aware that identities can also be rejected by those to whom they are applied. Or that these identities can be held back in reserve, as personal and private, rather than publicly paraded around as a testament to social change. The critically acclaimed actor, Riz Ahmed, argues that identity politics is almost always constricting for actors from a minority ethnic background. Writing about his own experiences with typecasting – as a British Pakistani-Muslim actor – Ahmed suggests that the portrayal of ethnic minorities through popular culture is like a 'necklace of labels to hang around your neck, neither of your choosing nor making, both constrictive and decorative' (Ahmed, 2016: 160). While it is possible to stretch and shape that necklace, to move beyond simplistic taxi driver/terrorist stereotyping, it is also almost impossible to entirely escape from it. Even subversive roles are linked, as a form of diametric opposition, to ethnic and racial stereotyping. For Ahmed, the opportunity to 'play a character whose story is not intrinsically linked to his race' is the 'promised land' (Ahmed, 2016: 160), in the sense that it is desired but almost always elusive. Perhaps because of this, Ahmed can often refuse to engage in a visible identity politics, politely declining to attend public engagements (such as charity functions) that might place a burden of representation upon him – he does not want to be 'just' a 'Muslim' or an 'Asian' actor but rather a professional and an artist looking to portray universal human stories. This echoes a point made by Mahmut Mutman, relating to an inherent flaw that runs through the anthropologies and sociologies of religion, suggesting that 'no one can avoid naming or writing Islam today' (2013: 178). With this in mind, I think it is necessary at the very least to caution against this presumptive and overweening tendency, even if I fall prey to this very same problem myself by choosing to analyse 'Muslim' media and popular culture throughout this book.

There are others, however, who use their art, talent and passion to more explicitly and intentionally explore their 'Muslimness' (i.e. their religious identity and the associated weave of everyday social behaviour) in a creative and public arena. There are multiple and often very personal reasons for doing so. For some, their art is a form of worship and devotion – such as the eclectic, Sufi folk-rock group, Silk Road, who speak eloquently about the spiritual nature of their performance and their desire to reach out and 'touch' their audience. Others are perhaps more interested in using popular culture as an accessible way to transmit religious, cultural and historical knowledge, as a form of *da'wah*, to enrich the learning of Muslims in Britain – from the teledawah *'ulama'* (see Chapter 4 for my discussion and definition of 'teledawah') through to the documentaries about contemporary Muslim life. And then there are those who explicitly grapple with contentious social, political and religious issues, whether seeking wider social change or engaging in intra-Muslim debates – from director Conor Ibrahiem, the award-winning director mentioned earlier, with his critical examination of Islamophobia through film, to female African-Caribbean rapping duo, Poetic Pilgrimage, who challenge pervasive stereotypes relating to Muslim ethnicity and femininity.

Ultimately, since 9/11 and subsequent events, Muslims have been thrust into the glare of public scrutiny, with repeated misrepresentation through both media and culture (Poole, 2002; Morey and Yaqin, 2011). This new era, saturated with images, metaphors and emotion, places a burden of representation on Muslims, but it also appears to have imparted a sophisticated understanding of the public sphere into a new generation of Muslim creatives. Thus, as I show throughout this book, while motivations for Muslim creativity, art and cultural production are varied – from the spiritual and ritualistic to the political and pedagogic – there is an awareness amongst many that popular culture and media activity can be an essential vehicle to generate new ideas, identities and forms of Muslim consciousness. I aim to look at the ways in which these expressions of Islam and Muslimness occur, from the explicit and the devotional through to the subtle and the non-religious.

Muslim cultural production and Muslim creatives

One of the challenges of this book has been in making sense of the actual research field. It is all very well to speak in broad generalities about 'Muslim media' and 'Muslim popular culture', but the reality is such that these phenomena are vastly diverse and do not constitute a singular style, industry or genre of activity. To take one example, the television sector is itself complex and varied, with numerous subcultures and subsectors. The BBC has a very different business model and culture of broadcasting, for instance, in comparison to the Birmingham-based, Urdu-language broadcaster, Takbeer TV. Similarly, individual professionals might be strongly associated with a specific industry or genre but at the same time can have a more wide-ranging involvement with other forms of cultural production, such as the rap duo, Poetic Pilgrimage, who, while known for their music, have been involved in multiple television and theatre projects. It is neither possible, then, nor appropriate to deploy terms and labels that are too rigidly defining. Instead, throughout this book, I use a looser and more inclusive language that refers to *Muslim cultural production* – outputs, styles and industries – and *Muslim creatives* – the varied individuals involved with this phenomenon, in both 'backstage' and 'frontstage' (or off-screen and on-screen) professions.

Defining the cultural industries has long been a problem for academics and policymakers (O'Connor, 2000; Power and Scott, 2004). They are simply too vast, complex, diverse and yet interconnected, to easily compartmentalize them into neatly defined realms of commercial and creative activity. Pierre Bourdieu's concept of different 'fields' of cultural production is perhaps more useful (Bourdieu, 1993), recognizing as it does that there are various arenas of partially autonomous cultural activity – such as fine art, pop music or reality television – that each possess their own distinct values and forms of 'capital' (Bourdieu refers to several different types of capital, including economic, social, cultural and symbolic). Through this reading, fields of cultural production are not necessarily defined by genre or style but more by the extent to which social and cultural groups are able to define themselves through the deployment and exchange of capital within these fields of cultural activity. For example, fine art and high theatre perhaps reside within the same field of culture – that is, they share the same or similar forms of capital – while graffiti and skateboarding inhabit another.

In this sense, then, Muslim cultural production refers to the diverse outputs and activities that are associated with Muslim creativity and performance culture in the UK. It spans different industries, genres and audiences. Tez Ilyas, for example, is mostly involved with the alternative comedy scene in Britain and with public service broadcasting, while Sami Yusuf has been the leading figure in the development of a *nasheed* (Islamic religious songs) industry, which appeals to predominantly Muslim audiences globally. Their professional lives are different to one another – their cultural activity and output are also very different. Yet, they are also situated within a shared field of cultural production – that is, a Muslim cultural economy – or field of cultural production, to use the language of Bourdieu – wherein there are common forms of capital that bind together Ilyas and Yusuf, just as they do with other Muslim artists and performers. These forms of capital might be symbolic – such as Islamic imagery, historical allusions or coded political references – social – in relation to shared religious networks, values, norms and identities – economic – relating to the commercial links that exist between Muslim organizations and groups – and cultural – with common or related forms of apparel, deportment and speech. In a sense, this book is concerned with analysing and interrogating these links and commonalities, while also recognizing that there are important differences. For example, Muslim television producers might share a similar passion in terms of attempting to articulate and disseminate 'authentic' Muslim stories and narratives, but individually they might face different pressures and barriers depending on the specific television sector within which they work (e.g. the BBC in contrast to the Islamic television sector).

Rather than launching into the fruitless and frustrating task of developing a systematic empirical cataloguing of Muslim cultural production – with clearly defined industries, audiences, institutions and areas of cultural activity – I instead take the looser and, admittedly at times, problematic approach of grouping all of this activity together in a broad field of Muslim cultural production. It is an analytical framework that uses religious identity as a lens through which to consider these different cultural producers and their areas of activity. Equally, if one were to rotate the analytic kaleidoscope, there are other ways – other paradigms – through which these eclectic artists and professionals could and should be understood (such as ethnicity, class, genre, etc.). They are not solely defined by their faith, even if this is the focus through which I channel my discussions within this book.

Similarly, while it is of course often appropriate to discuss individuals with reference to their primary activity – as a musician, an actor or a writer – I more often refer to those working within this field as Muslim creatives. This more inclusive term captures the wide-ranging and eclectic nature of these individuals – many of whom have varied interests – as well as recognizing that television production, or event organization, or camerawork are creative endeavours just as much as musical performance, or scriptwriting, or film directing. This cautious phrasing is not dissimilar to the way in which academics are required to approach the study of Muslims in Britain. To generalize about such a large and diverse group can be problematic, even if there are significant and formative commonalities that can justify such a grouping.

Muslims in Britain: Charting a changing country

Over the last two to three decades there have been gradual but increasingly significant changes to the sociological profile and public visibility of Muslims in Britain. Historically, the post-war Muslim demographic in the UK has been characterized by close-knit urban communities, low levels of educational attainment, poverty and important markers of ethnic distinctiveness (Ansari, 2004). The religious lives of Muslims have been shaped by a grassroots culture centred on the local mosque, alongside private worship in the home, which is also an important space for the activities of extended kinship networks. Religious ritual and belief have therefore typically been shaped in large part by the contours of community life, local religious leaders and the influence of family members. Mosque imams have fulfilled a specialist legal, spiritual and ritualistic role for the vast majority of Muslims in Britain, although their capacity to do so has long been a topic of fierce debate, with a 2008 study finding that only 8.1 per cent were British-born, raising questions about the pastoral abilities of imams, many of whom have lacked proficiencies in language and a sensitivity to the challenges of British social and cultural life (Geaves, 2008). Political representation has similarly often been confined to local Muslim politicians and elders – so-called 'gatekeepers' – who have sought to act as representatives of 'the community'. Women and young people have been – and often still are – excluded from positions of religious and political leadership. This is the picture that any scholar, or keen observer, will be most familiar with when considering Muslims in Britain over the last half-century.

This landscape has however started to change quite significantly and continues to do so at an accelerating rate. As Philip Lewis and Sadek Hamid argue in their book, *British Muslims: New Directions in Islamic Thought, Creativity and Activism*: 'change is on its way' (2018). Such change can be explained in large part by an upending amongst many of the demographic and social characteristics that I have just outlined. Muslims in Britain are gradually becoming more economically and socially advantaged, less a part of tight-knit communities, less constrained by traditional forms of leadership and are developing new avenues for the expression of autonomous religious identities and practices. These changes should not be overstated – the huge socio-economic challenges faced by Muslims are a pressing and immediate concern, with an estimated 50 per cent of Muslims living in poverty (Li, Heath and Woerner-Powell, 2018) – but the sociological trajectory is nonetheless quite apparent. It is a trend that continues to create new institutions and authorities, to encourage a greater degree of individualized religiosity and to fuel emergent forms of cultural and social experimentation. As I argue throughout this book, Muslim popular culture has been made possible in large part because of this sociological shift. There are three key areas where this changing landscape is most relevant for Muslim creatives: demography, individualism and leadership/representation.

Demographic change

Several key areas of demographic change are relevant for understanding the social and cultural profile of Muslim creatives. A 2015 report by the Muslim

Council of Britain (MCB), *British Muslims in Numbers*, has highlighted the improving socio-economic status of Muslims in the UK. The report makes a consistent effort to highlight ongoing issues of poverty and deprivation but partly concludes by stating:

> How have Muslims moved forward since 2001? The latest census indicates that a section of the Muslim population is prospering and making progress, as evident by representation in the higher socio-economic class and signs of social mobility. Muslims are also more educated than a decade ago. Many Muslims are small employers or self-employed. Research indicates the BME population is becoming less residentially segregated. (MCB, 2015: 68)

To substantiate this claim, the report provides a number of indicators from the 2011 census. About 22.7 per cent of Muslims work in managerial and professional roles, with a further 18.2 per cent studying full-time in further or higher education, of which 43 per cent are women. 24 per cent of Muslims already possess a higher education qualification, which is only 3 per cent below the British average. While still relatively concentrated in four urban areas – London, Birmingham, Manchester and Bradford – the report highlights research indicating that Muslims in Britain are becoming more geographically distributed, largely because of younger graduates moving out into the suburbs (Simpson, 2012). Furthermore, the number of one-person and single-parent households is perhaps surprisingly high, 135,000 and 99,600, respectively, together representing over 31 per cent of all Muslim households. While this raises potential issues concerning divorce and social isolation (Lewis and Hamid, 2018), it does also indicate that extended households are becoming less a feature of everyday Muslim family life, with the result that communities are perhaps becoming less cohesive – a trend towards smaller households which is very much a feature of Britain as a whole (McRae, 1999). This data is largely drawn from an analysis of the 2011 census. Given this trajectory, and supported by wider anecdotal evidence, we can expect these trends to be only further amplified within the findings of the 2021 census (which have unfortunately not been published at the time of writing). That is, the picture points convincingly towards the growth of a more segmented, highly educated and prosperous Muslim professional class, albeit as a demographic outrider for a disadvantaged majority. This has implications relating not just to the capacities and resources of this 'new elite' but also to their values and perspectives, which I argue often tend to be pluralistic and cosmopolitan in outlook (see Chapter 3).

Individualism

Linked to these demographic changes are more sweeping alterations to the way in which Islam is practised and understood within Britain. The inherent pluralism of Islam has often been noted in relation to the general lack of centralized hierarchical institutions, with, instead, a jostling and globalized marketplace of sheikhs, *pir*s (spiritual guides), *mufti*s (Islamic jurists), schools of thought and legalistic traditions. Of course, all global religions are diverse and contain competing voices, but Islam especially contains a degree of 'interpretive anarchy' (Robinson, 2009: 353). Peter Mandaville (2007) identifies three aspects that relate to the way in which Islam is interpreted and practised: functionalization, respatialization and mediatization. Broadly, Mandaville's claim suggests that, globally, Muslims are more and more likely to develop individualized interpretations of their faith. Muslims do this by becoming more and more likely to consider the functional role of their religious practice, by choosing from amongst a global landscape of competing Islamic authorities and by seeking new spaces of mediated religion. Such a shift is consistent with the common claim made by sociologists, following Anthony Giddens (1991), that the 'modern' world is characterized by a shift, whereby predetermined identities are now more likely to give way to the bricolage of individualistic behaviour and self-determination. Linda Woodhead has applied this understanding more widely to religion and belief in Britain, proposing that 'old religion' is becoming replaced by 'new religion'. Woodhead's claim is elegantly summarized by Davie:

> 'New style' religion moves away from the medium-sized membership structure towards more episodic modes of existence. Some are very large (festivals or gatherings), and some are very small (cell groups); the latter can exist within the former. In 'new style' religion, moreover, authority is dispersed and communication takes place through a wide variety of media; the agency of the individual is considerably enhanced. The stress lies in finding yourself rather than in a definitive form of salvation. (Davie, 2014: 225)

Through this reading, religion in Britain is becoming increasingly plural and decentralized, with a greater emphasis on diverse and mediated individual religious engagement.

Such trends appear to be evident in some respects amongst Muslims in Britain. For young Muslims in particular, traditional forms of authority and religious practice (old religion), centred around a cohesive local mosque-culture, are becoming replaced by more reflexive and individualized interpretations (new religion), which critically draw on a range of transnational scholars and other areas of globalized and mediated Islam. This is not a rejection of religious authority so much as it is a judicious process of sifting through competing authorities, beliefs and practices. Drawing on fieldwork conducted with Muslims in Britain, Amin summarizes this by stating:

> Who they deem as a 'true' scholar representing Islam in Britain was an essential, if not the most important aspect of the debate . . . the irony of religious authority is how in these discussions, most lay Muslims felt they could judge and decide themselves. (Amin, 2019: 12)

This process has created new avenues for the emergence of mediated Muslim authorities, not only in terms of Islamic scholasticism but also within other areas, from politics and lay professionals through to media, the arts and popular culture. In short, religious knowledge and practice is less likely to be governed or shaped by a narrow group of clerical actors, or by an inherited family/community tradition, but is instead becoming dispersed amongst a more diverse religious landscape that is informed by flows of globalized media and communication.

Leadership and representation

Another related area of change for Muslims in Britain concerns leadership and representation. Muslim leadership in Britain for much of the post-war period took the form of local mosque-based arrangements – such as the Muslim Council of Bradford – and the representation provided for migrant Muslims by countries of origin, such as Pakistan (so-called Embassy Islam) (Laurence, 2011). Transnational political organizations that were active in the UK, such as Jamaat-e-Islami, also played a role (Hamid, 2016). This changed dramatically in the late 1980s and 1990s, following the tumult of the Rushdie Affair (Werbner, 2002), which propelled Muslims into the public sphere in Britain. The fallout from the Rushdie Affair made clear a pressing need for national structures and leaderships that would be able to nurture a sense of collective religious identity and to advocate for the needs of Muslims in Britain. Significant organizations to emerge during the 1990s included the Islamic Society of Britain (ISB) and the MCB, both of which typically focused on 'community' rather than necessarily 'religious' concerns. Over the last two decades there has been a further flourishing of leadership and representation, visibly in national and international public debate, but also more quietly across professional and institutional contexts, as Sophie Gilliat-Ray and Riyaz Timol have summarized:

> Muslim leadership roles have seen further diversification in recent decades through incorporation into professions such as chaplaincy and youth work, while those British Muslims in senior positions within the media (such as Mehdi Hasan) or the third sector often function as influential spokespeople. Others who have succeeded in the public eye, such as Sir Mo Farah, CBE, Nadiya Hussain, MBE, or most recently, Liverpool footballer Mohamed Salah, act as 'role models' garnering followings among a wide cross-section of British society. (Gilliat-Ray and Timol, 2020: 559)

The key point here is that the 'Muslim public sphere' in Britain continues to diversify, with voices that project a range of concerns, rather than from amongst those exclusively anchored in Islamic piety, religious authority and religious-political activism. The result is a more textured and sensitive engagement with the social and cultural concerns of Muslims in Britain, relating to areas such as Islamophobia, cultural visibility/inclusion, securitization and the socio-economic status of Muslim communities. These new forms of leadership additionally serve to better include women and a younger generation of Muslims in Britain (Lewis and Hamid, 2018).

As these three areas indicate, the sociological profile and public visibility of Muslims in Britain have changed gradually, but decisively, over the few decades. The overall picture is one of greater diversity and confidence. Muslim creatives are an important part of this story. On the one hand, this new landscape has provided the conditions from within which Muslim media and popular culture has been able to thrive. On the other, Muslim creatives have helped to accelerate this reconfiguration. It is a virtuous cycle, whereby Muslim cultural pioneers, in the 1980s and 1990s, took advantage of emergent cultural spaces and forms of social capital in order to widen diversity and cultural experimentation. This has in turn fuelled the continued development of Muslim institutions, cultures and imaginaries. Muslim media and popular culture is a compelling field of inquiry precisely because it is bound together with these wider sociological and religious narratives of change.

Muslim media and popular culture: A research agenda

As I argue throughout this book, Muslim media and popular culture is multifaceted. For some popular culture fulfils specifically religious needs, for others it is a way of expressing universal human stories that may (or may not) be relevant for their personal religious or spiritual subjectivities. In Chapter 3,

I outline a typology that groups some of this complexity together within three broad strands: (i) Islamic, (ii) Islamically conscious and (iii) secular-civic. While these categories should not be considered hard or definitive boundaries, my claim is that Muslim popular culture can at times be associated with pietistic religion, but that it can also express itself through more spiritual, cultural and social manifestations, many of which are somewhat removed from traditional Islamic orthodoxies. These are tendencies that exist along a spectrum, then, rather than fixed categories – and individual Muslim creatives can express one or more of these tendencies, at different times, sometimes in combination, and in different contexts. Having said that, distinct genres of culture tend to gravitate towards particular locations along this spectrum. For example, Muslim comedians often reflect on Islamic practices – such as fasting – but do so in a way that explores their place within everyday British culture, playing for comedic value on the misapprehension and discombobulation of a wider non-Muslim public ('what, not even water?!'). This approach is in stark contrast with the teledawah *'ulama'*, who extol the divine blessings and spiritual virtues that are accrued during Ramadan. There are, then, always different motivations and perspectives at work within Muslim popular culture. To study Muslim popular culture is to consider the functional role that it plays within different aspects of contemporary Muslim life in Britain and to consider the varying semantic and symbolic arrangements – that is, the process of mediation – through which these tendencies are structured in cultural expression.

Religion has always been mediated – through texts, priests and materiality (Meyer and Moors, 2005) – but modern forms of technology and culture have placed a new emphasis on the way in which this mediation occurs. The expression of Islam and Muslim subjectivities, through popular culture, brings to the forefront questions about how contemporary forms of mediated communication can reconfigure belief and practice. There are many ways in which the link between media and Muslims could be examined, but, in this book, I work from the assumption that 'the very practice of everyday religious life is usually dependent on how [it] is mediated through different forms of media and cultural product' (Lynch, Mitchell and Strhan, 2012a: 1). In doing so, then, I accept that Islam in Britain has to some extent become 'mediatized' (see Chapter 3 for a full discussion about mediatization theory). Rather than simply highlighting the important link between religion and media, I claim that the everyday religious lives of Muslims in Britain are indelibly entwined with the logic, assumptions and processes of modern media and culture. As I demonstrate, media and cultural communication is having a decisive impact in restructuring Muslim institutions and authorities, in shaping identities and imaginaries, in regulating the circulation of symbols and beliefs and in generating new modes of religious practice. Consequently, the ways in which media and cultural communication occur – the form through which it is manifested – cannot be neatly or completely teased apart from the broader tapestry of everyday Muslim life in Britain.

Taken together then, throughout this book, I consider both the function and form of Muslim popular culture. I examine the function that culture assumes – the way in which it interlocks with other practices and beliefs, while also providing new and distinctive avenues for the expression of Muslim religiosity. And I also consider the form that it takes – the ways in which cultural and media communication penetrate and alter other aspects of the religious ecosphere. This shift can be registered across the whole expanse of Muslim religious life – from religious knowledge and authority, to practice and belief, through to political activism and identities, the reshaping of community and new forms of belonging.

The impact of Muslim popular culture has become increasingly evident within the realm of Muslim orthodoxy. If the *'ulama'* for many decades held a unique monopoly as the mediators of text and faith – as custodians and interpreters of both religious knowledge and law – their role has been challenged and changed somewhat in recent years by Muslim popular culture. Television provides an outlet for a new generation of media-savvy Muslim teledawah, but it also demands new competencies: an ability to articulate broader moral concepts, to engage in wider cultural conversations and to apply their knowledge to the social dilemmas faced by Muslims in Britain. They also compete in a more crowded marketplace, vying with scholars and teachers from across the Muslim world. Non-clerical cultural figures, from musicians to actors, can themselves play the role of religious interpreters, sifting through religious knowledge, sharing religious aphorisms and spiritual insights, as well as promoting favoured scholars via their social media channels and through other forms of cultural and media communication.

Religious nurture and learning amongst Muslims in Britain, for so many decades centred around the mosque and madrasa – with distinct forms of embodied and textual learning (Scourfield et al., 2013) – is now also shaped more significantly by cultural and media influences. This ranges from the explicitly educational, such as programming about prayer, Muslim history and the Qur'an – with Ali-Huda and Muslim Kids TV specifically seeking to educate children – through to the embodied piety of cultural role models, who perform their understanding of Muslimness for a vicariously receptive audience. The currents of intra-Muslim debate and schools of thought – confined in past decades to the jostle of organized reform movements (Geaves, 2013) – have reconstituted and re-embedded themselves in a wider cultural form, with vaguer attachments to one side or another of an 'Integrationist'/'Conservative Isolationist' (see Hamid, 2016) – or, as Muslim creatives sometimes understand it, a 'Sufi vs Salafi' – divide. It is impossible to consider the approach of different television stations, or to discuss music and art, without understanding the intra-religious currents and debates that, no matter how subtle, inform these practices and organizations (see Chapter 7 for a fuller discussion of these debates and schools of thought).

Muslim popular culture additionally plays a significant role in the everyday religious lives of Muslims in Britain. It certainly provides new avenues for the expression of religion, through consumption and commodification, through subjectivized forms of spirituality and through performed ritual and religious embodiment. The associated growth of an alternative Muslim lifestyle culture has been particularly evident in recent decades (Morris, 2016). While functional religious consumption has long been an important feature of Muslim life – from prayer mats and halal food through to hajj travel packages – a new wave of cultural experimentation has placed greater emphasis on forms of symbolic consumption, whereby non-functional but symbolically expressive religious identities are made manifest. Popular culture is the natural home for such an approach. Through material culture and art – from fashion and food to music and film – idealized 'Islamic lifestyles', promoted by a new generation of Muslim 'influencers' (see Chapter 5), are underpinned by ideological and ethical assumptions that are rooted in not just Islamic teachings but also in wider social and political views (Echchaibi, 2012). Thus, popular culture becomes another way through which highly individualized Muslim identities are constructed and made visible. These individualized expressions of Islam, through consumption and material culture, act in tandem with an increasing emphasis on spirituality – that is, on subjective, individualized experiences of the divine – rather than on externally authorized religion (Flanagan, 2007). This approach, which can be found across the discourses and outputs of Muslim creatives, gravitates towards an inclusive language and framing, whereby a focus is placed on the internal and the ecstatic, rather than the external and the codified.

This movement towards more individualized forms of Islam highlights the growing significance and influence of those involved in the production of popular culture. Grace Davie points towards the emergence of 'vicarious religion' in Britain, suggesting that religion is increasingly 'performed by an active minority but on behalf of a much larger majority' (Davie, 2007: 22). While this is a controversial claim – and, for some, without a solid base of evidential proof (Bruce and Voas, 2010) – it is nonetheless a tantalizing proposition that elevates a small number of religious actors as the chief interlocutors and performers of religion, on the behalf of a silent majority. While Muslims in Britain are largely religiously active at a community level (Gilliat-Ray, 2010), there is nonetheless a sense in which Muslim creatives can fulfil the role of influential performers and interlocutors, from the embodied piety of musicians and presenters to the televised ritualistic performances of teledawah '*ulama*'. In this way, Islam is performed by a small number of cultural producers, who compete with one another in a marketplace of religion, as a means to meet the 'vicarious' demands of a much larger Muslim audience.

Political and social issues also feature prominently within Muslim popular culture, which provides an outlet to address the 'equality gap' at the heart of Muslim citizenship (Elshayyal, 2018). Through this reading, it is recognized that Muslims face specific pressures and forms of discrimination, both from the state and across wider British society (Khan, 2019). These issues stem from a heightened political context, whereby Muslims are racialized, excluded and targeted, often through governmental securitization measures (Kundnani, 2009). There is furthermore a deeper cultural antipathy towards Muslims by many in the UK (Allen, 2010), including amongst the British media (Petley and Richardson, 2013). Muslim film-makers and comedians, in particular, can provide a counterweight to these distorted representations, as well as directly tackling issues of Islamophobia and discrimination. This occurs in part through the projection of complex and multifaceted Muslim experiences and identities through popular culture – including de-exceptionalizing Muslimness and making it 'ordinary' – in order to combat the one-dimensional and pathologized representation of Muslims in wider cultural and political imaginations. These attempts are most successful when they conjure universal narratives, incorporating specific Muslim experiences, but also exploring shared human stories relating to themes such as family and romance. Guz Khan, for example, in his BBC comedy series, *Man Like Mobeen*, shatters ethnic, class and religious stereotypes but maintains a clear focus on the humanity of his principal character, Mobeen, as he struggles to raise his younger sister and navigate the challenges of a deprived area in Birmingham. There are also more explicit attempts to critique or overcome forms of discrimination and Islamophobia. This can involve using popular culture to explore these issues, such as Conor Ibrahiem's film, *Freesia*, which examines the trauma of far-right violence against Muslim characters, or through the use of comedy, as with Ali Official, to draw attention to the often-farcical nature of security policies, such as the racialized 'stop and search' anti-terrorism measures.

Muslim creatives furthermore lead the way in a struggle to overcome barriers within their own professional lives. A sense of exclusion from the cultural mainstream is often raised by Muslim creatives, including a belief that funding and production opportunities are denied to Muslim professionals, in large part due to hidden forms of discrimination. While these experiences are not uniform – with some arguing that a diversity agenda in broadcasting and the arts can actually provide unique opportunities to 'minority' professionals – there are those who direct a scathing attack on the failure of the culture industries. Contained within these larger debates are specific issues relating to gender, such as the representation of Muslim women, but also in terms of gender imbalance amongst Muslim creatives themselves, as a group, and the specific challenges faced by Muslim female professionals. Muslim popular culture – as with music and broadcasting more generally (Oakley and O'Brien, 2015) – contains a distinct gender imbalance, with significantly fewer women operating in all areas of cultural production. Some of this relates to internal community censure, amongst some Muslims, concerning modesty and female performance. This is particularly the case for female musicians, with the 'voice' considered by some to be a part of female beauty (*'awra*) that needs to be protected from male, non-relatives. Yet Muslim women face further intersectional barriers relating to the ways in which their gender, ethnicity and religion are perceived within the wider public sphere. Notwithstanding these specific gender-based challenges, a successful cohort of Muslim women have risen to become not just noted performers and artists but have also been appointed to senior leadership roles in broadcasting organizations, including the BBC, Channel 4 and British Muslim TV. Consequently, while there is still much to be done, Muslim women are themselves making significant progress in resisting the many pressures and challenges that they face within popular culture.

Finally, it is notable that Muslim popular culture is impacting upon conceptions of community, belonging and identity. Diasporic attachments have historically been a central feature of cultural practice for many Muslims in the UK (Anwar, 1979; Werbner, 2006), although in recent decades these links have started to wane amongst a younger generation, or to be reconfigured through cultural experimentation and hybridity. Music is an important cultural vanguard in this respect. While South Asian music remains popular for some – such as Qawwali and Bhangra (Sarrazin, 2013) – younger Muslims are more likely to value it as a part of their childhood heritage. It is a nostalgic comfort, rooted in memory and family, while cultural evolution and pop-cultural practice drift in another direction, perhaps drawing on the cultural legacy of South Asian influences but looking towards a diverse expanse of (globalized) Western and other non-Western musical influences. A similar trajectory can be charted amongst other forms of popular culture. Urdu television stations, of which there are four in the UK, appeal to an increasingly niche diasporic cultural audience, but they only just about survive, competing in a broadcasting market that has shifted towards English-language content for a culturally British audience. These new English-language television stations, such as Eman Channel and British Muslim TV, make reference to diasporic culture, but as a celebration of heritage rather than as an active or dynamic influence. This is the critical point: diasporic culture becomes reconfigured as heritage and memory: an important legacy but a nostalgic vestige, nonetheless. The critically acclaimed film, *Mogul Mowgli* (2020), illustrates this claim. Starring Riz Ahmed, and co-written with American director, Bassam Tariq, the film explores issues of race and identity in contemporary Britain, but through the lens of remembered family history and the violence of the partition of Pakistan. Ahmed and Tariq juxtapose the contemporary struggle of a British rapper against the dreamlike haze of his family and cultural-historical memory.

This drift away from – and reconfiguration of – diasporic culture also raises a number of issues relating to cultural identity and belonging. Intra-Muslim debates about race are an uncomfortable and sensitive topic for many Muslim creatives, with some Black Muslims arguing that they can be overlooked or even excluded from the Muslim public sphere (see Morris, 2019a, for a discussion of this issue). The response amongst many Muslim creatives, from a variety of ethnic backgrounds, is to highlight and celebrate the racial and cultural diversity of Muslims in Britain. This can include placing an emphasis on the inclusivity of national and religious identities – of being a 'British Muslim' – rather than on the divisions and baggage of ethnic-exclusiveness. Muslim creatives are often therefore at the forefront of campaigns concerning, for example, inclusive English-language mosques (rather than those catering for a specific ethnic group).

Such divisions are also challenged with a turn towards more universal forms of Muslim identity and belonging, such as shared Islamic histories and the idea of a unified (or at least inclusive) global *umma* (Muslim community). Islamic storytelling and myth, which conjures the notion of a collective Muslim past, is a common feature within music and poetry, for example, which can recount the achievements of Muslim historical and spiritual figures, through to historical re-enactment on stage and screen, and with Qur'anic parables told on television in a narrative story form. It is no surprise, perhaps, that the standout television phenomenon of the last few years has been the Turkish historical drama series, *Diriliş: Ertuğrul* (2014–18), which recounts the dynastic and political history shortly predating the emergence of the Ottoman Empire. Available on Netflix, the programme has been widely watched and praised by Muslims in Britain, as it has been by Muslim audiences around the world. These stories, myths and retellings serve to construct fictions of Muslim unity and lineage, reorienting otherwise diverse Muslim groups away from ethnic and national division, towards conceptions of an 'imagined' Islamic fraternity. Similarly, new forms of Muslim belonging continue to develop, in relation to transatlantic connections between Britain and North America. Based on shared language, culture and experience, the 'Muslim Atlantic' is becoming a vital space where 'a broader set of conversations in which race, gender, immigration, belonging, identity, religion, and security are all woven together' (DeHanas and Mandaville, 2019: 3). Media and popular culture is a critical engine for generating this new transatlantic Muslim space, from the collaboration of American and British cultural producers through to the sharing of culture, institutions and overlapping transatlantic audiences (see Chapter 7).

Transatlantic culture is not confined to audiences or cultural spaces across Europe and North America. Muslim cultural producers play a key role in bringing Western values, ideas and cultures into dynamic interplay around the world. The Bloomsbury book series, *Islam of the Global West* – of which this book is a contributor – provides some theoretical structure to thinking through this exchange. This framing collapses the dichotomy between 'Islam' and 'the West', recognizing that Western concepts and institutions have been globalized, pluralized and to some extent geographically unhitched. It challenges the view that there is somehow an analytic difference or divide between Western culture, on the one hand, and Muslim 'interlopers' in the West, on the other. Writing elsewhere, I have argued:

> A spectrum of public opinion ranges from those castigating Muslim minorities as incompatible with Western norms and values (illiberal, unpatriotic, patriarchal, etc.) through to apologias that instead emphasise these very same features as part of a visible Muslim embeddedness (diverse, integrated, plural, etc.). These claims work from a similar premise: a 'matching up' between pre-existing Western political/philosophical paradigms, on the one hand, and Muslim *émigrés* on the other. Liberal democratic states might be shaped or altered by such contact, but again this is often understood in a reactive way – as a *response to* the presence of

Muslim minorities, rather than through Muslim agency per se. (Morris, 2019b: 23, emphasis in original).

As a theoretical framework, Islam of the Global West emphasizes the active involvement of Muslims (geographically located in North America and Europe, but also Muslims in other parts of the world) to pluralize 'Western' modernity. It partly dissolves conventional nation state analysis, pointing instead to complex global flows and connections, within which Muslims play a constitutive role. Muslim creatives are emblematic of this, as I argue, producing nuanced expressions of culture that are simultaneously Western, Islamic and diasporic. Throughout this book, then, I explore all of these themes and demonstrate how popular culture is providing new avenues for the expression and practice of Muslim religiosity. I will say it again – none of this should be overstated. The coming together of popular culture and religion is just one feature of contemporary Muslim life in Britain. For many Muslims, their religious lives are a small thread within a larger tapestry of everyday experience, whereby work, family, recreation and other factors take greater precedence. Also, for many, their engagement with 'Muslim popular culture' is limited, with tastes that instead gravitate towards the mainstream, from British soaps and Hollywood blockbusters to pop music and football. The idea that a majority of Muslims in Britain desire an exclusive religious-cultural space – at the expense of wider popular culture – is not accurate and, despite the focus of this book, I do not make this claim. And for many Muslims, their practice of Islam is confined to more conventional forms of religion, including, for example, prayer, collective worship and textual exegesis. However, as I argue, Muslim popular culture has become a phenomenon that in certain contexts can channel Muslim sensibilities and expressions as a means to reformulate existing religious ecospheres. It can also, just as importantly, provide a lens through which to examine the deeper social and cultural trends that underpin the practice of Islam in the UK.

Research methodology: Fieldwork and scope

The arguments and discussions that I put forward in this book are predominantly framed by concepts and theories from within the sociology of religion and British Muslim studies. I also draw in a more limited fashion from the disciplines of ethnomusicology, cultural studies, television, film and comedy studies. I hope that this multidisciplinary approach enables a fresh and distinctive analysis of

Muslims in Britain, as well as provide more general data for understanding the link between religion and popular culture.

My research findings are drawn from empirical fieldwork conducted between 2011 and 2020. This project initially began as doctoral research looking at Muslim musicians in the UK (completed in 2013), and some of the findings from that earlier phase of research have been discussed elsewhere. In 2016, I extended my fieldwork activities to include Muslim film-makers, comedians and those involved in television (as writers, actors, producers, commissioners, etc). My guiding principle has been to identify and work with Muslim creatives, many of whom operate across a broadly conceived Muslim 'cultural field' (Bourdieu, 1993). This includes not only cultural producers within very specific religious settings but also those who have risen to prominence within non-religious mainstream cultural settings (while nonetheless expressing a Muslim identity or Islamic themes throughout their work). While much of this activity is transnational in scope and impact – and I discuss these implications – I have confined my focus to British citizens and to English-language cultural production. This was partly a practical decision, but it also recognizes that national cultures and identities continue to predominate, even in an increasingly interconnected world. Furthermore, debates relating to national citizenship and belonging continue to be thrust upon Muslims in Britain, which means that Muslim cultural production is often conceptualized and expressed within this framework. However, the research findings discussed in this book will also have much relevance for considering Muslims in other minority Western contexts, particularly those in North America.

In total I conducted semi-structured interviews with forty Muslim creatives in Britain. Ten of these were women. The ethnic background of these participants broadly captures the diversity of Muslims in Britain, including those who identify as South Asian, Black, White British, Arab and North African – although these simplistic ethnic categories contain a certain degree of complexity within them, which I discuss in a later chapter. All of the participants and public figures discussed in this book are Sunni Muslim. While there are small but important Shi'ah communities in the UK, they have less public visibility and – at least as far as my research could establish – are not observable in the production of popular culture. The interviews were recorded, transcribed and shared with the participants. Anonymity is particularly tricky, because it is either not appropriate or even possible to anonymize all participants (i.e. individuals can often easily be identified by the nature of their artistic output). Most have been perfectly willing to forgo anonymity and are at ease with discussing their work and in making statements for public consumption. I have anonymized those working in less public or more sensitive positions, or when requested by the interviewee – this is indicated whenever these anonymized individuals are referred to directly. I also draw upon unrecorded and more informal conversations with Muslim creatives from across many years of conducting fieldwork.

In addition to these interviews, I have consumed and analysed a vast range of Muslim popular culture. This includes music and song, film, television broadcasts, comedy acts, plays and a slew of media commentary about these cultural products (including social media posts from both fans and commentators alike). Taken together, this is an almost bottomless well of cultural activity and I will have predictably made some notable omissions, especially given the rate at which popular culture becomes 'dated'. I can only hope that this research adequately captures a sample of Muslim popular culture that is both representative and analytically useful. This book should by no means be considered comprehensive – it is little more than a glimpse into a field that is vast, constantly changing and sometimes contradictory.

Chapter outline

This book is divided into two sections. The first section (Chapters 1–3) provides the empirical and theoretical context required for later discussions. The second section (Chapters 4–7) engages in a thematically organized discussion of the research findings.

Chapter 1 recounts the history of Muslims in Britain, from the early twentieth century through to the present day, with a narrative that is told through the specific lens of Muslim involvement in media and popular culture. In this chapter I show that contemporary Muslim popular culture has emerged from within a deeper historical context that has been long shaped by Orientalist tropes. I argue that despite widespread public antipathy and ignorance – and the often-deprived nature of migrant communities – Muslims have nonetheless managed to exert some degree of cultural agency over the last century or so. This has included not only the maintenance and development of grassroots musical and performance cultures but also an ability to use an awareness of developing communication and media technologies to better represent themselves (e.g. newsreels and television). I organize this history into four phases: early twentieth-century culture; post-war migration and settlement; the politicization of Islam during the 1980s and 1990s; and post-9/11 broadcasting.

Chapter 2 provides an empirical overview of contemporary Muslim media and popular culture and establishes an important contextual foundation for later discussions. I examine the emergence of a faith-based music culture for Muslims in Britain, looking at three key musical genres: contemporary *nasheed*s, syncretic music and hip-hop. I discuss the involvement of Muslims in minority theatre groups and across the wider television industry, before then looking at the rise of Muslim comedy and Islamic television. Finally, I consider the advent of digital media and the way in which this is enabling new forms of streamed television content. In this section, I discuss the dynamics of this evolving cultural landscape and Muslim agency within it. This includes providing vignettes of prominent Muslim creatives and a discussion of the institutional landscape of Muslim popular culture.

Chapter 3 examines theoretical dimensions relating to Muslim popular culture and engages in broader academic debates concerning religion, media and cultural production. This chapter has three principle sections and provides a set of ideas that can be applied more broadly to the analysis conducted within the second half of the book. I discuss the term 'Muslim popular culture' and provide a typology to make sense of this concept: (i) Islamic, (ii) Islamically conscious and (iii) secular-civic. This typology helps to organize and rationalize otherwise diverse forms of Muslim cultural production. I then proceed to apply mediatization theories to Muslim popular culture, looking at the ways in which Islamic institutions and practices are increasingly subject to a 'media logic' (Lynch, 2011). Finally, I explore the term 'Global Urban Muslim', first used by Navid Akhtar, the founder of the streaming service, Alchemiya. This term points towards a Muslim diasporic sphere that is characterized by relative economic privilege and international mobility. I introduce cosmopolitanism as a theory and framework to better understand this group, arguing that cosmopolitan attitudes and tendencies are made manifest within Muslim media and popular culture.

Chapter 4 considers the theme of religious authority and Islamic knowledge. The purpose of this chapter is to show how Muslim popular culture has disrupted established forms of authority and religious debate, as well as continuing to provide new avenues for the communication and mediation of Islam. I discuss the role of the *'ulama'*, suggesting that Muslim popular culture is a competitor to more traditional forms of religious knowledge – with Muslim creatives acting as interpreters of Islam – but that it has also opened up new avenues of influence for Islamic scholars, as well as demanding new competencies amongst the clerical elite. This is particularly evident when the role of popular culture is considered in relation to learning about Islam and the nurturing of Muslim sensibilities. I look at the way in which Muslim popular culture has become involved in such activity – something that was often confined before to the family, mosque and madrasah (religious school) – and the implications that this has for the education of Muslims about their faith. This includes the fierce debate around the religious permissibility of cultural practice – particularly in relation the music – and the way in which Muslim creatives attempt to navigate these challenging internal Islamic debates.

Chapter 5 looks at the role of popular culture in shaping and expressing religious sensibilities and attitudes. The purpose of this chapter is to turn away from religious elites and to instead consider the way in which media and popular culture can manifest ideas of 'everyday' and 'post-confessional' faith (see Ammerman, 2006; Dessing et al., 2016). I argue that Muslim creatives express highly individualized articulations of their faith, alongside a very clear and powerful sense of 'being Muslim'. In this sense, Muslimness is an identity and set of behaviours that are strongly held but only loosely defined. To support this claim, I look at three interrelated areas: the de-exceptionalizing of 'Muslimness' (of making it 'ordinary'), the expression of faith through brand and consumer culture (including Muslim 'influencers') and discourses of 'postmodern spirituality' amongst Muslim creatives.

Chapter 6 explores the professional challenges faced by Muslim creatives in the cultural industries – and the strategies that they adopt to overcome these difficulties. I argue that Muslim creatives face a context of expectation – a 'Muslim trap' – whereby they are simultaneously either excluded, typecast or, at times, included, but only on the proviso that they tell supposedly 'authentic Muslim stories'. I look at several key areas. First, the development of a Muslim cultural economy across the professional and institutional frameworks of the 'Muslim music' and 'Islamic television' industries. Second, Muslim involvement – in terms of both challenges and opportunities – across mainstream broadcasting and cultural production. Third, the demand, by Muslim creatives, for change and transformation across the cultural industries, including recent efforts to nurture and support emerging Muslim talent in film and television. This includes a discussion of various pathways to change that have been identified by Muslim creatives, both in this research and also independently elsewhere, such as through Riz Ahmed's 'Blueprint for Change'.

Chapter 7 discusses various transnational dimensions of Muslim cultural production in Britain. Turning away from the transnational links of ethnic diaspora, I instead focus on networks and imaginaries that are associated with other areas of Muslim transnationalism, most especially the 'Muslim Atlantic' – examining transatlantic links of industry, style, subculture and Islamic schools of thought/activism – and global Islam – with a focus on the notion of 'global Muslim culture' and forms of communal belonging and loyalty to the *umma* and the idea of an Islam of the Global West. As I argue, Muslim creatives have distinctly transnational lives – materially, economically, culturally and socially – and this transnationalism shapes both their artistic output and their emerging significance within Muslim societies and communities, not just in Britain but internationally.

On a final note, I repeat that this book is only a partial view of a diverse, changing and in some ways disjunctured cultural field. I have not been able to discuss every topic or issue in the depth that it often deserves. In not being able to include everything, I have attempted to be participant-led, writing about and discussing topics that emerged organically throughout the fieldwork process. This book is therefore in some respects little more than a starting point and a glimpse into a research field that will continue to change and diversify in the coming decades. In the ongoing effort to salve the political and social ruptures that have scarred Muslim inclusion within British society, Muslim creativity and cultural ingenuity will surely play a leading role.

Part One

Contextualizing Muslim cultural production

1

A cultural history of Muslims in Britain
From colonial newsreels to post-9/11 broadcasting

In this chapter I chart a history of Muslims in Britain, from the early twentieth century through to the present day, with a particular focus on Muslim involvement in broadcast media and popular culture. This chronology stretches from an era of Orientalist depiction, to post-war settlement and the social paradigm of multiculturalism, through to the overt politicization of Muslim identities in the 1990s, and finally the meteoric rise of Muslim media and popular culture over the last two decades. The history of Muslims in Britain has been covered in detail elsewhere (e.g. Ansari, 2004; Gilliat-Ray, 2010; Kalra, 2019; Lewis, 1994; Werbner, 1990), so there is no need here for a comprehensive summary. Rather, I aim to pick out key social and cultural trends in order to show the ways through which Muslim cultural agency has been embedded in wider historical developments. As I argue throughout this book, the recent surge of Muslim cultural activity should be considered the crest of a deeper swell in post-war economic, social and cultural change. I also point towards a perennial thread of cultural agency and media sophistication amongst Muslims in Britain. Or to put it another way, Muslims in Britain were attempting to shape media and cultural narratives long before the current generation of Muslim artists and performers took centre stage.

For much of the twentieth century, Muslim engagement with broadcast media and popular culture has been confined to newsreel footage and television broadcasting, on the one hand, and a grassroots Muslim musical culture, on the other. Because of their long-standing significance, these two forms of culture and media are the primary focus of this chapter (Muslim involvement in film, comedy and other forms of popular culture are more recent and will be discussed in the next chapter, along with Muslim involvement in contemporary broadcasting and music production). In many respects, however, broadcasting and music could not be more different from one another. Broadcasting culture (elite, institutional, national) has helped to shape perceptions of Muslims in Britain for a national audience, often providing little space for Muslim self-representation, while grassroots music cultures (accessible, local, diasporic) have enabled Muslims to carve out an artistic niche that has flourished over the decades. These two spaces are nonetheless both central in having shaped the cultural realities, representations and everyday experiences of Muslims in Britain over the course of the last century. Each in their own way, they highlight the dialectical struggle between dominant cultural tropes in Britain – concerning narratives of 'Empire' and 'Britishness' – and the attempt by Muslims to varyingly find a place within these discourses, to actively resist them or to otherwise find independent spaces for cultural self-expression.

The charting of a Muslim cultural history in Britain cannot really be conceived of without some reference to the symbiotic and formative relationship between 'British national culture' and the Orientalized 'Other'. As I allude to throughout, this relationship is long-standing, not just in the colonial period but also through to the present day. Writing about this link, with reference to the British Empire, Edward Said argued:

> the processes of imperialism occurred beyond the level of economic laws and political decisions, and – by predisposition, by the authority of recognizable cultural formations, by continuing consolidation within education, literature, and the visual and musical arts – were manifested at another very significant level, that of the national culture, which we tend to sanitize as a realm of unchanging intellectual monuments, free from worldly affiliations. (Said, 1994: 12)

Through this reading, Said deconstructs supposedly transcendental forms of national culture – from Shakespeare and Defoe to Austen and Kipling – and locates them very directly within the brute colonial machinery of empire. His argument is simple enough. That this rich period of literature was built upon and interwoven with the privileged positionality of these great writers, residing at the lofty summits of 'refined' British culture; and that this literature furthermore possesses fundamental assumptions concerning rulers and the ruled, the metropolis and the province, the 'cosmopolitan European' and the 'Oriental Other' – assumptions that accordingly helped to justify imperial enterprise and domination. As Said argues, these cultural epistemologies are not simply unfortunate historical detritus but remain very much alive in the cultural and media framing of Muslims today, particularly those centred upon the contemporary language of 'terrorism' and 'fundamentalism', which 'signify moral power and approval for whoever uses them, moral defensiveness and criminalization for whomever they designate' (Said, 1994: 375).

The real insight that can be derived from Said's thesis is not so much an analysis of the power imbalance, or the cultural violence, at the heart of imperial expansion (which is unquestionable) but the active and formative relationship, whereby British/European and non-Western self-understandings – on both sides – continue to be generated through this distorted hall of mirrors, with one breathing life and meaning into the other. The postcolonial era remains shaped by this dynamic, both culturally and politically. Salman Rushdie wrote – foreshadowing Gayatri Spivak (1988) – that 'the Empire writes back to the Centre' (see Ashcroft, Griffiths and Tiffin, 2002) and in doing so destabilizes colonial mythologies. Or, as we might now consider it, following sustained migration from the far-flung 'provinces' to the British 'metropolis', the 'Other' now writes from *within* and reformulates the centre. As Salman Sayyid argues, there has been a de-centring of the West, against which and within which these new narratives have emerged (Sayyid, 1997), whereby 'Western' and 'non-Western' – or 'British' and 'Asian' – are not so much fused together, as they are now 'a confusion of the possibility of both terms' (Sayyid, 2005: 7).

This chapter is a starting point, then, tracing the cultural history of Muslims, from the highpoint of the British Empire to the present day, with an emphasis on the continuing longevity of Orientalist framing through culture – and Muslim responses to this framing. I begin by considering the representation and the limited, although distinctly identifiable, cultural agency of Muslims in Britain during the first half of the twentieth century. This was primarily manifested for mass audiences through newsreel footage. I then progress to examine the rise of documentary television in the 1970s and 1980s, which, in relation to Muslims in Britain, was governed by paradigms of multiculturalism and the 'anthropological gaze', along with attempts by Muslims to preserve and replicate 'authentic' diasporic musical traditions. This is followed by a discussion of the overt and public politicization of visible Muslim identities in the 1990s – both by broadcasters and by Muslims in Britain themselves – followed by a consideration of post-9/11 broadcasting and the renewed hitching together of Islam with discourses of 'fundamentalism' and 'terrorism'. As I argue, this historical narrative is necessary to understand the context from within which Muslim creatives are still required to work. To draw a connecting line between, for example, Yemeni sailors engaged in a sophisticated performance, for the grainy newsreel footage of the 1930s, and – almost a century later – Muslim creatives seeking to disrupt and 'speak back' to an otherwise exclusionary and constraining national culture. Media and cultural technologies may have changed dramatically in this time, but, unfortunately, cultural and national imaginaries are perhaps more deeply rooted.

1900s–1945: Muslim pioneers in the age of empire

Muslims have visited Britain in small numbers since the height of the Ottoman Empire, in the sixteenth and seventeenth centuries (Matar, 1998), but it was during the late Victorian period that more substantial numbers of Muslims travelled to the UK. While this migration was diverse, from servants and students to envoys and teachers, it was for the most part propelled by the engines of empire, built on coal and maritime trade. This meant that by the early part of the twentieth century there were substantial numbers of non-British sailors residing in ports across the UK, many of whom had signed on to trading ships in places such as Aden, Calcutta, Bombay and Singapore. Known as *lascars*, these sailors were primarily drawn from Yemen, Somaliland, India and Malaya. While religiously diverse, including Hindus, Sikhs and Christians from India, a larger number of these sailors were Muslim. They were treated brutally aboard ship, where they worked as firemen, donkeymen and deckhands – arduous but relatively well-paid jobs compared to their prospects back home. By 1914, on the eve of the First World War, the number of 'foreign' seamen employed on British merchant navy ships had risen to more than 30,000 (Ansari, 2004).

These sailors formed transitory communities in London and large port cities such as Liverpool, Cardiff, Aberdeen and South Shields. They tended to stay in temporary accommodation during the time that they were onshore, so-called Arab boarding houses, but over time many of them married local women and settled more permanently in Britain. These more settled communities tended to be formed in port enclaves, which were not only diverse but also characterized by distinct ethnic communities living alongside one another. Many of these sailors were religiously observant and as far as possible they maintained Islamic practices, including communal prayer, halal slaughter and Islamic funeral rites (Lawless, 1995). During the interwar period new and additional Muslim communities began to be formed by South Asian migrants from rural backgrounds, working as peddlers, traders and textile workers, in cities such as London and Manchester (Ansari, 2004). A decline in maritime employment during the 1930s, alongside the growth of manufacturing, somewhat encouraged the redistribution of former sailors from port cities to the industrial heartlands of the Midlands and the North of England (Gilliat-Ray, 2010).

Alongside these working-class Muslim communities there was another more privileged and often less racialized narrative concerning Islam in Britain during the early part of the twentieth century. This was the development of notable convert and aristocratic Muslim communities. After remarkable archival research in recent years (Geaves, 2010; Gilham, 2020), we now know more about the most famous of these communities, formed by Abdullah Quilliam, in Liverpool, during the late nineteenth century. This community received little national recognition or popular media coverage at the time. Instead, more prominent in the public consciousness were two London-based communities, in Woking and Southfields. These were linked to a particular set of visiting Muslim dignitaries and upper-class English Orientalists. The first, in Woking, was centred around the Shah Jahan Mosque, which had been constructed in 1889 as a place of worship for students studying at the nearby Oriental Institute. The second, in Southfields, was linked to the wealthy and internationally mobile Ahmadiyya movement, and publicly backed by the eccentric British convert, Khalid Sheldrake, the founder of the Western Islamic Association. These communities were small and would normally constitute obscure historical footnotes, but the privileged class backgrounds of those involved ensured that they were at the forefront of projecting the public face of Muslims in Britain to a wider public.

This public visibility can be found most clearly amongst the silent newsreel clips that were popular from the early part of the century. Shown either in cinemas before a feature film or in dedicated theatres, newsreels were a form of mass media and documentary entertainment that reached millions across the UK. In many respects they were a precursor to television broadcasting (McLane, 2013). There are a number of newsreel clips that feature Muslims in Britain – dozens altogether, up until the 1960s, when newsreels became obsolete – suggesting that there was a steady, albeit modest, exposure of Islam in Britain to the public. Some early examples include (all can be accessed through the British Film Institute archives): *Woking – The Feast of Sacrifice* (Pathé, 1919), showing Muslims in prayer during Eid al-Adha; *Islam in London* (Topical Budget, 1926), showing the inauguration of Fazl Mosque in Southfields; and *An Oriental Atmosphere* (Topical Budget, 1928), again depicting Eid celebrations at Shah Jahan Mosque in Woking. For the most part these recordings focus on turbaned dignitaries from India, a juxtaposition of oriental exoticness against the leafy backdrop of London, along with footage of men knelt in prayer as their Muslim families (accompanying them from India) sit watching from behind, and a remarkable clip of a *muezzin* (official who leads the call to prayer) calling the *adhan* (call to prayer) from the minaret of Fazl Mosque. Muslims in London were the sole focus of these early newsreels, particularly at Woking Mosque, whereby there was a particular focus on aristocratic converts, visiting dignitaries and wealthy students.

These newsreel clips were selective in focus, privileging London-based Muslim elites, and they rarely featured the diverse, working-class Muslim communities that were located in manufacturing and port cities across the UK. It is difficult now to explore that hidden cultural history – almost all of these early Muslim migrants either died long ago or have since left Britain – but an oral history account of Yemenis in Cardiff suggests that they were close-knit communities, with a strong cultural distinctiveness (Mellor and Gilliat-Ray, 2015). There is evidence, for example, that early Yemeni and Somali sailors performed *dhikr* (ritual remembrance/recitation), and it is also likely that they brought with them diverse musical traditions from across Africa and the Arabian Peninsula (Lawless, 1997). Little of this has been recorded or preserved for posterity.

A rare exception to this otherwise limited portrayal of Muslims can be found in newsreel footage of an Eid procession in South Shields. Entitled *South Shields* (Pathé, 1937), the newsreel shows a procession of Yemeni men, accompanied by children, marching through the street, turbaned and robed, holding aloft banners inscribed with Arabic, before queuing to enter their mosque. A smaller procession of women, heads covered in fluttering white cloths, follow behind. These women appear to be of European heritage and are presumably the English spouses of the Yemeni sailors participating in the procession (Lawless, 1995). The footage of the march takes place from multiple angles, suggesting some degree of coordination and staging. Interestingly, the children cannot resist craning their necks as they walk past, to stare at the camera, while the adults remain with their gaze afront, marching in a resolutely 'natural' pose.

Another exceptional newsreel film, *Muslim Protest March in London* (Reuters, 1938), captures a march against H. G. Wells's *A Short History of the World* (this was a protest against references made in the book to the Prophet Muhammad, which were considered by some Muslims to be offensive). The march was organized by the newly formed Jamiat-ul-Muslimin, an organization comprised of South Asian working-class lascars and manual workers, who were campaigning for improved rights and for the accommodation of specifically

Muslim needs in Britain (Visram, 2002). The newsreel is fascinating because it shows these protesters arraying themselves before the camera with careful decorum, poised in dramatic suspense, aware of the need to present a favourable image to the camera. Given the staged and somewhat artificial nature of the march, it is also possible that the protesters contacted Reuters in advance, or somehow publicized the march, in order for organized filming to take place. This was therefore not just a protest, but it was also the sophisticated enactment of a media event, by working-class Muslims, for a mass media audience. Or put another way, it suggests a strategic understanding amongst Muslims in Britain of the need to utilize 'modern' methods of communication and media performance, in order to better represent themselves to a viewing public.

Footage of this kind was for the most part rare during the interwar period. Muslims in Britain were typically overlooked by the popular media and the general public. While the occasional newsreel did contain footage of celebrations, festivals and events at Woking Mosque, which acted as the public face of Islam in Britain until the 1960s, media producers and broadcasters instead preferred to portray Muslims as a people that existed far beyond the shores of the British Isles: as an exotic and potentially threatening dimension of empire and as something to be managed through the application of diplomatic, political and military power. This was largely because media producers of the time, most particularly the BBC, were in part an extension of colonial power. BBC officials came from the same social background and belonged to the same 'clubbable scene' as officials in the civil service and politics (Potter, 2012). They therefore carried with them an identical set of values and assumptions. Newsreels captured scenes of the imperial expanse, vividly connecting those at home to the adventure and danger of the far-flung provinces, with stunning visual scenes that ordinary Britons could never have hoped to witness before the advent of moving pictures. Typical newsreels included, for example, *Pilgrimage to Mecca* (Pathé, 1946), *Aga Khan's Platinum Jubilee* (Pathé, 1954) and *Egypt: Ramadan Fast Begins* (Reuters, 1956). This footage of Muslims focused on unfamiliar but visually evocative religious practices, or on political issues, with massed and sometimes agitated crowds, or exotic dignitaries and political-religious leaders, from India and Malaysia through to Egypt. A regular part of newsreel features in cinemas and theatres across the interwar and early post-war decades, this propaganda footage reinforced the assumption that Muslims were a subject people – tolerantly overseen by a benevolent British Empire – and therefore an inseparable part of the political and cultural edifice of colonial Britain.

1945–1980s: Settlement, survival and the anthropological gaze

Following the end of the Second World War, there were several important periods of migration into the UK. Ansari divides this into two phases, from 1945 to the early 1970s and from 1973 onwards (Ansari, 2004). The first phase, from 1945, was characterized by unskilled migration from Commonwealth countries, largely as a means to plug a labour shortage in Britain, but also resulting from so-called 'push' factors in the various countries of origin. This crucial phase attracted significant numbers of migrants, mostly young men, from both the Caribbean (known as the 'Windrush Generation') and South Asia (especially from Pakistan). While many of these migrants from South Asia were Muslim, their immediate experiences were not defined by religion, but rather by difficult working conditions, poor accommodation and widespread racial discrimination (Shaw, 2014). It was only in response to growing restrictions in the early 1960s that these South Asian migrants brought over their families to create permanent, settled communities, with a resulting emphasis on the communal aspects of ethnically conceived religion. The second phase, from the early 1970s, was typically a result of economic and political persecution, in countries such as Iraq, Iran, Uganda and Somalia. This created an influx of refugees, many of whom fled to Britain, further diversifying and adding to the already significant Muslim population in the UK.

For the largely low-skilled South Asian Muslim communities, this generation was defined and shaped not only by the immediate struggles of migration and settlement but also by diasporic attachments to the cultural and political imaginations of a distant homeland (Anwar, 1979). These new communities faced the task of providing for their families and children, not just at a basic economic level but also in terms of maintaining ethnic and religious traditions. This initiated a focus on the 'establishment of mosques, schools and other facilities in Britain that might help to transmit religious and cultural traditions to the next generation' (Gilliat-Ray, 2010: 49). While necessary at a basic functional level, relating to the requirements of religious practice, it was also in many respects a pragmatic and conservative approach, marked by a desire to maintain ethnic and cultural distinctiveness in a hostile environment. Yet this was not so much an unreflective reproduction of tradition but rather an attempt to reimagine and relocate this heritage in the new context of Britain – a process of adaptation that Seán McLoughlin has described as 're-traditionalisation'. According to McLoughlin, it is 'the solidarities resulting from re-traditionalisation that help groups to advance their own interests in competition with others in plural societies. In many liberal democracies, for example, such "fictions of unity" have been useful in binding migrants and diasporas together' (McLoughlin, 2010: 566).

This process was therefore more than just a form of 'strategic essentialism' (Spivak, 2013) – which suggests an outward show of unity for the purpose of claims-making – but rather it was an attempt to crystalize specific forms of South Asian Islam as a means to survive through internal group cohesion. These early communities lacked the economic, social and cultural resources to do anything more than survive in the hostile environment of 1960s and 1970s Britain. The emphasis was therefore usually on closed and inward traditions, rather than the open and outward possibilities of cultural and religious experimentation. This took the form of a diasporic language culture and the establishment of mosques and other community institutions based on a bounded ethnic-exclusiveness. Popular and artistic culture also tended to gravitate towards South Asia – from the film culture of Bollywood (Werbner, 2006) to the musical performances of Qawwali and Bhangra (Um, 2012). Yet rather than accusing this generation of 'backwardness' or 'conservatism' – they were after all migrant *pioneers* – it should be acknowledged that this was an effective and understandable strategy, which enabled tightly knit, working-class South Asian communities to develop the foundations necessary for future prosperity.

To further add to these class-based dimensions, it should also be noted that smaller Muslim communities, formed in the 1970s by often middle-class refugees, have followed a different path. These communities, such as those South Asians forced to flee from Uganda in 1972, brought with them sufficient social and cultural capital to quickly propel themselves into a more advantaged position in the UK. They were 'far more cosmopolitan in outlook than the Muslims of the South Asian subcontinent, and they already had a knowledge of English' (Ally, 1979: 3). These small migrant communities therefore soon became economically successful and more disproportionately represented in Muslim leadership roles – a pattern that has held somewhat true ever since (Ansari, 2004). The small indigenous convert community of the 1960s and 1970s had a similar and privileged middle-class position within the UK, although their contact with other Muslim communities tended to be quite minimal during these decades.

While post-war mass migration had dramatically reshaped Britain, it was not until the 1970s that this was reflected in the cultural consciousness of the nation at large. With regard to Muslims, there were two important cultural trends during the 1970s and 1980s. First, broadcasters began to reflect a growing awareness of 'multicultural Britain' through the depiction of minority communities in documentary television. Muslims in Britain were sometimes a part of this broadcast content, although 'race' was usually emphasized rather than 'faith'. Second, the size and permanence of Muslim communities in the UK (communities which now included large numbers of women and children) meant that Muslim cultural activity and agency became more widespread and pronounced. While Muslims were still excluded from the mainstream echelons of national culture and broadcast media, there were grassroots Muslim musical cultures that began to flourish in the otherwise hostile context of 'multicultural Britain'.

Newsreels lost their popularity in the 1960s, becoming rapidly replaced by broadcast television as the principal form of visual news and entertainment media. Stringent guidelines for television broadcasting in Britain ensured that there was a strong public service element to programming. This was reflected in the (admittedly sparse) broadcast media coverage of Muslims in Britain, which tended to gravitate towards television documentary in the 1970s. There were no popular entertainment broadcasting representations of Muslims during this time. Muslims were instead always an object of factual and documentary record, rather than subjects of dramatic representation, or complex characters with feelings and agencies of their own. An early example of documentary television looking at Muslims in Britain is the Thames Television production, *A Mosque in the Park* (1973), which was produced and narrated by Yavar Abbas, a Shi'i Muslim from South Asia, known primarily for his films looking at life in modern India, as well as his sideline in the recitation of Urdu poetry. In this television documentary, Abbas explores the lives of four South Asian families in London and Manchester. A humane and sympathetic production, it captures the ways in which migrant families strive to maintain cultural and religious distinctiveness, while also claiming, through the narration of Abbas, that 'the swinging London of the seventies is indifferent to, almost at home with, the Asian phenomenon in its midst' (Thames Television, 1973) (given the pervasive discrimination of the time this is perhaps debatable). Another example, later in this period, was *Schools for Moslems* (London Weekend Television, 1980), for the ITV religious affairs programme, *Creedo*, which examined the ways in which different schools were able to cater for a variety of faith backgrounds. Despite a supposed wider remit, the programme maintains a steady focus on the 'problem' of Muslim pupils. Filmed at the *Darul Uloom* (Islamic seminary) in Bury and at a multi-ethnic state school in East London, the film contrasts the difficulties faced by Muslim pupils (such as racist bullying, language difficulties, food, apparel and low educational attainment) with the success of an 'integrated' Jewish faith school.

These types of television documentary were notable for the way in which they subjected Muslims to an anthropological gaze. There was a desire to capture Muslim subjects in an 'authentic' state – to focus on 'backward' cultural and religious difference against the otherwise mundane yet 'modern' backdrop of everyday British life. The documentaries are clearly filmed and stylized to capture/create this distinctiveness, with Muslim participants performing in a state of feigned naturalness. These documentaries also reflected the developing agenda of multicultural Britain. This was typically framed as a debate concerned with the cultural and religious accommodation of minorities, particularly in the state sector. More importantly, however, documentary television provided an avenue for Muslims to communicate with a wider non-Muslim public. These programmes included Muslim participants speaking at length in their own words, although, again, these interviews would often be used by the programme producers to reproduce notions of anthropological strangeness and difference. This was most often done through framing shots and backdrops that placed a greater emphasis on activities or features that would be unusual, dated or even bizarre to most viewers, such as the practice of eating without utensils while seated on the floor (one can only speculate as to the reaction of ITV viewers to this on a Sunday evening in the early 1980s).

While broadcasting culture therefore either excluded or 'othered' Muslims during the decades following post-war migration, beneath the dominating façade of mass media there were vibrant forms of grassroots Muslim cultural production that took place in homes, communities and towns across the UK. This cultural activity was mostly in the form of South Asian musical traditions that had been brought to Britain as part of the migration process – and were part of the 'retraditionalisation' referred to by McLoughlin (2010) – although later, during the 1980s, minority theatre groups also began to develop. Notable musical practices included Qawwali, an intense form of celebratory Sufi music that is largely rooted in the Pakistani diaspora (Baily and Collyer, 2006); Bhangra, a non-religious music from the Punjab region (Roy, 2017); and *na'at*, a type of performance poetry that is often linked to Sufi remembrance of the Prophet Muhammad and South Asian *pir*s (spiritual guides). Migratory musical traditions could sometimes be hyperlocal, as with the small Khalifa community, from Gujarat, numbering only between 5,000 and 6,000 in the UK, but with a carefully preserved musical heritage (Baily, 2006). These musical histories were undeniably 'imported' and because of this they reflected the distinct experiences and imaginaries of migratory communities at that time. Such music was rarely, if ever, performed in English, while also in terms of content, meaning and style it replicated South Asian musical culture as a means to remember and preserve a migrant past. Music was therefore often the sonic manifestation of Anwar's 'myth of return' (Anwar, 1979) – that is, physically located in Britain but culturally and emotionally rooted in an ethnic homeland.

As these South Asian migratory communities became more settled in the 1960s and 1970s, there was a parallel though entirely independent and disconnected musical/spiritual movement taking place amongst a group of white countercultural folk musicians in the UK. Inspired by the spiritual yearning of the 1960s – and the rejection of a new brash consumer culture – artists and musicians began to look for a spiritual home beyond the confines of Christian Britain. While some looked towards the Vedic and Buddhist traditions of India, others were instead drawn to North African Sufism and the teachings of Islam. Prominent amongst these were the globally successful musicians Cat Stevens and Richard Thompson, in addition to the less well-known Ian Whiteman and Danny Thompson (from the folk-rock band Pentangle). These musicians converted to Islam and began to reflect their new religious sensibilities in their lives, music and art. Richard Thompson produced a trio of albums with his wife, Linda Thompson, in the early 1970s – albums that were laden with spiritual and Islamic tropes – before leaving the music business and moving to a Sufi convert community in Norwich. He later resumed a musical career, although one devoid of any reference to Islam. Meanwhile, Cat Stevens (known as Yusuf Islam since his conversion) rejected music for a time, in the late 1970s and 1980s, something that he now ascribes to poor Islamic scholastic advice, before beginning to perform *nasheed*s in the 1990s, and then newly written folk-rock songs in subsequent decades, with an underlying Islamic-spiritual-religious ethos. Ian Whiteman has progressed from music to become an accomplished visual designer, drawing on traditional Islamic art and typographies, while Danny Thompson has continued working as a successful session musician alongside his attempt to educate non-Muslims about Islam, such as in the 1999 BBC documentary, *Face of Islam* (BBC, 1999). These individuals are clearly all exceptional rather than typical – that is, they are successful public figures, ethnically privileged and they carry none of the burdens of migration – so their experience, while interesting, is for the most part uncharacteristic when set against the larger majority of ethnic minority Muslims in the UK. Yet, in their own way, they helped to share Islam with a wider British public and are undeniably part of the rich tapestry of Muslim media and popular culture in the UK.

1980s and 1990s: The politicization of Muslim identities

Towards the end of the 1980s, and during the 1990s, increasingly assertive Muslim communities in Britain, across a range of different Muslim traditions and schools of thought, began to push for greater recognition and an acknowledgement of their religious rights. This occurred alongside the rising visibility of Islam as an overt dimension of international politics, with a series of events that stretched from the Iranian Revolution, through to the Gulf War, and so-called Islamist militancy in the 1990s. These factors combined to give a newly emphasized political edge to Muslim identities in the public sphere – something that was replicated in both the growing cultural output of Muslims themselves and in the portrayal of Islam through wider broadcasting media. Of course, Islam had long been a dimension of colonial and postcolonial politics, but these decades brought a new impetus with the emergence of migrant identities that were visibly *Muslim* for the first time in the public sphere.

It was in particular the controversy over the publication of *The Satanic Verses* in 1989, by novelist Salman Rushdie, which propelled Muslim identities and mobilization into the political mainstream of British public life. Prior to the events surrounding the publication of *The Satanic Verses* there was little official recognition that 'Muslim' communities – as opposed to 'South Asian' – were in need of public recognition and political representation in the UK. The success of the race relations industry – that is, the way in which British political and educational institutions placed an emphasis on meeting the needs of ethnic minority communities in the UK – had almost paradoxically left institutional discourse blind to the importance of self-defined religious identities amongst the minority communities of Britain. Writing at the time, Jørgen Nielsen remarked:

> [There is] a long-standing dissatisfaction among members of the Muslim community leadership, who have felt that the structures of White British society are, at best, blind to the existence of a Muslim community in this country or, at worst, ignoring it by insisting on what are, from a Muslim point of view, divisive concepts of ethnicity or assimilationist concepts of race. Thus, it is felt, Muslims are viewed either as 'Pakistani' or 'Black', both of which contradict the Muslim ideal of one united Muslim community, the *umma*. (Nielsen, 1987: 384)

Nielsen captures here two important trends that were growing in the 1980s and subsequently ascendant in Muslim debates during the 1990s: an insistence on the incorporation of Muslim identities into British public life and the attachment by many (often through organizations and political groups) to a broader, if often patchworked, global Muslim *umma*. These both of course gave religious identity a primacy over other forms of mobilization and organization, with resulting implications for the development of Muslim institutions and networks. The Rushdie Affair, as it quickly became known, and the Gulf War in the early 1990s simply accelerated this latent tendency.

First, Muslim activists and public figures in the 1990s claimed that Muslim interests were overlooked or dismissed in favour of a multiculturalism based on race and ethnicity. The publication of *The Satanic Verses* highlighted two connected issues, both linked to what Khadijah Elshayyal has described as an 'equality gap' (2018). These were complaints concerning the privileges given to the Church of England and Christianity (e.g. protection through blasphemy laws) and the lack of anti-discrimination legislation for religious minorities other than Sikhs and Jews. Sparked by the Rushdie Affair, these issues gave rise to organized demands for the representation of Muslims in the public sphere, as well as an embedding of the idea of 'British Muslim' identity into political and social discourse. The legacy and impact of this era continues today through Muslim institutions, such as the Muslim Council of Britain, many of which were founded as a direct result of these activities.

Second, the emergence of a Muslim identity politics in the 1980s and 1990s was not confined to debates around governance and civic inclusion in Britain, but rather it extended to broader religious and political sensibilities within the context of Muslims and postcolonial international affairs. For example, Pnina Werbner provides a detailed ethnographic account of the way in which Pakistani Muslims in Manchester during this period were constructing a 'powerful, ideologically grounded allegory of their predicament as an enclaved Muslim community in the West, while simultaneously asserting their membership in a global diaspora' (Werbner, 2002: 153). This was the creative and negotiated combination of Pakistani and Muslim diasporic imaginations within the public space of everyday life in Manchester. In contrast, Hamid shows how a younger generation of Muslim activists were turning away from ethnic diasporic attachments to fashion new Muslim identities:

> the impact of international political crisis events in the 1990s, such as the first Gulf War and conflicts in Bosnia and Chechnya, became critical landmarks that had traumatic effects upon many young Muslims, causing them to ask why it was happening and why most non-Muslims did not seem to care . . . Islamic revitalization groups provided opportunities to express what French scholar Olivier Roy called a globalised 'deterritorialised' Islamic identity, that is to

say a decultured, universal Islam which expressed varieties of a born-again religiosity that transcended ethnicity, culture and space. (Hamid, 2016: 8–9)

Transnational Islamic revival movements and Islamist groups – many of which had been developing quietly throughout the 1980s – very quickly became attractive in the 1990s, mostly to a generation of young Muslims seeking to articulate internationalist Muslim concerns. While many of these groups actively sought to develop varying forms of British Muslim identity, they nonetheless often drew their impetus from international thinkers and organizations in the wider Muslim ecumene – ranging from individuals such as Abul A'la Mawdudi (b. 1903/d. 1979) and Khurram Murad (b. 1932/d. 1996) to political organizations such as the Muslim Brotherhood and Hizb ut-Tahrir.

These two trends – the recognition of British Muslims on the national stage and the growing relevance of transnational political Islam – were reflected in the broadcasting coverage of Muslims in Britain. This took place alongside a number of changes to the television market: the growth of satellite television, increasing competition between terrestrial broadcasters and a weakening of public service requirements. These changes inevitably forced documentary television – which in the 1990s was still the primary way through which Muslims featured on the small screen – to compete more directly with entertainment programming. All these factors combined to encourage a more sensationalist approach when it came to the broadcasting coverage of Muslims in Britain. Indeed, the number of documentaries about Islam exploded in the 1990s and has continued to remain buoyant ever since.

Typical documentary productions included *Voting for the Veil* (BBC, 1991), *Islam's Militant Tendency* (BBC, 1995) and *Islam Year Zero* (BBC, 1996). These television documentaries were produced for evening news programmes and focused on themes relating to security and rising fundamentalism. As Christopher Flood et al. (2012) argue, this coverage was overwhelmingly part of a wider turn in European discourse towards the securitization of Islam – that is, whereby Muslims are perceived to be a security threat to Western civilization, requiring extraordinary political, policing and legal responses. Of course, there were television productions that continued in an anthropological, rather than overtly political, documentary style, some of which focused on and gave voice to Muslims in Britain, including *The Spirit of Islam* (BBC, 1995) and *Rapping for Islam* (Roger Bolton Productions, 1997). But productions of this kind were vastly outweighed by the politicization and securitization of Islam in the public sphere. This discourse, amplified by Samuel Huntington's 'Clash of Civilizations' thesis

(1993), was in many respects nothing more than a variation of old Orientalist tropes concerning the violence and barbarism of Islam (e.g. as with Bernard Lewis's 'The Roots of Muslim Rage', 1990). In broadcasting terms, it continued a trend whereby mass media reproduced images and narratives about Muslims, rather than providing the space or resources necessary for Muslims to tell their own stories.

During this time, music continued to be an accessible and popular form of cultural activity for Muslims in the UK. It was perhaps the only cultural public space where Muslims could actually express their religious sensibilities in any meaningful way. Much of this activity in the 1990s was characterized by a grassroots tradition of *nasheed*s, *na'at*s (poetry in praise of the Prophet Muhammad) and other musical/poetic religious performances. This was often a mosque-based, paraliturgical tradition, more worship and ritual than entertainment, and so was part of a soundscape that encompassed the art of Qur'anic recitation and the *adhan*. It was this tradition that helped maintain a strong link between sound performance and the practice of Islam – something that was partly threatened by the rising tide of an austere, anti-music, Salafi-oriented Islam in the early 1990s (Hamid, 2016). Regardless, this form of paraliturgical performance continued to develop over the course of the decade and provided a grassroots foundation for the more recent development of a commercial *nasheed* industry (see the next chapter).

Yet music and performance culture also began to reflect the growing divisions and forms of consciousness that existed amongst and between minority ethnic communities. The growth of a 'Black Arts' scene in Britain – and a parallel anti-racism movement – helped to bring minority theatre, writing and music to a wider audience. Again, in line with the priorities of a multicultural agenda, these cultural movements had a tendency to overlook faith and to create essentialized racial identities. As I have already argued, there was a growing demand amongst Muslims for a recognition of their religious identities, rather than an assumption that they should be defined as Asian or Black. Music and performance reflected this long-standing concern, with many South Asian and Arab performers finding themselves wrapped up by anti-racism campaigners into an emergent 'Black music scene' (Kalra et al., 1996). The spiritual and religious aspects of performances, as with Qawwali, were often overlooked outside of the relatively private spaces of Muslim worship and devotion.

Alongside this, there was a small amount of Muslim musical experimentation at the edges – inspired by the cultural possibilities of 'Cool Britannia' (and partly as a rebuke to this otherwise politically diluted cultural age). This most notably included Aki Nawaz's Bradford-based band, Fun-Da-Mental. Combining a range of musical styles – including Qawwali, metal, rock and rap – Fun-Da-Mental were a politically aggressive band that challenged pervasive racial and economic inequalities in postcolonial Britain. While Fun-Da-Mental were in many respects self-consciously 'Islamic' (Swedenburg, 2001), with lyrics that referenced the Qur'an, they can also be understood as part of a broad liberatory movement that made use of Islamic motifs. Fund-Da-Mental were to some extent drawing on a cultural and political imaginary that had emerged vibrantly through postcolonial discourses that stretched from the oratory of Malcolm X through to the symbol-rich imagery of the Palestinian conflict. While Fun-Da-Mental had some impact on liberal, middle-class Muslims in the UK, they are better understood as part of an alternative multicultural music scene, rather than as pioneers in the development of a new and distinctively Muslim music culture in Britain. Fun-Da-mental – who released their most recent album in 2015 – were therefore a distinctive, if atypical, part of the cultural story of Muslims in Britain. Like Yusuf Islam, they were in many respects exceptional, closer to the mainstream music industry, and not particularly associated with the new wave of Muslim cultural production that emerged in the early 2000s. Nor were they mentioned by participants in this research or made particularly visible by contemporary Muslim media outlets (with the exception of the now-defunct *Q-News*, a magazine aimed at middle-class Muslims, which ceased publication in 2011). For this reason, they are mentioned here but do not feature in later discussions.

Broadcasting Islam in post-9/11 Britain

While the politics of Islam – and a Muslim identity politics – had been a rising theme of cultural production and broadcast media throughout the 1990s, it was the post-9/11 era that saw the rapid shift to a concern in popular culture with 'Islamic terrorism'. Aside from those concerned with news media, there have been no comprehensive or detailed studies looking at the representation of Muslims in television programming – and this despite the utter pervasiveness of Muslim stereotypes in popular culture. Yet even a cursory glance at British television since 2001 shows the predominance of a securitization discourse. There are too many to mention, but these programmes have ranged from the spy drama, *Spooks* (BBC, 2002–11), through to the more recent political thriller, *Bodyguard* (BBC, 2018). In this genre of production, Islamic terrorist tropes are so pervasive as to be almost unremarkable, but they do tend for the most part to be governed, as William Youmans argues (2019), by a 'good Muslim' and 'bad Muslim' dichotomy. This portrays Muslim characters as one-dimensional caricatures, whereby they are required to take a position either for or against an equally simplistic form of 'Islamic extremism', with little emotional or dramatic depth beyond this equation. As Evelyn Alsultany suggests, these polar positions are usually brought together in juxtaposition, with 'positive' representations of Muslims used in television dramas to 'offset the stereotype of the Arab/Muslim terrorist' (Alsultany, 2012: 14). There have been more sympathetic and/or complex attempts to portray Muslim characters, as with Peter Kominsky's drama *Britz* (Channel 4, 2007), featuring Riz Ahmed, which examines the parallel fortunes of a British Muslim brother and sister, who respectively join MI5 and a terrorist cell before facing off against one another in a climactic suicide bombing scene. While the two-part series is in some respects nuanced – criticizing the moral failures of the British government and wider societal Islamophobic attitudes, as well as those enacting terrorism under the badge of religion – the Muslim characters are nonetheless still defined by the way in which their Muslimness overrides all other aspects of their character.

Beyond television drama, there have been other attempts in Britain to portray Muslims on the small screen, mostly through factual and fly-on-the-wall documentaries. While many of these have been shaped by a discourse of securitization, such as *The Path to 9/11* (2006), a docudrama which features Muslim participants, but only in relation to their terrorist activities, there has also been a gradual turn over the last decade towards the idea of uncovering 'authentic' Muslim lifestyles in Britain. Ruth Deller (2012) has suggested that this form of documentary television can be understood through the metaphor of 'a journey' – that is, as a programme that transports the viewer through the unfamiliar and unknown. Since the early 2000s, in relation to Muslims, there have been a steady stream of these 'journeying' documentaries on television in the UK. Examples include those focusing on political themes, such as *Who Speaks for Muslims?* (Channel 4, 2006) and *What Muslims Want* (Channel 4, 2006) – documentaries that explored the 'real' views of Muslims in Britain – through to social and cultural documentaries, such as *Great British Islam* (BBC, 2005), which examines the challenges faced by three Muslim converts, and *Gay Muslims* (Channel 4, 2006), looking at the pressures that homosexual Muslims face from their 'own community'. The thread that most often connects these documentaries is the way in which Muslims are exceptionalized, either through the misconstrual of everyday narratives and views or through the decision to focus on valid but unrepresentative cases. A balanced and complex representation of Muslims in Britain has usually been lacking – as has the actual involvement of Muslims in creating television content.

A new wave of documentary television has started to partially address some of these shortcomings. This is often pitched as programming that has been commissioned to shatter stereotypes, by including more 'authentic' footage of 'real' Muslims, filmed from a fly-on-the-wall perspective. Crucially, these programmes provide greater agency and voice to Muslim participants through the intimacy provided by a longform documentary format. A notable example of this is *Extremely British Muslims* (Channel 4, 2017), a three-part series which filmed Muslims in Birmingham over the course of a year, examining in turn the issues of Muslim dating, masculinity and religious practice. This is a sympathetic documentary that provides Muslim participants with the space to represent themselves and their own stories over an extended period, with an attempt to capture the diversity of Muslims in Britain for a wider audience. However, despite the partial self-representation and agency of Muslim participants, the series is still framed by the conceptualization and editing of the producers, whereby Muslims are exceptionalized and homogenized for a 'journeying' non-Muslim audience.

This overview of post-9/11 broadcasting is far from comprehensive – such an endeavour would take a book-length project itself – but it does capture the prevalence of certain themes that have dominated the cultural environment within which a current generation of Muslim creatives have come of age. Writing in 2012, Peter Morey and Amina Yaqin's assessment of television portrayals of Muslims remains valid a decade later:

> What all these shows have in common is that 'Muslimness' exists for us largely through performance and is only guaranteed by its juxtaposition with surrounding cultural values that are different, more familiar, more 'Western'. (Morey and Yaqin, 2012: 176)

There are two critical points to this evaluation. First, 'Muslimness' has been (and still often is) constructed through popular culture and media as a type of performance – that is, as a demand for Muslim faith identities and practices to be publicly displayed and surveyed, in a dramatic manner, in a way that is often disconnected from the textured realities of daily life. Second, that these acts of performance are conceived as a dark mirror, held up against the perceived normality and superiority of Western values, lifestyles and cultures. Through this framing, in the public imagination, Muslims are utterly defined by this positioning: whether as backwards barbarians, bearded and robed; or as symbols of forward-thinking *apologia*, suited and carefully spoken, emphasizing the compatibility of Islam with Western modernity; or, perhaps, as a tormented and discombobulated figure, grappling with an existential choice between these two divergent worlds.

Morey and Yaqin direct this commentary at post-9/11 television broadcasting, but, as I have argued throughout this chapter, it is a critique that resonates across the entire cultural history of Muslims in Britain. Those early newsreels and their depiction of oriental exoticness – framed either by the loyalty of grateful colonial subjects within an imperial expanse or by the submerged potential for irrational Muslim violence – contain many of the same themes, encapsulated around the notion of civilizational difference, that, as Said argued, reinforces a belief that we are 'only, mainly exclusively, White, or Black, or Western, or Oriental' (1994: 407–8). The veneer of cultural sophistication may have changed over the course of a century, as newsreels have become replaced by Netflix, but in relation to the depiction of Muslims, popular media and culture remains stubbornly and depressingly rooted in many of the same impulses that animated Edwardian Britain. The challenge – and indeed partly the whole basis for this book – is to consider how Muslim creatives are able to subvert and ultimately overcome this framing:

> It is no longer a matter of a 'positive images approach' or of who gets to produce the stereotypes. Rather what is needed is a recognition of the ubiquitous cultural interpenetration that has always marked relations between Islam and the West, and an attempt to work this realization into the mainstream representational landscape, and into both cultural and political views of Muslims as something more than just a strategic problem. There *are* ways beyond the frame, as we have seen, but it will take effort, openness, and a new vision of what politics can be to make these meaningful. (Morey and Yaqin, 2011: 207)

In subsequent chapters I explore the attempt by Muslim creatives to move 'beyond the frame'. Such efforts are not a straightforward narrative quest for 'authentic Muslimness' (whatever that might mean) but rather a series of contextual strategic and tactical choices, made by Muslim creatives, in an attempt to clear a space for creative freedom. I begin this discussion by examining, in the next chapter, the growth of contemporary Muslim cultural production, from new and innovative genres/styles of Muslim cultural expression through to the supporting industries and institutions that are helping to engender greater degree of Muslim cultural agency in contemporary Britain.

2

Sound and vision

From reciters and rappers to the Muslim Netflix

As I discussed in the previous chapter, until the end of the 1990s and the early 2000s, Muslim engagement with popular culture and media broadly took place in two different ways. First, Muslims were often the subject of cultural representation, with a framing that was characterized by themes of alterity, strangeness, violence and civilizational incompatibility. At times, Muslims were able to subvert this misrepresentation, but they were ultimately outmatched against an elite broadcasting culture and widespread cultural antipathy. Second, Muslims nurtured and preserved forms of grassroots culture – often performance and music based – that were typically rooted in the experiences of diaspora and an ethnic-exclusiveness. Whether in the early experiences of migration or the anti-racism struggles of the 1980s, cultural production gravitated towards ethnicity and race, rather than overtly manifesting aspects of faith and religious identity. Of course, Islam can very much be a part of ethnic or national culture – for example, with practices such as Qawwali and Urdu poetry. However, these expressions of culture were anchored in the racial paradigms of multicultural Britain, whereby localized ethnic communities were expected, or perceived, to maintain cultural cohesion and difference.

This has changed dramatically over the last two decades and there are now multiple avenues for the expression of diverse Muslim subjectivities through media and popular culture. There are two principal reasons for this. First, many of the Muslim creatives discussed in this book came of age during the events following the Rushdie Affair and then subsequently in the post-9/11 era. These events thrust Muslims into the glare of public scrutiny, often with damaging and discriminatory consequences, but also in a way that encouraged Muslims to explore and project their faith into public debate. Second, with increasing forms of social and economic capital, Muslims have developed an interlocking network of faith-based institutions to better meet their public and private needs.

From charities and political pressure groups, to education institutes and media organizations, through to professional networks and standards bodies, the range and scope of Muslim institutions across the UK continues to grow. Muslim popular culture has emerged from within this context, whereby new institutional and organizational resources are hitched together with an increased confidence in the exploration and articulation of faith-based identities. This has created a dynamic Muslim public sphere: mediated and diverse spaces, wherein Muslim public figures and organizations engage in a politics and culture of religious/communal identity (Meyer and Moors, 2005). Of course, the Muslim public sphere is not hermitically sealed, but rather it is in constant dialogue with other publics and discourses, both in the UK and indeed globally.

In this chapter I outline the genres of Muslim cultural production that are a feature of the Muslim public sphere in Britain. My aim is to provide an empirical overview, looking at not just individual cultural producers – such as musicians, actors and comedians – but also at the organizations that provide an institutional framework to support cultural production – such as television stations and production companies. This is far from a comprehensive overview, but it does outline in broad strokes the shape of performance-based Muslim creativity in the UK.

Reciters, rock stars and rappers: Muslim music cultures in Britain

Three styles of music have emerged to significantly shape distinctly Muslim soundscapes and music cultures across modern Britain: contemporary *nasheed*s, syncretic music and hip-hop. Driven by the confidence and cultural impetus of second- and third-generation Muslims, these musical styles have drawn upon cultural traditions from across the Muslim world and the Global West – including American and British pop music – as well as developing new and hybrid sounds. As I argue, part of the distinctiveness of these new styles – in comparison to earlier forms of music – is that they are self-consciously 'Muslim' and 'British'. That is to say, musicians have deliberately incorporated aspects of their religious and national identities into music that resonates with the spirit of a post-Rushdie era. This is a phenomenon that has occurred alongside the emergence of the Muslim public sphere in Britain. Musicians have contributed to the media institutions and cultures that have been part of this process – from magazines to television (Ahmed, 2005) – including through the development of music-oriented production and recording companies (many of which also release other religious/Islamic recordings, such as Qur'anic recitation and speech/oratory productions). To understand this landscape better it is helpful to consider these emerging musical genres in turn.

The contemporary *nasheed* style emerged in the late 1990s, with notable acts such as Shaam (from 1997) and Aashiq al-Rasul (from 1998). These groups drew on the traditions of the Arabic *nasheed* and South Asian *na'at* styles – as well as other diasporic sounds – with the aim of expressing Islamic themes in the English language. It is a musical style that locates itself as part of an Islamic aesthetic that includes calligraphy, poetry and architecture, but with a corresponding desire to transpose this heritage to the UK for a Muslim audience. Many of the musicians involved in this emerging musical and artistic milieu are grounded in a largely (but not exclusively) mosque-based tradition of performed scriptural cantillation. There is a natural progression from the art of Qur'anic recitation, with an emphasis on the subtleties and technicalities of vocalized sacrality, through to the controlled and devotional sound of the contemporary *nasheed*. While there is some debate over the correct application of the term 'nasheed', the general consensus appears to be that it refers to music that is non-instrumental or percussion-only (such as with a simple hand drum) – a restriction that aligns the sound with conservative religious proscriptions (see Chapter 4) – along with lyrics that focus upon praising Allah and the Prophet Muhammad, or other similar paraliturgical content. This is a musical tradition that dates to the early years of Islam, in the Arabian Peninsula, although contemporary *nasheed*s are an evolution of this style: they move away from the simple replication or preservation of a *nasheed* tradition through to something that is more experimental. This includes the elaborate use of membranophones – including dense polyrhythms, with instruments such as the *tabla*, *doumbek* and *djembe* – as well as complex vocal percussion and a cappella performance.

Birmingham-based group Aashiq al-Rasul are exemplars of the contemporary *nasheed* style. Influenced by South Asian and Arabic drumming styles – and drawing on lyrical traditions that include *qasida* (Arab poetry), *na'at* and *nasheed* – Aashiq al-Rasul produce fresh-sounding *nasheed*s for a British and international Muslim audience. With two percussionists, using instruments such as an electric drumkit, *tabla* and *doumbek*, they incorporate interlocking polyrhythms with handclapping, humming and other forms of vocality. The group is a collective, with a rotating membership of up to around eight members, headed by Amran Ellahi, operating from a converted building that is used as both a community centre and a Sufi *tariqa* (Sufi order/school).

Another good example of a contemporary *nasheed* performer is Amir Awan. With professional voice training at the Institute of Contemporary Music and Performance, in London, as well as additional training in Qur'anic recitation from Safar Academy, Awan performs a range of classically influenced yet resolutely modern *nasheed*s. Awan maintains scholastic restrictions concerning non-percussion instrumentation and instead uses complex vocal sounds and computer sampling to produce a sound that stylistically draws from eclectic influences, such as contemporary R&B and other pop music sounds, with Michael Jackson highlighted as a particularly key influence.

The second genre, *syncretic music*, has developed alongside and often within the *nasheed* tradition, yet is distinct enough to warrant analytic separation. It is notable that many musicians performing in this style are often strategically and emotionally located within the so-called '*nasheed* industry', although I would argue that syncretic music might often better be described as pop music with inherent and sometimes subtle Islamic themes (or 'Islamic pop', although this term is controversial and rejected by many as trivializing religious content). This music often takes Islamic themes as primary subject matter, but it also explores broader religious and spiritual subjectivities, as well as touching on social and political content. Syncretic music can draw on a wide range of musical styles, from R&B, funk, folk-rock and classical guitar playing, through to Qawwali, Sufi drumming and Arabic *maqamat* (modal systems). As with contemporary *nasheeds*, the performers of syncretic music emphasize the need to reach out to young Muslims in the English language, but they are also more likely to argue that their music is capable of penetrating the musical mainstream and therefore of communicating to a non-Muslim audience.

Sami Yusuf is not only the most preeminent musician to perform syncretic music, but he is also one of the most successful Muslim musicians worldwide, with accolades from media outlets such as the BBC, *TIME* magazine and *Rolling Stone*. An ethnic Azeri, Yusuf was born in Tehran but raised in London where he was trained in both Western and Middle Eastern classical musical traditions. This background influenced his early music and in 2003 he released his first album, *Al-Mu'allim*, which combined the use of membranophones and classical Middle Eastern styles with Western melodies and lyrics in both English and Arabic. Since then, Yusuf has released a series of albums, with his tenth, *Ecstasy* (the name references a state of Sufi spiritual experience), released in 2022. Over the years Yusuf's music has gradually taken on more of a pop sound – with piano riffs and stringed accompaniments – to develop into something that he has labelled 'spiritique' (Tusing, 2010) – a type of spiritually inclined pop music. Stylistically and semantically, Yusuf has gravitated towards a more mainstream audience, although he remains overwhelmingly popular with audiences across the Muslim world, from Indonesia and Egypt to Canada and the UK.

A different but equally fascinating act is Pearls of Islam, a female duo from London, who similarly perform in a varied syncretic style. Rabiah and Sakinah, the children of converts from an African-Caribbean background, draw on a range of musical styles – including *nasheed*, folk, rock and rap – to produce soulful and poetic music that is laden with spiritual and reflective themes, citing musical influences such as the Malian heavy-blues group, Tinariwen, and the funk and roots-rock American musician, Ben Harper. With lyrics that often dwell on ideas of spiritual journeying and personal transformation, Pearls of Islam translate their Islamic beliefs into universal themes that resonate for both Muslim and non-Muslim audiences alike.

The third style of music is *hip-hop*, which references both the style of music (rap) and wider hip-hop cultural references (including art, apparel and language). From the early 1990s there was growing interest in Islam amongst African-Caribbean communities in Britain, partly inspired by Spike Lee's 1992 biographical film *Malcolm X*. With an increasing number of conversions amongst this ethnic group (Reddie, 2009), hip-hop, with roots in Black America (Rose, 1994), began to be incorporated into an emerging Muslim youth culture in the UK. Early performers included The Planets – fronted by Ayman Raze, of Syrian heritage – and Mecca2Medina, a collective described as a '*nasheed* hip hop' group, centred around African-Caribbean convert Rakin Fetuga. Hip-hop, as a poetic-musical style – with an emphasis on self-expression, truth to power and the idioms of urban life – folds neatly into the increasingly activist tendencies of Muslim youth, particularly when faced with the rising tide of anti-Muslim prejudice following 9/11. It was in the 2000s that so-called 'Muslim hip hop' became a modestly successful cultural phenomenon in the UK, with a growing number of acts beginning to emerge, such as Mohammed Yahya, Quest Rah, Blakstone and Poetic Pilgrimage, and a series of visible events, such as the 'I Am Malcolm X' tour in 2009. This tour was funded as part of a roadshow organized by the Radical Middle Way, an influential, partly UK government-funded, organization that was created following the 7/7 London bombings with the intention of bringing an accessible, 'moderate' and classically informed version of Islam to Muslim youth (Jones, 2013) – it was therefore notable that music (specifically hip-hop) was seen as one of the key ways through which to do this (Khabeer, 2016).

One of the reasons for the success of hip-hop as a genre is that it can be performed without instrumentation, thereby becoming acceptable for those Muslims who have concerns about the Islamic permissibility of music. There is also the sense that hip-hop, which partly originated with Black Muslim Americans, *belongs* to Muslims across the world: a claim which has prompted references to the idea of a 'global hip hop umma' (Aidi, 2004; Alim, 2005; Ackfeldt, 2012), as part of a cultural and indeed religious lineage that stretches back to the ancient traditions of Islamic poetry. The idea of a distinct 'Muslim hip hop' movement in the UK began to recede, following a high watermark of excitement and interest in the late 2000s, and it has in many respects now been folded into a wider hip-hop subculture, where religious and spiritual themes are in any case relatively commonplace.

Poetic Pilgrimage are perhaps the most visible and assertive Muslim hip-hop and spoken word group in the UK. The act consists of two female converts, Sukina and Muneera, both from Bristol, and of Jamaican heritage, although they have lived in London since their student days in the early 2000s. They combine fiery lyrics, tackling issues from female empowerment, through to the moral failure of political leaders in the West and the Middle East, as well as reflecting on spiritual journeying and faith. Stylistically they have drawn on Jamaican reggae and Ska as well as a range of American soul and rap artists, from Erykah Badu and Lauryn Hill through to Nas, Mos Def and Common.

In stylistic contrast, another notable hip-hop performer, emerging in 2003, is Quest Rah. An articulate Londoner, with an Egyptian and English heritage, Quest Rah combines dense electronic beats and blended sampling with his own lyrical rapping and production polish. Drawing on classical Arab music (specifically often Egyptian) Quest Rah brings this together with hip-hop influences such as Gang Starr and Tribe Called Quest, prompting descriptions of his work as 'East Coast meets Middle East'. His lyrical content ranges from a sharp critique of global politics – especially following the 2003 Iraq War and associated 'War on Terror' – through to softer, more spiritual content, which weaves together historical, religious and mythological themes with a personal reflection on self-knowledge and identity.

Treading the boards: Muslims in theatre

An overlooked but vibrant area of cultural production and performance for Muslims in Britain has been the emergence of minority theatre groups and the wider involvement of Muslims in drama and performance. There is a history to minority theatre that stretches back to the 1980s, when Black and South Asian theatre groups – so-called constituency theatres – were established as part of an effort to project ethnic, gender and radical political identities (Saunders, 2015). Much of the aesthetics and creativity within this upsurge of theatre was inspired by the Black Arts Movement, originating in the United States, which brought together a range of art and culture that celebrated movement and voice, from dance and song, to poetry and spoken word, as well as sharp, narrative plays set within a postcolonial framework (Bailey, Baucom and Boyce, 2005). Muslim involvement in theatre is therefore often correspondingly wrapped up within expressions and explorations of intersectional racial identity. There is an extensive and complicated history surrounding this rich theatre scene in the UK (see David and Fuchs, 2006; Tomlin, 2015), but it is nonetheless possible to highlight some of the Muslim organizations and playwrights who have played a leading role in making Muslim subjectivities and identities visible through theatre and drama. Muslim involvement in theatre is a particularly fascinating area for consideration because, perhaps more than any other cultural form, it sits across a creative nexus that brings together literature, film, performance, poetry and visual art.

The most well-established Muslim theatre group in the UK is Khayaal Theatre Company. Khayaal was founded in 1997, by Luqman Ali, the current artistic director, with the aim of bringing 'the rich aesthetic, artistic and literary traditions of Muslim cultures to mainstream popular culture' (Khayaal Mission Statement). Within this remit, Khayaal has overseen a number of productions, performed at venues across the UK, from theatres and museums through to community venues and schools. These productions have been varied but share common themes relating to the reimagining of Muslim folktales and poetry, as well as expressing contemporary issues of identity and belonging. Along with this artistic and aesthetic endeavour, Khayaal has sought to foster interfaith and cross-cultural dialogue, as well as to generate cultural capital amongst Muslim communities, often as a way to challenge social and political issues relating to Islamophobia, securitization and misrepresentation. Khayaal is in many respects the leading light of Muslim theatre, with wide-ranging national scope, an accolade of international awards and high-profile productions that have been featured by national broadcasters and performed for high-profile luminaries, including Prince Charles.

Beyond the national presence of Khayaal, there are also a range of alternative constituency theatres that now provide a space for distinctive Muslim voices and productions. These theatres are located in cities across the UK and have long been important artistic venues for minority ethnic groups. Over the last decade or so, religion has become an increasingly important theme for some of these theatres, with dedicated productions that celebrate Muslim narratives, as well as supporting aspiring Muslim writers, directors and performers – many of whom use this opportunity to begin a career in both playwrighting and screenwriting. These theatres include Freedom Studios (Bradford), Rich Mix (East London) and The Edge Theatre (Manchester). A vital role fulfilled by these constituency theatres is the support that they provide to young Muslims, nurturing a new generation of artistic talent. Aside from dedicated theatres, a vast array of community arts venues also provide accessible spaces for performance, although many of these centres struggle for survival following a decline in public funding over the last decade. A notable example was Ulfah Arts, in Birmingham, which was tragically unable to rebuild after a racially motivated arson attack in 2014.

While dedicated theatre and art venues are an essential space for aspiring Muslim artists, there are other routes into theatre for Muslim creatives. This is particularly the case for Muslim playwrights whose numbers are increasing. Ishy Din, for example, began his writing career while working as a taxi driver in Middlesbrough, with his first play, *Snookered*, commissioned at the Bush Theatre in 2012. He has since written a series of acclaimed plays, performed on both stage and BBC Radio, many of which explore themes of ethnicity, class and northern English identity. Aisha Zia, a graduate in creative writing, has worked productively with the Bradford theatre company, Common Wealth, to write and produce *Our Glass House* (2012), examining domestic violence, and has received accolades for *No Guts, No Heart, No Glory* (2014), which tells the story of the first female Muslim boxer – and former UK champion – Ambreen Sadiq (starring as herself during the performance).

A common thread that connects this large and diverse landscape of Muslim theatre production is the way in which these productions are able to grapple with sensitive political and social issues. This is often about creating a new space for debate, in challenging misrepresentation, and in enabling more authentic narratives to shine through. Asif Khan, for example, most noted for his acting pedigree, published his first play, *Combustion*, in 2019. The play explores the stories of four Muslims in Braford, each individually navigating the pressures placed upon them by wider British society: to be quiescent and 'integrated', alongside an expectation that they should somehow publicly oppose 'radical Islam' and perform visible acts of national loyalty. Such plays make use of the capacity that 'high art' theatre has to be subversive and challenging, sometimes with controversial and unexpected consequences. In 2015, the play *Homegrown*, written by Nadia Latif and Omar El-Khairy, was cancelled ten days before the first performance, by the National Youth Theatre, which cited issues of 'quality' and 'safety' but gave little official reason beyond this. The play, which has since been published, explores issues of radicalization and so-called 'jihadi brides' – with a focus on school-age children – and it is resolutely critical of police and government interventions through the counter extremism Prevent programme. It offers a nuanced and difficult reading of British Muslim experiences within the ambit of state securitization measures. Those involved have since complained that the play was cancelled because it was deemed to be too sensitive and controversial, with El-Khairy suggesting that this amounted to little more than censorship.

While controversy and sensitive themes, such as those around radicalization or gender-based violence, more readily gain national media attention, there are also examples of performance levity and family-oriented theatre production. The charity Penny Appeal has notably been pioneering a series of performance-based tours across the UK. These have included not only music performances and film screenings but also theatre productions, including *The Great Muslim Panto*, which was first performed in November/December 2017. This sell-out show has been performed at cities across the UK and retells traditional pantomime stories (such as Cinderella) with jokes and references aimed at a Muslim audience. An inclusive and light-hearted series of productions – wildly successful – which act as a reminder that most Muslims in Britain are more interested in fun and entertainment than forever grappling with political controversy or with intra-Muslim religious tensions and social debate.

Muslim professionals and the mainstream television industry

Muslim involvement in mainstream television production (i.e. public service broadcasting and flagship commercial television) during the 2000s and early 2010s was seemingly limited and confined to acting roles, most of which were small walk-on parts – a picture that is consistent with wider ethnic minority participation in television production (Malik, 2013). It is very difficult to assess the number of Muslim actors working in television during this time – it is after all a large and complex cultural industry – however, anecdotal testimonies from Muslim television professionals suggest that the number was not high. Examples of actors still working today include Mina Anwar, Mazhar Munir, Hajaz Akram,

Jan Uddin and Kayvan Novak. The acting credits for these individuals during the 2000s mostly include small appearances on prime-time British television staples, such as *Doctor Who, Spooks, The Bill, EastEnders* and *Casualty*. There are very few Muslim professionals currently working in British television who built their careers during this decade, suggesting that Muslim television actors were rare during the 2000s and early 2010s. The only prominent and widely known Muslim actor to emerge from this period is Riz Ahmed, who developed his career with critically acclaimed appearances in various mini-series and television films, such as *The Road to Guantanamo* (BBC, 2006), *The Path to 9/11* (ABC, 2006) and *Britz* (Channel 4, 2007). This lack of inclusion and representation was widespread, with minority ethnic actors tending only to be provided with incidental parts (Campion, 2005), despite attempts by publicly funded broadcasters (the BBC and Channel 4) to increase the on-screen representation of minority ethnic groups (Saha, 2012). And of course, while Riz Ahmed's breakthrough roles were all prominent leads – a rarity for minority actors and otherwise unheard of for Muslim actors – they were, initially at least, all roles linked to Islam and the paradigm of violent terrorism.

The inclusion of Muslim television professionals in backstage positions – especially in senior production roles – has been even more dire than that of Muslims on-screen. It is difficult to uncover much evidence of Muslim involvement in the writing, production or commissioning of television programming during the 2000s and early 2010s. Noted writers and producers, all of whom are still active today, include Faisal Qureshi, Afi Khan and Ishy Din, yet their role in television production tends to have been as supporting experts (in research and writing), with a particular remit around faith and ethnicity, rather than as creative leads with primary writing or production credits. During this time, television production about Muslims – whether fiction or non-fiction – is almost entirely written and produced by non-Muslims, with Muslim professionals at best playing a supporting role in conception, writing and production. There are two notable exceptions to this otherwise widespread exclusion.

The first is Aaqil Ahmed, who started a career at the BBC, in the 1990s, as a producer of documentary television, making an early name for himself with *Trouble Up North* (BBC, 2001), which explored the events and significance of the 2001 summer riots in Burnley, Bradford and Oldham. Ahmed was then appointed as the Commissioning Editor of Religion and the Head of Multicultural Programming at Channel 4 between 2003 and 2009, with high-profile programmes that included *The Qur'an* (Channel 4, 2008) and *Christianity:*

A History (Channel 4, 2009). In 2009 Ahmed was appointed as the 'first Muslim' Head of Religion and Ethics at the BBC, sparking concerns amongst some, including from the Church of England, that Christianity was being sidelined in favour of minority faith groups (Khan, 2009). Ahmed served in that role before it was abolished in 2017. In 2019 he was appointed as a non-executive director for the regulator Ofcom (alongside other roles in the media industry). The second senior Muslim to work in television is Fatima Salaria. Again, she built a career as a producer at the BBC, during the 1990s and 2000s, with prime-time productions that included *Andrew Marr's History of Modern Britain* (BBC, 2007). In 2016 Salaria became the Commissioning Editor for Religious Programming at the BBC and was responsible for productions such as *Muslims Like Us* (BBC, 2016) and *A Vicar's Life* (BBC, 2018). As with Ahmed, Salaria's appointment was met with howls of outrage from some quarters. Newspaper coverage in the right-wing press focused on Salaria's faith background rather than her undoubted professional pedigree, with dog whistle headlines, such as in *The Express*: 'BBC puts Muslim in charge of religious television shows' (Mansfield, 2017). In 2018 Salaria was appointed as the Head of Specialist Factual at Channel 4, with a remit that focuses on the arts and history, as well as religion.

The rise of Ahmed and Salaria to senior production and commissioning roles has taken place alongside a more general increase in the number of Muslim professionals working both on-screen and backstage. This includes Muslim actors, such as Abdullah Afzal, Arsher Ali, Wasim Zakir, Asif Khan, Imran Yusuf and Guz Khan. While still hugely underrepresented across the television industry, these actors are nonetheless being offered more significant roles, including on major television dramas, such as *Line of Duty* (BBC, 2016) and *Ackley Bridge* (Channel 4, 2016). More striking is the increasing visibility of Muslim presenters on television programming, including, since 2015, figures such as TV chef Nadiya Hussain, former solider Adnan Sarwar and beauty blogger Mehreen Baig. These presenters all bring a blast of charisma and charm in their attempt to represent British Muslims in a positive, authentic and sometimes understated way on-screen. Backstage there are an increasing number of Muslim producers and writers, although, again, underrepresentation is still a pressing issue. Recently established producers and writers include Ahmed Peerbux, Fozia Khan and Sarah Ahmed, who between them have worked on a range of popular mainstream programming, including shows that have depicted Muslims in Britain, such as *Muslims Like Us* (BBC, 2016) and *Extremely British Muslims* (Channel 4, 2017), but also a broader range of non-religious programming, from *Bond's Greatest*

Moments (Sky Movies, 2013) through to *Posh People: Inside Tatler* (BBC, 2014). A new generation of Muslim writing talent is also starting to emerge, often with the support of writing foundations and networks, such as Taiba Amla, who after a string of writing competition awards – including winning the 2018 Northern Writers Award for Best TV Drama – has been commissioned by the British film industry to write her first feature film with Finite Productions.

However, perhaps the most significant and well-known new Muslim creatives in the television industry – both on-screen and backstage – can be found through the ascendency of 'Muslim comedy' in Britain.

The rise of Muslim comedy

Since 2010 Muslim comedians have become a familiar sight on screens and stages around the UK, with comics such as Guz Khan and Tez Ilyas becoming well-known celebrities with their own radio and television programmes. 'Muslim comedy' itself encompasses a wide range of performers, writers and styles, from stand-up to sitcom, and crucially it can be aimed at either an internal Muslim audience or for wider popular consumption (or both). There are dozens of Muslim comedians working across the UK comedy circuit, making it one of the most important forms of popular culture for Muslim performers and writers. What makes it significant as a genre – as 'Muslim comedy' rather than as just 'comedy' – is the way in which Muslim comedians use humour to explore wider social concerns for Muslims and to explicitly perform aspects of their ethnic and religious identities. Or, put another way – following Palmer's assessment that comedy is 'a signifying process and a social process' (Palmer, 1987: 204) – Muslim comedians create, communicate and embody symbolic features of Muslimness for mainstream popular consumption.

While Muslim comedy is mostly a relatively recent phenomenon, there are two important pioneers who have paved the way for a current generation of Muslim comedians: Shazia Mirza and the American comedic trio, Allah Made Me Funny (AMMF). These two acts have been the forerunners for a new generation of Muslim comics in the UK, breaking down barriers and providing a stylistic model for Muslim comedy in Britain. This particular style of comedy can be understood as a 'social gesture' (Bergson, 2013), whereby Muslim comics recreate the deadly absurdities of the modern world and the manifold expectations loaded onto Muslims living in the West. Laughter becomes a corrective, whereby some of this anti-Muslim hysteria can be defused.

Shazia Mirza began performing stand-up comedy in 2000, combining a mix of personal and family humour with political satire. Her career flourished quickly in a post-9/11 era. Regularly billed by promoters and venues as 'the world's only female Muslim comic', during her early performances, in the 2000s, Mirza performed in hijab and brought her biting wit to bear on aspects of everyday life, as a Muslim woman, with jokes that demolished popular myths concerning arranged marriage, terrorism, veiling and sexual repression. Her most recent stand-up tour, in 2016, entitled *The Kardashians Made Me Do It*, satirized the so-called phenomenon of 'Jihadi brides'. With her own trademark controversy, Mirza stretches these difficult issues into the absurd and in doing so provides an important corrective to the way in which they have typically been dealt with in public debate.

Azhar Usman, Bryant 'Preacher' Moss and Mo Amer – otherwise known as the AMMF Trio, from the United States – provide a far gentler and self-deprecating look at Muslim cultural attitudes, social practices and everyday experiences. Their humour tends to be based on gags and an anarchic, free-flowing comedy of disorder, whereby they drive themselves forward with self-parody and relentless charisma. Their humour is observational, telling stories that resonate for many Muslims in the Global West, from beard grooming and fasting during Ramadan through to more serious issues, such as the implications of airport security for those who are visibly Muslim. The trio began performing together in 2004, before touring widely from 2005 at Islamic events across North America and Europe, as well as with performances in South East Asia and the Middle East. Faced with criticisms from some Muslims concerning the permissibility of mixing Islam and humour, they received a *fatwa* (religious ruling) from the Grand Ayatollah of Iraq, in response to a question from the Shi'a community of Vancouver – a ruling which permitted them to keep performing (Van Nieuwkerk, 2008). Since 2006, they have encountered mainstream success, performing at comedy venues around the world, with reviews and interviews across a range of television and print media titles.

These comedians were all pioneers in the sense that they introduced the idea of 'Muslim comedy' to both Muslim and non-Muslim audiences. Since the success of both Mirza and AMMF, a fuller range of Muslim comedians have broken out onto the UK comedy scene, including Abdullah Afzal, Ali Official (also known as Ali Shahalom), Bilal Zafar, Jay Islaam, Abdul Rashid, Humza Arshad, Prince Abdi, Imran Yusuf and Shaista Aziz. Most of these comics perform for Muslim audiences – at Islamic events, conferences and on Islamic television channels – as well as for a more diverse crowd at comedy clubs, festivals and other cultural events. Their humour varies, as one would expect, but it usually draws on both the satirical and the self-deprecating observational styles of Mirza and AMMF. For the most part these comedians operate in the niche area of Muslim comedy, rather than for a broad national audience, and in doing so contribute towards a partially self-contained Muslim comedy scene. There are however Muslim comedians who have broken through to mainstream television broadcasting in the UK. Most notably, and somewhat controversially, this includes the writer, comedian and actor, Adil Ray.

Birmingham-born Adil Ray began his broadcasting career in radio during the 1990s, gradually working his way from a pirate station in Huddersfield, through to commercial radio, and then to the BBC Asian Network in 2002. A popular and lively radio presenter, Ray's increasing prominence and broadcasting experience provided him with the opportunity to branch out in 2011, with a co-written situational comedy, *Citizen Khan*, following the lives of Mr Khan (played by Ray) and his family, set in the Sparkhill area of Birmingham. The programme was successful over a total of five seasons, running until 2016 and attracting a regular audience of between 2 and 3 million in the UK. Yet the show was also hugely controversial, dividing opinion amongst South Asian Muslims in Britain, many of whom felt that the sitcom reproduced damaging ethnic and religious stereotypes. Mr Khan himself is portrayed as pompous, buffoonish and self-important – a stereotypical South Asian 'community leader' – while members of his family navigate a web of community and family censure, such as Mr Khan's daughter, Alia, who reads fashion magazines from behind the concealing cover of a Qur'an. As Rupa Huq argues, *Citizen Khan* seems redolent of boorish 1970s comedy, showing 'Asian-Muslims to be ridiculed as backward philistines, rather than offering humorous treatment of the contradictions in everyday situations that second generation Asian viewers and the viewing public at large can readily identify with' (2013: 82). For all the criticism levelled at *Citizen Khan*, it has at the very least opened up an avenue for a form of gentle, situational comedy whereby everyday aspects of Muslim life in Britain are explored for a wide and diverse audience. Yet, in every other respect, it has provided a model *against which* other Muslim comedians attempt to define themselves.

The backlash from *Citizen Khan* provoked a debate in the BBC and wider broadcasting circles about the representation of ethnic and religious minorities on-screen (Miles, 2015). This was coincidently timed with the appointment at the BBC of a new Controller of Comedy, Shane Allen, in 2012. Allen strode into his new role with a desire to end the dominance of White men in comedy and to bring greater diversity to the BBC. For Muslims, this was realized, in

2015, with the British Muslim Comedy series, launched in June, at the start of Ramadan, as part of the annual celebration in Britain. The series involved five short videos/sketches produced by British Muslim comedians. The videos were highly successful and three of the comedians involved in their development have subsequently proceeded to build more substantial broadcasting careers with the BBC: these are Guz Khan, Tez Ilyas and Sadia Azmat. In a sense, the 2015 British Muslim Comedy series represents the point at which Muslim comedy began to significantly broaden out as a distinct and self-defining genre in British broadcasting.

Guz Khan has explicitly set himself against the 1970s-style sitcom humour of *Citizen Khan*, stating, 'I just think 30 or 40 years on when you have characters playing those same stereotypes [in *Citizen Khan*], something's wrong' (Jeffries, 2018). Instead, Khan has developed a brand of humour that explores complex dimensions of class, ethnicity and faith, alongside a broader social commentary on modern Britain. A former secondary school teacher from Birmingham, Khan began performing comedy in 2014 and gained rapid publicity following his appearance at a BBC Asian Network event. In 2015 he created a short film, *Roadman Ramadan*, for the BBC British Muslim Comedy series, alongside his own comedy videos that gained viral status on the internet in both the UK and the United States. This breakout success was picked up by Steve Coogan – a long-standing and hugely successful British television comic – and under Coogan's production company, Baby Cow, Khan's comedy was subsequently piloted on BBC Three, before being developed into a full series, entitled *Man Like Mobeen*. Set in Birmingham, the series follows Mobeen (played by Khan), a former criminal now working in a care home and acting as a surrogate parent for his young sister, Aqsa. In contrast to the outdated stereotypical portrayals of *Citizen Khan*, Guz Khan has developed a set of characters that defy stereotypes by navigating the messy, contradictory and irresolutely human nature of everyday life in an ethnically diverse, working-class area of Birmingham.

The stand-up comic, Tez Ilyas, while stylistically very different, nonetheless engages in a similar form of humour that attempts to problematize and satirize stereotypes, rather than reinforce them, à la *Citizen Khan*. Originally from Blackburn, Ilyas had a career as a civil servant in London, in the 2000s, during which time he began attending comedy workshops. He attended a six-week stand-up comedy workshop in the spring of 2010, followed by his first performance that summer, before achieving notable success in 2011, when he became a finalist at the prestigious BBC New Comedy Awards. Ilyas subsequently toured comedy venues and events, such as the Edinburgh Fringe Festival, before breaking out, like Guz Khan, into broadcasting with a short sketch, *The Fast and the Fool*, for the 2015 British Muslim Comedy series. Following this exposure to a wider broadcasting audience, his comedy tour, *Tez Talks*, was developed into a series on BBC Radio 4, in 2018, to critical acclaim, and in 2019 Channel 4 began broadcasting *The Tez O'Clock Show*, a late-night comedy news programme, fronted by Ilyas, with a satirical look at current events in Britain. Citing comedic influences such as *South Park*, Ilyas combines observation and critique, often playing out stereotypes in order to shatter them through their own absurdity, or with humorous yet educational narrations, whereby misconceptions about Islam and Muslims are directly addressed.

Sadia Azmat is another Muslim comedian who has gained mainstream broadcasting success following her contribution, the short film, *Things I Have Been Asked as a British Muslim*, to the BBC's British Muslim Comedy series in 2015. A former call centre worker from Essex, Azmat began performing in 2010 and launched her first comedy show, *Please Hold – You're Being Transferred to a UK Based Asian Representative*, at the Edinburgh Fringe Festival in 2011, followed by another show, *I Am Not Malala*, in 2014. Following her success with the 2015 comedy short, Azmat developed and then launched a BBC podcast, *No Country for Young Women*, in 2018, with co-host Monty Onanuga. A comedic but informative programme, it explores the experiences of young ethnic minority women in Britain, with guests who discuss everything from Ramadan fasting, headscarves and body positivity to pornography, dating and fetishes. The show is not only fun and light but also provocative and combative in the way that it upends stereotypes about ethnic minority women in Britain.

Islam TV: A crowded and growing market

Broadcasting was revolutionized in the 1990s with the emergence of widespread satellite television viewing. Until this time, as Jean Chalaby explains, television 'was often tied up with the national project and no other media institution was more central to the modernist intent of engineering a national identity' (Chalaby, 2005: 1). This ensured that Muslims in Britain, along with other minority groups, were excluded from television content, which often blandly reinforced ethnic, cultural and religious norms. Satellite television shattered this arrangement by creating new transnational and diasporic television cultures. The sheer number of channels available on satellite television – which in the UK was operated by Sky Television – began to cater for every niche audience and interest, including for language cultures that stretched across national borders. Consequently, a number of diasporic channels became available in the 1990s, such as Zee TV, Sony Entertainment Television Asia and Bangla TV, some of which appealed to Muslims in the UK, although mostly as a form of cultural rather than religious programming (Tsagarousianou, 2001). The only exception to this cultural-linguistic focus was the launch in 1994 of Muslim Television Ahmadiyya (MTA), which continues to be broadcast in many countries around the world, including the UK. It is an advert-free channel, funded by donations and the international Ahmadiyya movement and aimed at the transnational Ahmadiyya community.

The relative absence of Islamic programming from satellite television ended in 2004 with the launch of Islam Channel. Described as the first English-language Islamic television station, it was followed in quick succession over the years by a number of smaller competitors. At the time of writing there are twenty-nine self-declared Islamic channels available on satellite frequencies in the UK. All of these channels are available in other parts of the world, seventeen of them include English-language content, only six are broadcast from the UK (these are listed in Table 1) and many are aimed at a wider diasporic/religious audience, rather than specifically at Muslims in Britain per se. Bethat TV, for example, was launched in 2017, is broadcast from Pakistan and has solely Urdu-language content aimed at a transnational Pakistani audience (which will no doubt include some UK viewers). There are seven principle Islamic channels that broadcast English-language content in the UK, either in full or as part of a multilingual offer (an eighth, Blackburn-based Ummah Channel, ceased broadcasting in 2017). It is

Table 1 A Summary of English-language Television Channels in the UK

Channel Name	Launch Year	Language	School of Thought*	Broadcast Location
Islam Channel	2004	English	Scholastic Traditionalism	London
Noor TV	2006	English/Urdu	Barelwi Sufism	Birmingham
Peace TV	2007	English	Salafi Political Reformism	Dubai
Madani Channel	2009	English/Urdu	Barelwi Sufism	Karachi
Ummah Channel	2009**	English/Urdu	Barelwi Sufism	Blackburn
Takbeer TV	2010	English/Urdu	Barelwi Sufism	Birmingham
British Muslim TV	2014	English	Liberal Reformism	Wakefield
Eman Channel	2016	English	Salafi Reformism	London

*This is based on Tariq Ramadan's typology of different Muslim schools of thought (Ramadan, 2004). See Chapter 7 for a full discussion.

**Ceased broadcasting in July 2017.

impossible to understand the landscape of Islamic television in Britain without considering the various dimensions of intra-religious debate, ethnicity, language and transnational activism/religious authority that underpin and inform these channels. These are summarized in Table 1.

It is not the aim of this book to provide an exhaustive account of Islamic television in the UK, but it is worth noting a couple of important points. First, Islamic television cannot easily be separated from competing forms of Islamic activism in the UK. I discuss these intra-religious trends in greater depth in Chapter 7, but it is often the case that Islamic television stations reflect some kind of school of thought or activist tendency. This can either be explicit, with broadcasting as a form of activism (Madani Channel, for example, is a platform for the Sufi activist group Dawat-e-Islami), or, more subtly, usually in terms of the views and sentiments that are expressed in the broadcasting content. Second, there is clearly a growing Islamic television market, with new Islamic/Muslim television stations appearing across the UK. While most of these are small and low cost (the barriers to satellite broadcasting are minimal), this does suggest that there is a demand, both nationally and internationally, for English-language Islamic television content – although whether this is sustainable remains to be seen. In contrast, despite its size, the United States has not developed an even remotely comparable network of Islamic television stations, although this might be changing with the launch in 2020 of the Chicago-based Muslim TV Network. American Muslims have instead largely been reliant on international channels and programming, including those that are broadcast from the UK (Malik, 2016). While speculative, this might suggest that Muslims in Britain are developing the infrastructure and resources required to become a cultural and broadcasting hub for a wider English-speaking Muslim world. Or, at the very least, that the model of UK-based Islamic broadcasting will influence developments in other Muslim-minority contexts, including North America (see Chapter 7 for an examination of these transatlantic links). This is particularly the case given that these television channels, once reliant on satellite frequencies, are now finding a more natural broadcasting home through the internet.

Islam Channel remains arguably the most dominant Islamic television station in the UK, claiming to have over 2.1 million viewers in Britain alone. There are no independent viewing figures to verify this claim and it has only a small social media following (29,000 followers on Facebook at the time of writing), but it is likely that a spike in Ramadan viewing provides it with an inflated audience during a time when many Muslims focus on their faith over other aspects of their lives (a time for more Islam Channel and less Netflix). It was established in

2004 by Mohamed Ali Harrath, a Tunisian activist and exile in Britain. Harrath has a background in Islamist politics across the Middle East and North Africa, including helping found the Tunisian Islamic Front in 1986. Islam Channel positions itself as non-divisive and ecumenical, drawing from across a spectrum of Islamic scholasticism, although on core matters of faith it is largely anchored in what might be described as a conservative lean, with teledawahs from across Deobandi and reform-minded Salafi traditions. This core religious programming is largely funded through the sponsorship of a sister charity, The Dawah Project, which was set up in 2009 by Harrath. However, across its programming as a whole – particularly on lifestyle and political shows – Islam Channel draws on a wide range of speakers and guests, including from heterodox Sufi and liberal traditions. While produced in the UK, Islam Channel promotes itself around the world as the premier Islamic television station. This transnational approach is evident in its programming, with historical, political, social and cultural content from across the Muslim world, although with a noticeable weighting towards European and North American Muslims.

British Muslim TV (BMTV) is the closest rival to Islam Channel in the UK. Launched in 2014, by business entrepreneur, Adeem Younis, BMTV is self-evidently aimed at a British Muslim audience, rather than at an international audience (although it can be accessed abroad), with a strapline 'confidently Muslim, comfortably British'. In terms of viewership, BMTV commissioned a survey by the Broadcasters Audience Research Board (BARB), in 2015, which suggested that it had upwards of 400,000 views a month. There are no reliable figures since this time. It also has the largest social media following of all the Islamic television channels, with 258,000 followers on Facebook at the time of writing, suggesting a dedicated interest amongst a large swathe of Muslims in Britain. The channel is different from other Islamic television stations in the UK because it focusses less on dedicated religious content – with little, if anything, in the way of Qur'anic exegesis, prayer, recitation, etc. – but rather it offers a broad array of lifestyle content that delves into 'Muslim culture', including shows based on music, cooking, film, cartoons and chat shows. The small amount of dedicated religious programming on the schedule tends to focus on interfaith debates and wide-ranging discussions with Islamic scholars and speakers, such as the Deobandi-trained Sheikh Ibrahim Mogra; Munir Ahmed, former president of the Islamic Society of Britain; the Sufi scholar Sheikh Ahmed Babikir; and Sarah Joseph, former editor of *emel* (the now-defunct Muslim lifestyle magazine). International scholars/speakers are occasionally featured, although usually drawing from transatlantic Muslim networks, including a notable series that hosted the lectures of the charismatic American televangelist, Hamza Yusuf. A common criticism of BMTV is that it is perceived to be the advertising arm of the charity, Penny Appeal. There is certainly no doubt that the two organizations are tightly connected – both were founded by Younas and until recently their offices were adjacent to one another in Wakefield. This claim has been rejected by both organizations, arguing they have a 'normal' commercial relationship, although Penny Appeal does promote itself heavily through BMTV, including with regular sponsorship, and in doing so provides the primary stream of funding required to ensure that the channel is commercially viable.

Peace TV was founded in 2006 by the Indian Islamic televangelist, Zakir Naik, and is reputed to reach 200 million viewers worldwide. This extraordinary and unverifiable figure seems unlikely, although Peace TV does broadcast three different language versions (English, Urdu and Bangla) and is available across most of the world. Peace TV is funded through a linked charity, the Islamic Research Foundation, and it is an advert-free, non-commercial venture that is funded largely through donations. In terms of content, Peace TV programming consists of talks by Islamic teledawahs, largely on topics of scripture and Islamic practice, with some discussion of comparative religion, all based on a conservative and literalist approach to Islam. Given that regular presenters include Zakir Naik (India), Bilal Philips (Canada), Abdur Rahim Green (Britain) and Abdullah Hakim Quick (United States), it is reasonable to characterize Peace TV as a media platform for a network of influential Salafi scholars from across the English-speaking world. Peace TV largely avoids any discussion of overtly political issues, usually framing talks as moral discussions that contain political and social implications, but it does regularly host speakers with a more strident pedigree of political activism, relating, for example, to calls for the creation of a pan-Islamic caliphate. It also has a strong message of social conservatism that has led to it being censured by various regulatory bodies, including in both the United States and the United Kingdom. It has been banned from broadcasting in both India and Bangladesh following allegations that it incited terrorism. By way of contrast, it was nominated for the Responsible Media of the Year award at the British Muslim Awards in 2013 (organized by the cultural events business, Oceanic Consulting), following a widespread call for nominations from Muslims in Britain, and thereby receiving a seal of approval from a section of the Muslim establishment in the UK.

Eman Channel was launched in 2016 with the stated aim of producing entertainment and factual programming for Muslims in the West. With high-quality, professional production and distribution techniques – including an app for mobile and tablet devices – Eman Channel is a well-funded and ambitious entry to the growing market of Islamic television in Britain. It broadcasts traditional religious programming – such as Qur'anic exegesis, televised prayer and motivational speaking – alongside a smaller selection of lifestyle programming, ranging from cookery (recipes include Beef Wellington and Lamb Shoulder) through to children's adventure activities, which are often linked to physical feats drawn from Muslim history (archery, horse riding, etc.). Broadly speaking, Eman Channel can be described as a form of neo-traditionalism (Esposito, 2016), with a particular emphasis on scholastic legalism, personal piety and an exemplification of the Sunnah, but with the aim of making this traditionalism relevant and accessible to Muslims leading a Western consumer lifestyle. Contributors to its religious content are not drawn from any exclusive school or tradition, but rather they sit across a broad spectrum of conservative Islamic scholars and speakers, ranging from Salafi figures, such as Wasim Kempson (UK), through to the motivational speaker and Grand Mufti of Zimbabwe, Ismail Menk. While produced in Britain, Eman Channel is less explicitly aimed at a British audience but rather seeks to appeal to Muslims across the English-speaking world.

The Barelwi Sufi channels, broadcast in Urdu and English, offer a unique service to an important part of the Muslim demographic in Britain, but with falling rates of Urdu-language use in the UK (Anderson, 2008) it is likely that these channels will serve an ever-older and ever-shrinking audience. Of course, the diasporic links between Britain and Pakistan continue to be important. However, the closure of Ummah Channel in 2017 suggests difficulties within a crowded market of Urdu-language Islamic television. That being said, given the way in which Islamic television is typically associated with a certain school of thought or 'participation orientation' (see Hamid, 2016) – and (with the exception of BMTV), the fact that there is a general exclusion of Sufism from English-language programming – it might be anticipated that there is a gap in the market for high-quality content focusing on British and transnational Sufism.

Muslims and film

Muslim involvement in film production is relatively limited, with only a small number of Muslim writers, producers and actors working in the British film industry. This is partly explained by the many barriers to entry in a competitive industry (such as high production costs), but also, as with television, relating to the way in which institutions have been guided by the imperatives of racial rather than religious diversity – such as through the promotion of 'Black British film' (Nwonka and Malik, 2018) and 'Asian British film' (Korte and Sternberg, 2009). There are however growing signs of Muslim involvement in film, as a new generation of cultural producers develop artistic proficiencies and a growing reputation. This growth is occurring in two parallel ways: across mainstream popular film and with the halting emergence of an independent 'Muslim film culture'.

The impact of Muslim creatives on mainstream British film is still largely to be registered, despite the fact that Muslims have routinely been represented through the medium of film (Bolognani et al., 2011). There are two notable exceptions. Riz Ahmed is the first. As I have already mentioned, he is clearly exceptional in many ways, having achieved considerable mainstream recognition and impact. A prolific actor, writer and artist, with an extensive television pedigree, Ahmed has appeared in a long list of successful films, both in Britain and, to much acclaim, in several Hollywood blockbusters (including *Rogue One*, in 2016, part of the *Star Wars* franchise, and the 2018 superhero film, *Venom*). More recently he has gravitated towards leading roles – a recognition of his success – including in films such as *Sound of Metal* (2019), for which he was nominated as Best Actor in the 2021 Academy Awards, which tells the story of a drummer who begins to lose his hearing. Ahmed's early career was often marked by typecasting – in films such as *The Reluctant Fundamentalist* (2012), which looks at radicalization, albeit in a subtle and arguably non-sensationalized way – yet with a growing reputation he is beginning to develop increasing creative control over his artistic output. This is most notable with the film *Mogul Mowgli* (2020), which he has co-written and produced. The film is Ahmed's most striking attempt to represent authentic ethnic and religious narratives, drawn from his own personal background, exploring contemporary issues of belonging through remembered family history and the partition of Pakistan. Ahmed's widespread and sustained success across film and television led to him being included in *TIME* magazine's 2017 list of the 100 most influential people.

Faisal Qureshi has also had some success as a screenwriter and producer, with recent credits that include *Leaving Neverland* (2019), a documentary film examining the sexual abuse claims made by survivors against Michael Jackson. Qureshi's most noted contribution towards British film – and the representation of Muslim narratives – was as an associate producer for the 2009 film *Four*

Lions (which also starred Riz Ahmed). Directed by Chris Morris, the film was a satirical and farcical look at Muslim radicalization in the UK, which attempted to defuse some of the hysteria around the 'War on Terror' by suggesting that 'radicalised Muslims' were fringe and eccentric individuals, to be laughed at rather than feared. Morris spent several years researching the topic and Qureshi's involvement was important as a means to more accurately include Muslim views and experiences in the production of the film. When interviewed for this research, Qureshi spoke highly of the experience of working with Morris but was otherwise resolutely negative about the prospects of Muslim and minority ethnic inclusion within British film. He has since turned his professional activity towards the North American film market, which he argued is more inclusive and less straightjacketed by racial paradigms (see Chapter 6).

Alongside this limited involvement of Muslims in mainstream commercial film, there have also been small steps towards what might be described as an independent Muslim film culture in the UK. By this I mean a genre of film over which Muslims have creative control, with the aim of better representing explicit and authentic Muslim narratives. This includes films specifically aimed at a Muslim audience and/or overseen by Muslim production companies, but it also includes commercial and independent films, which can be produced for a wider audience, while still being rooted in the experiences and creative expression of Muslim filmmakers. 'Muslim film culture' is therefore a loose and deliberately vague genre, much like 'Black British film' (Malik, 2019), and is an attempt to recognize the creative space where 'authentic' Muslim stories, aesthetics and discourses are told by Muslims through film. Such films are currently rare – and in some respects it is premature to even discuss the notion of an independent Muslim film culture in the UK – but there are three notable films that arguably fit the criteria. Whether this is the first wave in a distinctly Muslim film culture – or an outlier – remains to be seen. The launch in 2021 of Riz Ahmed's *Blueprint for Change* – an initiative designed to nurture Muslim involvement in film – will perhaps accelerate this otherwise slow-moving trend (see Chapter 6).

Finding Fatimah (2017), directed by Oz Arshad, is a light-hearted romantic comedy that tells the story of Shahid, who seeks new love following a recent divorce. Shahid turns to a Muslim dating site, where he meets Fatimah, an assertive and ambitious medical doctor, and the film explores their growing relationship alongside the various personal challenges that they each face. In some respects, the film is a universal story of love and romance, which happens to feature two Muslim protagonists. Yet the film also expresses themes that will resonate specifically for a Muslim audience, such as intracultural issues relating to the stigma of divorce, as well as Muslim dating culture. *Finding Fatimah* is the clearest example of independent British Muslim film culture. Partly because of the references within the film, but also because it was directly funded by the Islamic charity, Penny Appeal. As Arshad explained, several restrictions were attached to the funding provided by Penny Appeal: that the film be suitable for a Muslim family audience, that a talent show be featured in the film and that the story explore the non-physical aspects of the relationship between Shahid and Fatimah. While the film was picked up for widespread distribution by Icon, it was most widely watched through a Penny Appeal charity fundraising tour across the UK. In many respects the film was shaped by the agenda of Penny Appeal, which was founded by Adeem Younis, the CEO of SingleMuslim.com. The inclusion of online dating and a talent show was not coincidental given the entrepreneurial activities of Younis.

Freesia (2017) is a feature-length film written and directed by Conor Ibrahiem. An acting school graduate, Ibrahiem established the social enterprise, Arakan Creative, in 2009, following his frustration in finding suitable acting parts within British film and television. With funding from the Joseph Rowntree Charitable Trust, Arakan Creative was tasked with producing three artistic explorations of Islamophobia and interfaith dialogue: a play, a film and a comic book series. The second of these, *Freesia*, recounts the story of three characters in Bradford: Yusif, the son of a Muslim scholar; Zac, a White working-class boy influenced by far-right radicalization; and Khadija, a young politics graduate with professional ambitions that are hampered by pressures relating to her gender (from her overbearing brother and wider societal expectations). The film brings these stories together around the fallout from a violent Islamophobic attack (perpetrated by Zac) and a local media scare concerning sexual grooming. The film is a sympathetic portrayal of all three characters, exploring their unique personal perspectives and backgrounds, in an attempt to uncover the human stories running throughout otherwise charged political debates. It received several awards, including 'Best Director' and 'Best Original Screenplay' at the International Filmmaker Festival of World Cinema, in 2016, and has been made available on the streaming service Amazon Prime.

Blessed Are the Strangers (2016) is a documentary film written and produced by Ahmed Peerbux and Sean Hanif Whyte. The film was an independent project, partly self-funded by Peerbux, but also reliant on fundraising through individual donations. The film examines the history of a convert community in Norwich, formed by the Scottish playwright, Abdalqadir as Sufi (formerly Ian Dallas), and an eclectic group of converts, in the 1970s. Their vision is for a self-supporting 'Muslim village', motivated in part by a countercultural turn against the perceived over-consumerism of wider British society. During the 1980s, the community begins to attract a growing number of African-Caribbean heritage converts from West London. The film examines the struggles, dynamics and heritage of this remarkable story, with a focus on the cultural diversity and spiritual utopianism of the community. It is beautifully produced, with interviews and archival footage that are brought together to recount a compelling historical story. Themes of cultural diversity and spiritual journeying are brought to the forefront, creating a subtle Muslim counternarrative against wearying public discourses that more often pathologize Muslims through media and popular culture.

Streaming Islam: Muslim media audiences in the age of Netflix

The advent of 'streamed' television in 2010, pioneered and popularized by Netflix, has rapidly changed the television market over the course of the last decade. By providing viewers with a catalogue of programmes to watch 'on demand' rather than 'live', Netflix has helped to redefine the notion of the television audience, shifting it away from a passive and linear communal experience (albeit over multiple channels) to a fragmented kaleidoscope of individual viewing moments and niche audiences (Jenner, 2018). This is largely because the sheer volume of television content, available instantaneously at any time, has pluralized viewing habits, eroded the idea of simultaneous audience viewing and encouraged television communities and subcultures to cohere around genres rather than channels (Barker and Wiatrowski, 2017). Following Netflix, other providers, such as Amazon Prime Video, Hulu and Now TV, have helped to boost the market for streamed television. This shift should not be overstated. In 2018, Ofcom reported that 71 per cent of television viewing time in the UK was still spent on traditional broadcast content (as opposed to online streamed television), but that this figure dropped to only 46 per cent amongst those aged sixteen to thirty-four (Ofcom, 2018). This trend suggests that traditional broadcast television is under threat due to a generational change in viewing habits – a change that carries with it a number of implications concerning new media communities and institutions, particularly relating to television production and consumption.

For Muslims, these implications are already being felt through the gradual emergence of bespoke streaming services aimed at Muslim audiences. These new online streaming services are in many respects an alternative to traditional forms of Islamic television, and they mirror the wider trend towards bespoke television viewing. Given that Islamic television channels in the UK are already governed by the demands of diverse religious and linguistic Muslim audiences, the possibility of new television providers further opens up the possibility of Muslim micro-audiences and subcultures, both in Britain and transnationally.

The first Muslim streaming service to be launched in the UK was Alchemiya, in 2015, by Navid Akhtar, a broadcasting stalwart with a background producing documentary programmes on Channel 4 and the BBC. Akhtar argued that Islamic television in the UK – or '*dawah* TV' as it is sometimes pejoratively referred to – fails to cater for an audience of mostly young and educated Muslims. This audience, according to Akhtar, does not want to be 'preached at' but rather it is interested in the artistic and cultural heritage of Islam. Akhtar outlined this view at a public lecture series in 2014, where he coined the term 'Global Urban Muslim' (see Chapter 3) to refer to this arguably underserved and growing audience (Akhtar, 2014). Described widely across the media as the 'Muslim Netflix' – almost certainly a cunning marketing strategy – Alchemiya works by bringing together a curated collection of content about the Muslim world. In May 2018, the Alchemiya catalogue held a collection of fifty-three programmes and films, from *A Beginners Guide to Andalusi Calligraphy* (2017) to the film *Salaam Dunk* (2011), about an Iraqi women's basketball team. The collection is mostly English-language but with a small selection of subtitled content (languages include Arabic, Turkish, French, Swedish and Italian). Alchemiya was originally made available as a unique service with its own streaming platform. This required users to access Alchemiya through an internet browser, making the viewing experience cumbersome and not easily watched through a standard television set. This changed in 2017, when Amazon Prime Video approached Alchemiya and asked them to join a growing collection of independent channels (such as the production company HBO) that were becoming available through the Amazon platform as add-on packages for a small additional premium. As Alchemiya continues to grow, with a planned expansion into the South and East Asian television markets, this arguably represents the development of a new transnational audience characterized by class, religion and language – or put another way, it is becoming a platform for the cultural expression of a new Anglophile, global Muslim elite (see Chapter 7).

While Alchemiya is to date the only example of a Muslim streaming service aimed at adults, there are new providers emerging within the area of children's television. Two streaming services, Muslim Kids TV and Ali Huda, were respectively launched in 2014 and 2017, both with the aim of providing educational and entertaining content for children (both also regularly labelled the 'Disney for Muslim kids'). While neither are based in the UK, they have been heavily promoted in Britain and elsewhere in the English-speaking world. Muslim Kids TV is a Canadian venture, based in Edmonton, and fronted by the Canadian interfaith speakers and Islamic scholars, Jamal Badawi and Navaid Aziz. Ali Huda (*'ali* 'High' and *huda* 'Right Meaning' – the Shi'i connotations of the names are coincidental) is based in Denmark, but culturally and linguistically it leans towards North America, with programmes that feature American presenters (such as the comedians Omar Regan and Baba Ali). Several of the individuals behind Ali Huda have also endorsed Eman Channel (such the Salafi speaker Bilal Phillips) and it has a similarly conservative outlook. The content on both channels is largely animated (which is relatively low cost), although some programmes (e.g. storytelling and poetry) involve a filmed performer. Typical content includes programming aimed at basic Islamic pedagogy, such as learning Arabic, verses from the Qur'an, how to pray, how to greet people, etc., but there is also a selection of fictional narrative programming that draws from Islamic history and mythology (such as *Saladin*), as well as portraying children's characters in animated stories about everyday dilemmas and moral quandaries (such as *Alif and Sofia*).

Muslim streaming services are still in their infancy, but they do point towards important trends. It is notable that, globally, the only streaming services that offer Islamic programming are English language (with some Arabic content). There are no doubt commercial benefits to this, given the widespread use of English, but it further boosts the significance of Muslim voices located in the UK and North America, mostly at the expense of traditional sites of Muslim power and influence (i.e. the Middle East, South Asia and North Africa). Furthermore, just as Netflix has widely been accused of turning out a mass of original but also very generic American-centric programming, it will be important to chart the rise of Muslim streaming services and the cultural assumptions that underpin them. What audiences will these streaming services gather around them? How diverse will they be? How will they enable the communication of Muslim values and ideas across national borders? And do they represent a new frontier in the exemplification of an Islam of the Global West?

This tension between homogenization and pluralization is arguably a central issue when considering the developing phenomenon of global Muslim streaming services, as indeed it is with all forms of Muslim cultural production. Accordingly, I turn in the next chapter to a theoretical analysis of Muslim cultural production, providing a typology and conceptual framework that can be used to organize these cultural forms, industries and networks. As I suggest, Muslim cultural production is diverse and contested, but there are a series of observations that can be made about the form, function and animating impulses of contemporary Muslim cultural production.

3

Understanding Muslim popular culture
Islam in the media age

In this chapter, I engage with wider academic literature concerning religion, media and popular culture (e.g. see Hoover and Lundby, 1997; Hoover and Clark, 2002; Deacy and Arweck, 2009; Horsfield, 2015) to theorize Muslim cultural production in the UK. Such literature has typically considered how forms of social and cultural change are driven by media and popular culture – much of which is transnational, global and transgressive beyond established borders and boundaries – with the implication that religion itself, as a concept and a set of codes, traditions and institutions, is somehow in a process of reformulation. The impact of these changes can be felt widely across various religious phenomena, from the circulation of religious symbols and ideas in the public sphere through to everyday practice and social behaviour. As Gordon Lynch, Jolyon Mitchell and Anna Strhan argue (2012a), contemporary forms of media and culture have enabled the 'deregulation' of religion, creating diverse religious subcultures and modes of communication, many of which are beyond the control of historically rooted religious institutions and elites. This bustling marketplace of mediated religion therefore informs a new type of religious consumer: one that is not only animated by individual agency and experience but also corralled and constrained by emergent modes of communication (e.g. new technologies and cultural expressions) and contemporary structures of mediation (e.g. new industries and institutions).

For Muslims in Britain, popular culture is a sphere of activity where these trends are becoming manifest and where traditional religious phenomena are either being challenged, synthesized or reformulated. A grassroots mosque-based and *'ulama'* religious culture – which has been dominant in the UK since post-war migration – is facing competition from a generation of lay Muslim elites. This includes Muslim voices from politics, business, education and – notably for my arguments in this chapter – from within the arts, media and popular culture. While formal religious discourses and institutions remain important, as they do for all religions, these social and cultural changes indicate a flourishing of new religious perspectives amongst Muslims in Britain. In this chapter I provide some theoretical insight into these changes. In later chapters, I consider some of the many ways in which Muslim subjectivities and practices are changing; however, the reasons for this shifting religious and cultural landscape can in large part be explained – or at the very least better understood – by considering the more fundamental social and cultural underpinning discussed throughout this chapter.

Religion and popular culture: A typology of Muslim creativity

Throughout this book I use the terms 'Muslim popular culture' and – a little more neutrally – 'Muslim cultural production' (the terms are almost synonymous). At a basic level these terms refer to forms of mass culture and media that are produced by Muslims, with the intention of expressing or developing a religious identity, experience or sentiment. The problem with this definition is that it runs into the very same ethical dilemmas that I outlined in the introductory chapter – that is, a dangerous tendency to 'name' Islam in a way that overemphasizes and exceptionalizes religion (Mutman, 2013). While acknowledging this warning, I do attempt in this book to outline and explore the relationship between Muslims in Britain and popular culture/cultural production. My aim is to show how Islamic practices and Muslim identities are lived and experienced through popular culture in ways that are socially and culturally significant. The terms that I have settled on to capture this field of study – Muslim popular culture/cultural production – refer to a set of activities and meanings that are both diverse and complex. Many might not even be considered 'religious' in any normative sense but are nonetheless more subtly influenced by religious subjectivities. In organizing this field, then, I consider it helpful to propose that Muslim popular culture has three varying tendencies or functions: (i) as 'Islamic' (concerned with explicit Islamic practice and knowledge), (ii) as 'Islamically conscious' (expressing more subtle and less direct religious and spiritual subjectivities) and (iii) as 'secular-civic' (relating to secularized forms of social identity and a wider cultural politics that draws heavily on religious-ethnic identities). I examine each of these in turn in this chapter.

More generally, the task of defining 'popular culture' and 'religion' – and exploring the theoretical link between the two – has been commendably attempted before by both cultural theorists and scholars of religion (e.g. Cobb, 2008; Lyden, 2019; Lynch, 2005; Storey, 2018; Tanner, 1997). This task is difficult in part because both popular culture and religion are continually in motion. These examinations have however helped to establish some working definitions and to justify the fraught linkage of religious identity and cultural production. They have also teased out some of the ways through which the study of popular culture can enable a more rounded understanding of everyday religion and the formation of new religious imaginaries. What they share is a recognition that the study of religion should not be isolated or exceptionalized – this is certainly not how religion is practised or understood in everyday social and cultural life. As Lynch argues, this approach to the study of religion and popular culture contains within it not just 'a concern for how we might describe the structures and practices of contemporary society' but also 'far-reaching questions about cultural values and cultural politics' (Lynch, 2005: 19). To better understand Muslim engagement with popular culture is by extension to have a firmer grasp of the currents of religious, social and political change – many of which are shaping not just Muslim communities but also a wider British firmament.

Following Williams (1983), I use the term 'popular culture' as a way of referring to a set of artistic and intellectual practices, objects and beliefs. These are signifying activities – that is, they create shared social meanings – and are widely encountered in ways that are both mediated and immediate. This can include everything from entertainment and sport through to slang, news and fashion. For the purposes of this study, I am principally interested in music, television, film, comedy and (to a more limited extent) theatre (i.e. performed entertainment culture). Yet this amorphous and creeping definition means that it is very difficult to isolate specific aspects of popular culture. Where, for example, does television end and the internet begin? The trick it seems is not to worry too much about what properly constitutes popular culture but rather to consider the processes of signification contained within it. As Stuart Hall has suggested, while there may be as many problems with the term 'popular' as there are with the word 'culture', we can nonetheless recognize that it is – at the very least – an 'active reworking' of existing traditions, behaviours and products (Hall, 2006: 477–8). In this sense, popular culture might better be defined as a dynamic cultural force that shapes, reconfigures and reinforces fundamental social values and politics within society at large. This 'active reworking' can be conservative or reactionary;

it can be consumerist or superficial; and it can be radical or revolutionary. More often it is a mixture of all three. It also operates across and within a churning mix of cultural forms, from tattoos and television to parkour and performance art. Despite the chaotic and motley nature of popular culture, it is a driving force that has for decades decisively shaped cultural and social politics. This can relate to social and political identities – such as gender, class, race and sexuality – or to our understanding of everyday activities – from home life and health to the use of technology. In this sense, popular culture is a deeply political concept because it cuts to the core of human meaning-making. Or as Bryan Turner argues, it is a critical 'site where the everyday construction of everyday life may be examined' (Turner, 2003: 5). When considering Muslims in Britain, then, the task at hand is to consider not just the ways through which popular culture can rework Muslim identities and values but also the capability that Muslims have, through popular culture, and through an increasing involvement in the public arena, to engage with and shape a wider cultural politics.

When examining the relationship between popular culture and religion, Bruce Forbes and Jeffrey Mahan (2005) suggest a fourfold typology: (i) religion in popular culture, (ii) popular culture in religion, (iii) popular culture as religion and (iv) religion and popular culture in dialogue. (These categories make sense of religion and popular culture by considering them as distinct and separate realms that nonetheless overlap and interact in interesting ways – that is, these categories all work by *appending* religion to popular culture.) This approach is often favoured in scholarly work, with areas of study that vary, for example, from 'Hindu cinema' to 'Jewish hip-hop'. In this way, religion often becomes a segmented part – or a distinctive 'flavour' – of wider cultural trends. It also subtly suggests that religion might be perceived of as a set of historically rooted traditions that sit in contrast to, or are otherwise distinct from, modern popular culture: 'old' religion that can be freshened up and made relevant through 'new' forms of popular culture.

However, as Kathryn Tanner (1997) suggests, we might also consider that religion is not so theoretically different or distinct from popular culture as a phenomenon, in the sense that religion, like popular culture, is first and foremost concerned with meaningful action and with symbolic signification. This latter approach is useful because it blurs or perhaps even eliminates the boundaries between religion and popular culture, recognizing that they are – and have both always been – vital forces engaged in human meaning-making. In this sense, religion, like popular culture, can be considered just one more thematic category within a wider system of signification, alongside other forms that might include, for example, democratic politics, cartography and medicine. They are all modes of behaviour and fields of discourse that, regardless of their empirical basis, are influential frameworks of human meaning-making. This view is sympathetic to scholars who have problematized the very concept of religion itself, as an historically contingent term that conceptually isolated Christianity, in order to universalize it, and in so doing to elevate it as existing 'beyond' culture (McCutcheon, 1999). While we might therefore acknowledge the distinct properties or qualities of religion – such as in reference to the sacred or the transcendental – this approach resists the tendency to overly narrow or compartmentalize religion, which is often done by placing it solely within the hallowed spaces of the temple, or the text. Rather, we might instead conceive of religion as a set of (sometimes loosely) connected symbols and narratives that are reworked and enacted within 'popular culture', as much as they are elsewhere.

The study of Muslims in Britain has tended to gravitate towards an examination of ritualistic and educational spaces, such as the mosque and the *madrasa*, or towards networks of authority and learning, and to expressions of devotion, such as prayer and pilgrimage. In contrast, by adopting the approach outlined above, it is possible to recognize that Muslim imaginaries, pedagogies and acts of devotion can occur just as much within the everyday spaces of culture as they can in 'traditional' spheres of religion. To understand, for example, that an expressive musical performance, or a stand-up routine, or a carefully crafted film, can all be forms of devotion and knowledge, created in supplication before the greatness of God, much as one might offer up a prayer, a testimony or a charitable donation. My aim in this book is to examine the ways in which these everyday cultural activities might contain dimensions of religion and belief for Muslims and to consider the ways through which Muslim religious subjectivity is reconstituted around networks and spaces of popular culture. In order to make sense of this otherwise complicated field of study, I propose organizing Muslim cultural production into a typology of three categories: Islamic, Islamically conscious and secular-civic. It is not my intention to label or categorize specific cultural producers – as if to designate this musician as 'Islamic', this film as 'Islamically conscious' and this stand-up routine as 'secular-civic'. Rather, I aim to suggest that these are tendencies, or subjectivities, that are made contextually manifest across a broader tapestry of Muslim cultural production. By understanding this we can better analyse and document the continued evolution of Muslim beliefs and practices within the UK, and indeed in other minority-/majority-Muslim societal settings.

Muslim popular culture as Islamic

There are instances where Muslim cultural production in Britain might be considered a form of core Islamic practice and belief. This refers to activities that exclusively target communal and religious spheres of activity – usually relating to religious ritual, pedagogy and experience – in a way that reinforces the moral coherence of a distinct and devout Muslim community. Examples include religious programming on Islamic television stations, such as phone-in shows with religious scholars, or live prayer around the Kaaba, or cartoons that emphasize elements of an Islamic habitus for children (e.g. accurate Qur'anic pronunciation or correct posture and movement during prayer). It might also encompass forms of recitation and music (such as *nasheeds*) that are paraliturgical, in the sense of being ritualistic rather than simply entertaining or even 'just' spiritual. The function of Islamic popular culture is therefore not only to strengthen communal religious solidarity and identity through shared beliefs, histories, practices and values but also sometimes to act out forms of mediated ritual and religious activity.

Describing any form of popular culture as 'Islamic' can be controversial. Such a designation is not always accepted by Muslim creatives themselves. There can be a desire to keep the material and potentially profane world of human activity more clearly demarcated from that which might be traditionally conceived of as sacred. This is particularly the case with 'suspect' forms of culture, such as music and comedy, which are perceived by some to be lesser forms of activity – that is, lacking the seriousness of forms of conventional devotion, such as prayer – and possibly even *haram* (religiously forbidden) because of their perceived association with a 'morally dubious' secular mainstream. Yet for others, popular culture can be infused with the religious and moral urgency of Islam. Definitions vary, but usually the notion of whether popular culture can be considered 'Islamic' relates to the functional role of the activity or product – and the intention behind it. The musician Amran, from the *nasheed* group *Aashiq al-Rasul*, neatly captures this when discussing the concept of 'Islamic music':

> Intention is central in a Muslim's life, in whatever we do, if your intention is sincere, your prayer is accepted. . . . [So] if I were to give a definition of Islamic music, it would be focusing on the words and meanings of the lyrics. . . . Vocally, there are certain words which you could say are through and through Islamic. They remind or educate the listener about God or Prophet Muhammad, Peace Be Upon Him. (Amran, musician, January 2011, Birmingham)

This was an unprompted response, suggesting that the need to defend or clarify the descriptor 'Islamic' is important for some Muslim creatives. It also captures the essence of 'Islamic' culture: to make a deep and explicit connection to Allah and the Prophet, much as one might do through other forms of orthodox practice. Across a panoply of popular culture that might be categorized as Islamic, there are four central themes that emerge:

- The use of popular culture as a form of devotion – almost analogous to prayer – in order to praise Allah and the Prophet Muhammad.
- To reaffirm core religious values and to subjectivise these as explicitly 'Islamic'. This includes values that relate, for example, to modesty, deference (e.g. to a spiritual teacher), respect (e.g. to an older relative) and to gender roles (particularly the centrality of gendered motherhood).
- To celebrate and enact forms of core Islamic practice. This includes, for example, Ramadan and Eid, marriage, fasting, charity, prayer and pilgrimage.
- Reference to Islamic history, tradition, and religious life worlds, including historical and religious figures of importance, or Islamic religious discourses and theological debates.

Of course, these broad areas of discourse and practice are diverse and contested – there are certainly few settled interpretations of correct Islamic values or practices – but this is a starting point to consider how popular culture might slot into frameworks of existing Islamic orthodoxy and orthopraxy.

Muslim popular culture as Islamically conscious

Islamically conscious culture is driven by a desire to universalize the beliefs and values of Islam. This involves drawing on Islamic teachings and a Muslim world view, but in a way that will resonate with both Muslims and non-Muslims alike, relating, for example, to broader spiritual experiences and to ethical values that are rooted in Islam, but, crucially, with a sense of their wider applicability. This is an approach that stretches and reshapes the traditional borders of religious belonging. It is less concerned with strengthening internal Islamic orthodoxies or forms of Muslim communality but rather in making these subjectivities relevant for a wider audience. Cultural producers motivated by this approach will often avoid forms of 'exclusive' Islamic symbolism, language and conceptualization. They will also typically reject – or at least carefully manage – any form of labelling that places them squarely within an Islamic or Muslim cultural genre, preferring instead to identify themselves as expressive artists, with a rich array of personal and ethical experiences, all of which can be reflected within their oeuvre. This is usually manifested in one of two different ways: by an emphasis on political and social values or through the expression of spiritual subjectivities.

The actor and director, Conor Ibrahiem, captures the first of these points when discussing the motivation for his work:

> Injustice is really my key driving factor. . . . I really just wanted to emphasise that to the wider world, and to us. To the wider world to say, look . . . we should think of our non-Muslim neighbours and the issues that they're suffering. Internally, you are doing a disservice by not upholding the laws of the Qur'an and the examples in the Hadith, of peace and love, and being selfless in your journey in life. Because power comes into it, money comes into it, misogyny comes into it, all those little evil things in a way take over what is right and wrong. So it's a message both ways. Because I'll always look both ways. (Conor, film-maker, July 2018, Keighley)

Ibrahiem envisages his work as looking 'both ways', with a set of ethical values that are rooted in Islam but that are expressed more loosely – couched in a more expansive cultural and political language – to both a Muslim audience, on the one hand, and to non-Muslim audiences, on the other. While core Islamic teachings and values are always a central motivation for Ibrahiem, they are channelled into a moral discourse that relates to ideas of injustice and social conflict.

For others, their art enables them to express a spiritual subjectivity that, while rooted in Islam, is nonetheless relevant for a non-Muslim audience. The musician, Sami Yusuf, is emblematic of this approach, with his self-titled genre of music, 'spiritique'. Shying away from the exclusive Islamic/Arabic references that inevitably led to his earlier work becoming labelled as both '*nasheed*' and 'Arab', Yusuf has gravitated towards universal themes, reflecting on, for example, human rights, spiritual journeying and the nature of human existence.

Whether in relation to political morality or spiritual experience, Islamically conscious culture therefore places an emphasis on individuality and personal expression, in contrast to the often communal and ritualistic functionality of Islamic popular culture. Both are infused with the teachings, values and the aesthetics of Islam, but Islamically conscious popular culture brings these beliefs and subjectivities to play within wider cultural and political conversations. In this sense, Islamic and Islamically conscious cultural expressions both look to transmit Islam in their own way, but to different audiences and through the use of distinct symbolic frameworks.

Muslim popular culture as secular-civic

The third tendency within Muslim popular culture is something that I refer to as secular-civic. Less concerned with the expression of normative religion, secular-civic culture relates to the contemporary landscape of secularized and multicultural public life in Britain. It is through this prism that – in public discourse at least – Muslims have become a racialized political and cultural group, rather than one necessarily defined by religious practices and beliefs. It is this which dominates public media discourse and popular culture in Britain. 'Islam' – in relation to the sacred, spiritual, revelatory and transcendental – becomes somewhat peripheral, while 'British Muslims' are instead viewed through a framework of a social politics and attendant issues of cultural diversity. Crucially, this framing often has distinct class and racial – rather than religious – characteristics. In relation to cultural production, this is manifested as a focus on themes of everyday Muslim life in Britain, from marriage, fashion and food through to airport security checks and Islamophobic abuse. These forms of culture are 'secular', because they de-emphasize normative religion, and 'civic', because they focus on aspects of identity and belonging in multicultural Britain.

Public broadcasters such as the BBC are at the vanguard of promoting forms of secular-civic Muslim culture in Britain. As Nasar Meer and Tariq Modood have argued (2009), there is continuing widespread institutional confusion about where religion fits in amongst a competing and overlapping array of ethnic, cultural and class identities. This seems particularly evident within broadcasting and media circles. While religious literacy amongst broadcasters has declined precipitously since the 1980s (Knott, Poole and Taira, 2016), there has in recent years been a renewed focus on promoting diverse ethnic, class and gender identities through broadcasting. For secular broadcasters, therefore, the nuances of Islamic belief and practice – of religion – are neither familiar nor seemingly relevant for a wider audience. Meanwhile, cultural diversity, social anthropology and political discord are all parts of a familiar and active media agenda. As such, the breakthrough Muslim broadcasting stars of the last decade, such as Guz Khan and Tez Ilyas, have tended to focus on the ways through which the everyday cultural and social aspects of Muslim life – which are often understood through class or race – can 'bump up' against non-Muslim expectations and understandings. A good example, presented in Brummy street-lingo patois, might be Khan's comedic introduction of Ramadan, in the BBC comedy short, *Roadman Ramadan* (2015), to a recent convert: 'It's about way more than abstaining from food, bro.' It transpires that the 'way more' refers to the avoidance of swearing and flirtatious behaviour, as well as the requirement to make charitable donations – in essence, Ramadan is framed as a moral and cultural, rather than only a spiritual, endeavour.

Beyond broadcasting, this tendency can be found amongst musicians, film-makers and playwrights who reflect British Muslim identities and subjectivities in a way that engages with the social and cultural aspects of the everyday. For example, Ishy Din's play, *Snookered*, which examines friendship and belonging amongst a group of young Muslim teenagers. Or the rap duo, Poetic Pilgrimage, who consider the experiences of Muslim women in Britain. In each of these cases, Islamic subjectivities can be entirely hidden from view, while the human dilemmas of Muslim life are brought forward. Muneera, from Poetic Pilgrimage, explains this tendency:

> we may not always reflect Islamic themes, but us being Muslim, it is a Muslim perspective, we're talking about love. When I'm talking about what I'm looking for in a husband, we're still reflecting that from a Muslim perspective. (Muneera, musician, February 2011, London)

Of course, a 'Muslim perspective' will usually always contain dimensions of Islamic belief and practice, but through the expression of secular-civic culture these religious connotations become hidden, or de-emphasized. Instead, a spectrum of universal human experience is explored and expressed, with both positive and negative connotations: love and friendship, growing old and coming of age, grappling with poverty, cherishing family life and encountering alienation or discrimination. These are of course all important and valid experiences, but there is a sense in which this cultural framing places an emphasis on aspects of civic belonging, rather than 'religion' as a lived and ritualistic experience, and in doing so therefore enacts something of a secularization of Muslim social identity.

The Mediatization of Islam in Britain

The typology that I have outlined in the preceding sections (Islamic, Islamically conscious and secular-civic) broadly relates to the intentions and subjectivities of Muslim creatives, but there are also structural changes occurring at an institutional level for Muslims in Britain. As I argue in this section, these changes can be understood through theories concerning the mediatization of religion (see Hjarvard, 2008, 2011, 2013; Hjvard and Lövheim, 2012, 2019; Lövheim, 2014; Lundby, 2018; Moberg, 2018). Academic interest in the link between religion and media is long-standing, with a diverse field of inquiry that was opened up largely thanks to the work of Stuart Hoover (e.g. see Clark and Hoover, 1997; Hoover, 2006). While the field of religion and media has seen a number of approaches, mediatization theory is perhaps the most provocative because it proposes that contemporary religion is defined by the assumptions, values and processes of modern media. According to this claim, religion, rather than existing as a separate and distinct field of activity, is so imbricated with forms of mass and digital media that it is difficult to consider it an independent social institution. Gordon Lynch refers to this as the growing presence of a 'media logic', but he also rightly critiques the theory by suggesting that there is insufficient evidence to apply it beyond the secular and Northern European/ Nordic Christian backdrop from within which it first emerged (Lynch, 2011). There is therefore a need to continually test this theory against a range of contexts and to consider how the mediatization of religion might be manifested in other, more wide-ranging cases (Lövheim and Hjarvard, 2019). In opening up this research field, Stig Hjarvard states:

> Through the process of mediatization, the media come to influence and change religion at several levels, including the authority of the religious institution, the symbolic content of religious narratives, and religious faith and practices. A theory of the interface between media and religion must consider the media and religion in the proper cultural and historical contexts, since the mediatization of religion is neither historically, culturally, nor geographically a universal phenomenon. (Hjarvard, 2013: 80)

With this in mind, I am interested in examining the extent to which Islam has become mediatized in contemporary Britain. To what extent have Islamic institutions and fields of activity become defined by this 'media logic'? And what are the implications of this for religious authority, for the circulation of Islamic symbols and beliefs or for changing religious practices, mythologies, imaginations and identities, and the restructuring of Muslim institutions?

The Muslim public sphere in Britain has been dominated for much of the post-war period by institutions and discourses that are centred upon the 'ulama', Islamic reform movements and a mosque-based community culture. Even a cursory glance at research on Muslims in Britain can point towards the centrality of these sources of authority and organization for everyday religious practice (e.g. see Lewis, 1994; Gilliat-Ray, 2010). However, over the last two decades this status quo has been weakened and somewhat replaced by a diverse Muslim public sphere, within which new voices and institutions jostle for prominence. In this emerging media landscape, for example, rather than *muftis*, sheikhs and community leaders, there are instead new Muslim public figures who interface more directly, and perhaps more relevantly, with the everyday religious lives of Muslims in Britain – such as Islamic teledawah, Muslim comedians and Sufi singers, to name just a few. This is not to deny the importance of traditional sources of Islamic authority but rather to suggest that the Muslim public sphere in Britain is increasingly dominated by these 'new interpreters' (Anderson, 2003) – that is, by Muslim elites that have emerged from business, politics, academia and the realm of cultural production. The task, then, is to consider the extent to which the creative industries are mediatizing Islam in Britain and to ask what the implications of this are for three key areas: (i) religious authority and institutions, (ii) everyday religious practice and belief and (iii) Muslim political and cultural identities.

Mediatization: Religious authority and institutions

One of the most important claims made by mediatization theory is that traditional religious institutions are losing their prominence as the sole arbiters and communicators of religious knowledge. Through Hjarvard's reading (2013), in the Scandinavian context, this claim suggests that clergy-based, church institutions are losing their responsibility for circulating and interpreting religious ideas and symbols. This role is, according to Hjarvard, increasingly being fulfilled by a variety of media, from journalism and broadcasting to popular film, television and the internet. While much of this media might be secular – with secularizing tendencies – he suggests that religious media institutions controlled by non-clerical religious actors are also playing an accompanying role. This includes, for example, not only religious broadcasters and newspapers but also forms of digital religious media, from social media through to video streaming services. The key point here is that lay religious actors and institutions – utilizing both 'new' and 'old' forms of media – have entered the marketplace of religious communication – and that this is somewhat in competition with traditional sources of religious authority. There is a similar process at work for Islam in Britain, on an institutional level, with implications for understanding the changing nature of communication about religion, on the one hand, and the consumption of religious knowledge, on the other.

The emergence of Muslim religious media institutions is perhaps the most critical development in relation to the institutional landscape of Islam in the UK. These institutions take a number of forms, from Islamic recording companies and television stations to online and print media publications. Islamic television stations are the most visible and publicly significant of these, with seven now operating across the UK television market, but there are a wide variety of Muslim organizations that provide a cultural platform for the communication of religious knowledge. These range from cultural giants, such as Awakening Music, which oversees a portfolio of musicians and *nasheed* artists, to smaller organizations, such as the Khayaal Theatre Group, streaming service Alchemiya or the influential cultural blog sites, *The Muslim Vibe* and *Everyday Muslim*. The key point here is that these organizations are institutionalizing a dynamic and diverse Muslim media and cultural sphere in Britain, across television, film, theatre, publishing, music and the digital world. In doing so, they create new institutional frameworks for the communication of Islam and for the formation of Muslim communities and identities. These institutions are becoming sites of religious and cultural authority in their own right, with an increasing ability to define, prioritize and communicate ideas and symbols about Islam.

Hoover (2016) argues that this phenomenon is widespread across many different religious groups and traditions in the late modern era, with religious authority often being generated by charismatic actors in media spheres, rather than from amongst those rooted in scriptural chains of tradition and memory. For Muslims in Britain this is perhaps partly true, but with some important caveats. Islam does not have the same centralized, church-based hierarchies that have typically characterized Christianity. Furthermore, Muslims have always placed far greater emphasis on teacher/student relationships and on the respect given to those in traditions of learning, that is, an emphasis on charismatic and traditional authority (see Weber, 2004). Salvatore describes this as an emphasis on 'civility' – as a social value or moral code in Islamic societies – rather than on the Western arrangements of 'civil society' – that is, as a set of social and cultural institutions (Armando, 2016). For Muslims in Britain, then, it is vital to recognize that these new media institutions are somewhat less of a break with tradition and instead provide new avenues for both traditional and charismatic authority. For instance, teledawah *'ulama'* are rooted in chains of traditional authority, but they also find new ways to communicate on-screen through Islamic programming (i.e. a new form of charismatic religious authority). Or, less directly, Muslim musicians and film-makers, as charismatic authorities in their own right, who engage with a selection of handpicked Islamic scholars in order to reproduce religious knowledge and, in so doing, to stamp their work with recognized seals of traditional religious authority (see Chapter 4 for a fuller discussion). Consequently, rather than established Islamic authorities simply being replaced by emergent forms of Muslim media, there is instead a reconfiguration through which these established authorities adapt by engaging with changing forms of media communication. This creates a generation of religious leaders who are as much media figures as they are religious scholars. It also creates contemporary figures of Muslim media authority – such as musicians, film-makers, producers, writers and editors – who are responsible for these new media institutions, and in doing so become charismatic religious with their own audiences and remit of influence.

Mediatization: Religious practices and subjectivities

It is important to also consider the impact of changing media upon everyday religious practices and experiences for Muslims in Britain – and in particular to consider the implications of this for the agency and religious consumption associated with individual Muslims. In his work, Hjarvard demonstrated an interest in everyday religion, but this was manifested as a discussion of the ways through which media can create a set of secular rituals and practices to satisfy the communal and spiritual needs of a largely non-religious society (Hjavard, 2013). Hjavard terms this 'banal religion': mass media events, such as televised royal weddings and funerals, provide new social bonding rituals, while film and books (e.g. *Harry Potter* or the *Da Vinci Code*) have become a popularized means through which people engage with the supernatural and the spiritual. Clearly, the problem with 'banal religion' is that it relies on a sweeping assumption of secularization and therefore glosses over the enduring functions of established religious traditions. Consequently, some of the most fruitful discussions of mediatization theory involve its application to specific religious groups or phenomenon, ranging from global Christianity (Martino, 2016) to events such as Catholic World Youth Day (Hepp and Krönert, 2009) or the public visit of Pope Benedict to Berlin (Knoblauch, 2014). These studies are helpful because they ask how mediatization theory might explain aspects of religious change, for religious traditions and discourses, in a media-saturated era and, moreover, what this might mean for individual or group religious practice.

The key question, then, is to ask how rituals and religious experiences might be reconfigured for specific communities, particularly in light of the growing significance of mass media.

For Muslims in Britain this takes the form of new mediatized practices, centred upon prayer, pilgrimage and charity, as well as a wider trend towards individualized religious consumption. Less an erasure or replacement of traditional Islamic practices, this rather represents the growing significance of a media market culture, whereby individual religious experiences and agencies become prioritized in place of, or alongside, shared or communal experiences. Through this form of mediatization, core religious practices are woven together with media experiences. Or put another way, religious and spiritual experiences become media events: documented, recorded, shared, broadcast, sold and consumed.

In 2018, for example, the film *One Day in the Haram* was released and screened through a sold-out tour across the UK (subsequent tours followed in 2019 and 2020). Produced by a British director, Abrar Hussain, the film was marketed by the charity Penny Appeal and received widespread media attention across television, radio and digital media. It was billed as a way for Muslims to witness the Kaaba and was aimed, in particular, at those unable to participate directly in the Hajj, that is, most Muslims in Britain (McLoughlin, 2019). The marketing pitch dwelled on the deeply emotional nature of the film, claiming it will 'move you to tears' as the 'brilliance of Hajj unfolds before you'. Accompanied by 'vox pop' testimonies from viewers, the marketing campaign emphasized the personal transformation – spiritually and educationally – that occurs for those individuals able to watch the film on the big screen. Simultaneously, during Ramadan and across Islamic television channels, a series of programmes facilitated everyday Muslim involvement with not just the holy month itself but also the events and activities surrounding the Hajj. For example, Ramadan Live, on British Muslim TV, broadcast hours of live footage from the Kaaba, while taking on-air donations from individuals who were subsequently thanked (live and on-air) with prayers from the presenters and attendant religious scholar. Meanwhile, for those wanting to get their *barakah*s (blessings) in early, it was possible to participate in fundraising challenges before Ramadan – from mountain hikes and long-distance bike rides to 10k city runs – all documented by short video clips and inspirational photos, ideal for sharing on social media and as promotional material for Islamic television programming.

Consequently, what once might have been a private or communal act – prayer, pilgrimage or a charitable donation – is now an individualized public performance – and a 'product' that slots into a basket of mediatized and individualized religious experiences, rather than necessarily being linked to established group activities (i.e. in the mosque, community or other sites of collective religious practice). It is a 'product' because media is 'sold' to and consumed by the individual in an à la carte fashion, drawn from a buffet of mediatized religious experiences, rather than being confined to traditional group prescriptions around collective prayer, fasting, etc.

Mediatization: Political and cultural identities

Mediatization theory also helps us to understand media as a key driver of political change for Muslims in Britain. The notion of 'change' has long been central to theories of mediatization, so much so that Andreas Hepp defines mediatization as 'a concept that seeks to capture the shifting interrelationship between change, on the one hand, and socio-cultural media-communicative change, on the other' (Hepp, 2013: 31). Or put another way, wider changes within society and culture are fundamentally driven by changes in media communication. To study the social world around us, then, requires an understanding of the decisive role of media. Mediatization studies have applied the theory in such a way, ranging from analysing the mediatization of politics (Asp, 2014) and play (Hjarvard, 2013) to the mediatization of economics and education (Hepp, Hjarvard and Lundby, 2015). The central theoretical assumption that governs each of these studies is the claim that changes in media communication decisively affect other areas of social and cultural behaviour. For Muslims in Britain, then, the impact of changing media communication is not just felt in relation to religious institutions, authorities and everyday religious practices but can also be registered throughout wider forms of political and social engagement. Historically, Muslim political and social attitudes have been tightly linked to local and national political institutions and elites, whereby Muslim political leaders have given voice to 'community' concerns – the so-called gatekeepers of the 'Muslim vote'. This has however changed somewhat in recent years, with new forms of political communication – most notably through social media and a diversifying online media market – that have enabled diverse Muslim narratives to emerge. In short, evolving forms of media and cultural communication have enabled Muslims to sidestep established political elites and hierarchies. Muslim creatives are very much a part of this phenomenon.

This occurs in two primary ways. First, Muslim creatives are for the most part often engaged, as public figures, in political and ethical debates relating to issues such as racism, securitization and military intervention in Muslim-majority societies – all of which resonate specifically with Muslims (see Chapters 6 and 7) – as well as wider issues of national concern, for example, relating to poverty, homelessness and the use of food banks. Second, many Muslim creatives explore themes of cultural memory and social identity, typically relating to ethnicity, religion and national belonging. This positioning is important when the broader political and social currents of the UK are considered. Britain, like many parts of the world, has become increasingly subject to the growing divisions of 'identity politics', whereby social characteristics and cultural belonging play an increasingly vital role in informing political attitudes and affiliations (Fukuyama, 2018). Crudely put, in the UK, the tensions of this political landscape have bubbled up as the manifestation of a discourse concerning 'liberal internationalism' arrayed against a form of 'nativistic patriotism'. With Muslim creatives firmly placing themselves in alignment with the former view – one that emphasizes civic belonging, pluralism and international cooperation – there is a good reason to believe that these views are being encouraged and reinforced amongst Muslims in Britain more widely. Muslim creatives are public figures with an enormous capacity to influence their audience and respective communities – their opinion matters, and it is through their extensive media presence that this opinion is transmitted on a daily basis.

'Global Urban Muslims' and cosmopolitan culture

Research on Muslims in Britain has in the past often focused upon general deprivation of Muslim communities – including issues such as overcrowding, low educational attainment and poverty – but there has been a growing awareness that 'pockets of prosperity' are creating a generation of socially and economically capitalized Muslims in the UK (Muslim Council of Britain, 2015) – a demographic that I have described elsewhere as an 'emerging Muslim middle-class' (Morris, 2019a). As my findings in this book outline, the culture and entertainment industries are a key area where this newly capitalized generation continues to make a decisive impact. This includes through the establishment of businesses and networks in the culture industries, an engagement in public and political debate and more expansively through art and creativity. Muslim creatives are therefore very much a part of this emerging middle class and are almost without exception well-educated professionals with a high degree of social and cultural capital. Those that are not engaged on a full-time professional basis in the culture industries are nonetheless engaged in other professions, such as teaching, management or finance. These high levels of education and professional attainment inevitably have implications relating to the world view of these individuals – particularly around ethical values, political beliefs and behavioural norms – as well as raising questions about the influence that they exert on their audience. As I argue, many of the views held by these Muslim creatives are formed in part because of their sustained engagement with transnational networks and the sense of inhabiting an interconnected, globalized world: the horizon of their cultural, religious and political lives is therefore undeniably internationalist in scope.

In 2012, the journalist and broadcaster, Navid Akhtar, produced a series of articles and a BBC Radio 4 documentary that explored the emergence of this new, transnational Muslim class. He summarized this social group in the following terms: 'Global Urban Muslims, highly educated, well-travelled, often with families spread across different continents, they are increasingly seeking out goods and services that respect and reflect their needs as Muslims' (Akhtar, 2012). According to Akhtar, this new demographic – internationalist and with money to spend – has not been sufficiently catered for in the UK. It was unsurprising then, when only a year later, in 2013, Akhtar founded the streaming service, Alchemiya, as a way to partly meet the cultural demands of a new Global Urban Muslim consumer market. Interest in this so-called 'halal global economy' is not new, but its rapid and sizeable growth has been notable: estimated from $150 billion in 2009 to somewhere between $2 and $3 trillion in 2019. While the economic dimensions of this growth are important, interest also relates to the social and cultural aspects of this emerging global Muslim consumer culture, much of which is rooted in Muslim popular youth culture – a group described by Shelina Janmohamed as 'Generation M' (2016) – which utilizes consumption as a way to develop and reshape what it means to be a Muslim in Britain. Crucially, however, as Akhtar recognizes with the Global Urban Muslim nomenclature, this group is 'globally' connected, both willing and able to draw on social and cultural connections with not just a wider Muslim ecumene – from Turkish fashion through to American hip-hop – but also with 'global culture' more widely.

Global and transnational networks have been theorized by Arjun Appadurai (1990) as a series of 'flows' that relate to ideology, finance, technology, media and ethnicity. Appadurai's central point is that these global cultural flows are better understood as 'scapes' (e.g. ideoscapes, financescapes, etc.) and are encountered much as one might traverse a landscape – that is, our unique perspective and positioning within each 'scape' determines how we see, experience or engage with these flows. Muslim creatives in Britain are extensively involved in many of these transnational networks and globalized forms of popular culture. They are in almost every way an exemplar of the Global Urban Muslim archetype outlined by Akhtar (2012) – or more theoretically, following Appadurai (1996), they might be described as a distinctive 'diasporic sphere': one with a shared set of concerns and characteristics that are constituted in large part by class-based global/transnational Muslim connections. Yet we need to better understand the dimensions and inflections of this group. To what extent does their unique position within wider global and transnational contexts inform their values and beliefs? And to ask what it might mean to be a Global Urban Muslim in Britain?

The turn to cosmopolitanism in the academy (for a summary see Rovisco and Nowicka, 2011) has provided a set of ideas that can be used to analyse this Global Urban Muslim public sphere. I have discussed this at length elsewhere (see Morris, 2019b) but look to examine some of these ideas here, within the context of Muslim cultural production. Cosmopolitanism, as a framework of values or virtues, has existed in various guises throughout history, from late Vedic pluralism in India and the proto-democracies of ancient Greece through to Kantian world peace republicanism and twentieth-century ideas of global governance (e.g. Archibugi, 1995; Held, 1995). In more recent articulations, cosmopolitanism has been the utopian search for a universal ethic or political arrangement, as a bulwark against the dark lure of exclusive ethnic and national identities. Theoretically, cosmopolitanism is additionally understood as a disintegration of clear-cut national cultures and societies in a global age (Robbins, 2006) – provoking a call by Ulrich Beck for sociologists to equip themselves with a new methodological paradigm for the 'age of cosmopolitanization' (Beck, 2012). My interest in cosmopolitanism reflects this theoretical direction, and I draw from Gerard Delanty's notion of 'critical cosmopolitanism'. This proposes that we view cosmopolitanism as a social process occurring 'when and whenever new relations between Self, Other and World develop in moments of openness' (Delanty, 2009: 52–3). This carries the presumption that cosmopolitanism is not so much an abstract ideal, but rather that it is constitutive of social activity in a real and lived sense. Furthermore, that we should understand these processes as rooted and, in each case, uniquely specific, in the sense that they draw from the social and cultural resources that happen to lie at hand (Appiah, 1998). For Global Urban Muslims in Britain, then, I argue that these unique resources at hand correspondingly include Islamic beliefs, values and practices – all of which are framed by Muslim creatives as inherently plural and cosmopolitan, which includes actively resisting exclusivist interpretations of Islam – along with transnational networks and ethnic/cultural traditions that are linked to 'global Muslim culture' (see Chapter 7). Furthermore, given the deep civilizational rifts that are seemingly made manifest by the Orientalist imagination, cosmopolitanism is a natural ideological tendency through which to resist the enforced reductivity of 'Islam vs the West'. Or, to reverse the paradigm, as a way in which an Islam of the Global West can be exemplified and made manifest.

Of course, Muslims in Britain are a diverse social group with many competing and sometimes paradoxical views. A global and internationalist perspective in and of itself is no guarantee that cosmopolitan or pluralist views will be developed by specific individuals or groups. As scholars such as Hamid (2016) and Werbner (2002) have demonstrated, the entanglement of Muslims on the global stage, coupled with perceptions of Western persecution against Muslims, has in the past encouraged young, educated and socially mobile Muslims to develop forms of political and religious consciousness that have been labelled as 'Islamist'. This sweeping designation conceals broad differences amongst and between different transnational Islamist networks/traditions, all of which contain varying political and religious beliefs (usually 'radical', sometimes conservative, very occasionally militant). For some young Muslims, Islamism was a form of social activism and intellectualism that dominated the 1990s and 2000s. While diverse, it was typically held together by a framework of ideas (usually anti-colonial and critical of Western nation state dominance) that made sense of the modern world. While some of this was organized through activist groups and networks – with the structural features of membership, leadership and organizational resourcing – much of it was (and still is) largely a series of interconnected ideas, narratives and philosophies that have shaped social and religious engagement, which have been (often crudely) labelled with the catch-all term 'Islamism'. While debates will no doubt continue about the use of the term 'Islamism' – particular after its political weaponization by Western governments and political leaders – it does certainly have a great deal of value in reference to specific and historically rooted political and social trends within contemporary Muslim societies (see Esposito, Rahim and Ghobadzadeh, 2017).

In the same way, cosmopolitanism is a loosely bound framework of ethical and cultural beliefs, which, I argue, animate the very section of society that Akhtar has described as Global Urban Muslim. These views are prominent amongst Muslims involved in the cultural industries, and this must inevitably have an impact upon their audience. This is a mostly young and middle-aged generation that polling company Ipsos MORI identified, in a 2018 poll, as being more liberal and educated than their parents and grandparents, as well as possessing higher levels of religious commitment and greater confidence in expressing a strident British Muslim identity. After decades of negative political rhetoric in the West – whereby Islam has often been denigrated as a pre-modern, anti-democratic and anti-liberal religious tradition – these Muslims pose a counternarrative. One whereby Islamic beliefs and values – and the specific experiences that Muslims often have relating to discrimination and disenfranchisement – are entwined with philosophical and political debates concerning pluralism, internationalism and human rights. (Muslim) cosmopolitanism seems to me to be a useful way to frame this counternarrative. It is not a movement or an organization but rather a set of discourses and an ethical framework that appears to be animated by the pluralism that is inherent in a postcolonial world, marked by migration and new forms of global communication.

Cosmopolitanism draws attention to two social tendencies manifested by Global Urban Muslims: their cultural expansiveness and their ethical world view. The first point refers to the fact that Global Urban Muslims often reside at a point of contact between Western, non-Western and Islamic cultural traditions. They are naturally well placed to draw from a remarkable range of cultural resources, from American hip-hop and South Asian cinema through to Turkish television and classical Arabic poetry. Their cultural horizons are vast, as well as varied, and therefore necessarily promote a series of encounters with 'the Other'. They possess the critical ability to step away from their own perspective – which they often do – and to consider the lives of others, both Muslim and non-Muslim alike. The second feature associated with Global Urban Muslims is that of a more expansive ethical world view: of moral commitments that are obviously internationalist and transnational in scope but that also ferment grander ideas relating to a universal and humanitarian ethic. While such commitments are illustrative of cosmopolitan virtues in general – described by Turner (2002) as irony, reflexivity, scepticism, care for others and hybridization – they also uniquely belong to Global Urban Muslims precisely because they *draw from* and are *filtered through* a framework of Islamic values and beliefs. Indeed, cosmopolitan virtues are seen by many Global Urban Muslims to be inherent to Islam and moreover to have been developed in the Islamic tradition long before the Western world finally 'caught up' through the Enlightenment. Regardless of their provenance, cosmopolitan ideas – as I will show in later chapters – can be found circulating in a number of ways within contemporary Muslim cultural production: in relation to pluralized religious knowledge, individual autonomy and universalized experience, expansive cultural agency and belonging and through transnational networks and globalized imaginaries.

In the next section (Chapters 4–7) I look to build on the contextual and theoretical discussions of this and previous chapters in order to provide a thematically structured analysis of Muslim cultural production. As I will demonstrate, many of these themes – relating to the functional role of culture, mediatization and a class-based cosmopolitan politics – can be found within the discourses and cultural/social practices of Muslim creatives. This is only part of the story but as I suggest, Muslim creatives are critical voices of change at the forefront of very recent historical and social-significant developments that will continue to shape Muslim Britain in the decades to come.

Part Two

Muslim creatives in contemporary Britain

4

Voices of authority
The changing landscape of Islamic knowledge

A man from the audience, an elderly gentleman, a scholar and a leader amongst our local Muslim community said, 'I've never been to a concert in my life', and he'd never listened to Islamic music either, because he thought it was wrong. He said, 'this is the first time ever I've heard you guys perform or heard any Islamic music. I closed my eyes and listened, and I thought, is this haram or halal? Is this taking me towards God, or is this taking me away from God?' And he said, 'It brought me closer to God, so I smiled, opened my eyes, and enjoyed the evening'.

Amran, musician, January 2011, Birmingham

Muslim creatives interpret, mediate and defer to religious authority in different ways: through the artistic expression of religious ideas and knowledge, by providing an accessible commentary on Muslim values and beliefs, and as students, sitting before the feet of the *'ulama'*. There is also a very real sense in which Islamic scholars themselves use media and culture to extend their influence and reinforce their status, most especially through the broadcasting genre of teledawah. Yet the relationship between popular culture and Islamic authority is complicated. This is nothing new. Throughout Islamic history there have always been conservative and influential religious discourses that have looked askance at 'culture', perceiving it to be a natural home for deviant and forbidden practice (Shiloah, 1997): whether as a lure into the world of illicit pleasure – such as intoxication and sexual promiscuity – or as a form of *bid'ah* (religious innovation), which can draw true believers away from the *sunnah* of the Prophet Muhammad. So, while cultural and religious contexts may have changed over the centuries, this fundamental tension – religion/culture – has essentially always existed, since the time of the early Muslim community in the seventh century, when pre-Islamic practices were evaluated against the dictates of scriptural revelation, and continues to do so in the modern period (Otterbeck, 2008). Yet as Amran (lead musician for Aashiq al-Rasul) indicates in the opening passage, the dividing line between the secular and the sacred – as well as the forbidden and the permissible (the *haram* and the *halal*) – is a grey area, constantly navigated and negotiated, not just by lay Muslims, and Muslim creatives themselves, but also by the *'ulama'* and others in a position of traditional religious leadership. Thus, extensive Islamic scholarship dating back to the Middle Ages, with frequent religious and moral debates concerning music and aniconism (Frishkopf, 2009), has led into more finely grained debates about the functional merits of popular culture: from spiritual sound cultures to religious cartoons, teledawah and educational or devotional film. Purist discourses, driven by conservative forms of Wahhabism and Shi'a Islam, are still very much a part of the global Islamic ecosphere. Yet for many the fundamental question can more pragmatically relate to a matter of individual judgement: how does popular culture and media advance religious knowledge and devotion?

The individualization of religious authority amongst Muslims has been charted and debated now for several decades (e.g. Tezcan, 2005; Peter, 2006; Kaya, 2010; Amin, 2019). Writing about Muslims in a minority context, Jocelyne Cesari argues that established traditions of authority have been dissolving away in response to the context of diverse and plural Western democracies. Cesari suggests that the 'social adaptation process of Muslim minority groups has placed Islam within the three interrelated paradigms of secularization, individualization, and privatization' (2003: 260). The result is that religious authority becomes relativized within a marketplace of competing 'truths' – and that the personal autonomy of individual believers is correspondingly prioritized. As I will show, for Muslims, media and popular culture play a vital role in this process, but this does not necessarily entail the diminishing of traditional lineages of religious authority, which, for Islam, typically reside within the institutions and networks of the *'ulama'*.

Yet this thesis also implies that established religious authorities are required to respond to the conditions of a dominant media and cultural landscape. That is, to reformulate and recast their message in an effort to connect to a changing public – to become more charismatic and more attuned to the way in which knowledge must now be communicated. As Stuart Hoover argues, media and culture also enable religious authorities to generate new forms of knowledge about religion:

> Religious authority is now, and will continue to be, fluid and elastic. The terms and boundaries of authority are no longer fixed by law, tradition, or the

exceptional characteristics of charismatic leaders or systems. In the motile and fluid marketplace of religious symbols, selections, generativity, and circulation are determined not just by the aspirations and prerogatives of the received but by the affordances and products of practice. (Hoover, 2016: 34)

While media and culture therefore create the prevailing conditions within which existing religious authorities are required to navigate (new competencies, forms of communication, institutions, etc.) – and this relates very directly to my earlier arguments concerning mediatization (see Chapter 3) – they also create original and emergent forms of religious knowledge. In doing so they are constructing alternative spaces of religious authority. This ranges from the creative process of cultural production itself – for example, writing and producing a film – through to consumption practices – such as watching that film, interpreting it and then discussing it with friends. Both acts – production and consumption – are capable of transmitting and interpreting religious knowledge in a way that might often at times be beyond the control of traditional religious authorities. Yet, as Hoover suggests, traditional religious authorities are not so much being replaced as an institution, or even undermined, as they are faced with new conditions, competitors and collaborators. As I argue throughout this chapter, the power and influence of the *'ulama'* has become weakened in some ways, but strengthened in others, and they are still a vital institution when it comes to enabling authorized discussions of Islam. The stamp of scholastic approval and the expertise of jurists is widespread and deeply rooted in Islam – a religious tradition that, after all, has for 1,400 years (Brockopp, 2017) placed almost unmatched emphasis on the formal traditions of religious learning. Furthermore, the *'ulama'* are finding innovative ways to extend their influence directly, such as through an emergent genre of teledawah. In this chapter, then, I examine this changing landscape for Muslims in Britain, specifically considering the nature of the relationship between Muslim creatives and Islamic religious authority in the UK.

Lay Muslim creatives: 'New interpreters' of Islam?

As I indicated in the opening section, perhaps the most compelling academic debate on Islamic religious authority has concerned the changing nature and status of the *'ulama'*. In an influential publication, Jon Anderson argued that a generation of lay Muslims have emerged as the 'new interpreters' of Islam (2003: 47). Anderson points towards Muslim professionals, in the United States, who have utilized their proficiency of digital technology to provide a critique of, and commentary on, Islamic religious knowledge. The claim is simple enough: that these individuals have eroded the dominance of traditional Islamic scholars, many of whom are ill-equipped to engage with a rapidly changing global information economy. In contrast, Larsson (2011) has highlighted the ways in which the *'ulama'* have started to make use of the internet and other forms of global knowledge exchange (including television and lecture tours). These claims are both valid: the *'ulama'* are operating in a more crowded and competitive field of religious discourse, but their critical role as the custodians of religious knowledge remains paramount. As I argue, Muslim creatives have emerged over the last two decades to become important figures within this bustling marketplace of Islamic discourse. Before exploring this claim, it is helpful first to make two general points about the role of Muslim creatives in relation to religious authority.

First, it should be acknowledged that there is considerable diversity in relation to how creatives communicate religious knowledge. The typology of Muslim popular culture that I outlined in Chapter 3 broadly reflects these different approaches (i.e. Islamic, Islamically conscious and secular-civic). This ranges from an explicit engagement with scripture through to the complete avoidance of religious discourse and debate. For example, there are musicians and writers who cite scripture, channelling Qur'anic insights into their work, while there are others who have little or no interest in overtly discussing or expressing orthodox 'religion'. This reinforces a central claim that I make in this book. Muslim popular culture is functionally diverse: it expresses different motivations and perspectives, only some of which are relevant for the changing nature of religious authority. It is those Muslim creatives who are explicitly and specifically engaged in a form of *da'wah* – that is, projecting knowledge and instilling religious education/practice – that are relevant when considering religious authority. This primarily includes those producing 'Islamic music' and those involved in 'Islamic television' – both forms of cultural production use their output as a vehicle to convey religious knowledge. Muslim creatives that lean towards entertainment, or social and political critique, are less 'religiously' significant in this regard, but this does not mean that they entirely lack influence: their public promotion of selected scholars, or their embodied realization of Muslim piety and practice, can also transmit important signals that inform authorized interpretations of Islam.

Second, the transmission of religious knowledge and discourse is not always seen to be appropriate for some cultural genres and styles. For instance, comedy is not typically perceived to be an appropriate forum to discuss the life and example of the Prophet Muhammad, but gently poking fun at everyday Muslim religious experience – such as the family dynamics of Eid or funny and awkward situations during communal prayer – is considered acceptable. Music, in contrast, is seen to be particularly evocative for spiritual experience and transformative self-knowledge, while documentary film lends itself to an intellectual engagement with the history of Islamic ideas. This suggests that there is a spectrum of religious knowledge and discourse: from the sacred and the protected through to the lived and the experienced. This is significant when considering the continued role of the *'ulama'*, because there are realms of sensitive religious knowledge that are understood to be inviolate and therefore requiring specialist treatment from authorized figures of religious learning. This is a manifestation of that deep-rooted tension between 'religion' and 'culture', and it places a limit on the extent and reach of lay Muslim authority (including that by Muslim creatives). There will always therefore be a unique role for the distinct religious authority of the *'ulama'*.

Rather than considering Muslim creatives as autonomous and independent creators of religious knowledge, then, it is more accurate to describe them as emergent interlocutors within deeper traditions of Islamic learning and knowledge. This engagement can be understood in three different ways: as interpretation, mediation and deference.

Muslim creatives can in certain contexts be understood through Anderson's paradigm of 'new interpreters'. Discussing the changing nature of global Islamic discourse, Anderson argues:

> This larger public sphere is marked by a coming into public view, and discussion, of interpretive practices between the high textualism of *'ulama*, marked by super-literacy of an interpretive elite, and more mystical, participative expressions of the non-literate sometimes identified as 'folk' Islam. (Anderson, 2003: 46)

Drawing on Hodgson (1974), Anderson continues this line of argument by suggesting that, rather than this being an historical rupture, it is 'more of a continuum' that reflects long-standing fractures between '*sharia*-minded and Sufi-minded Islam'. This division points towards the inaccessibility of text-based religious knowledge for audiences that lack developed religious literacy, and the consequent need, for these audiences, for a non-literary-based and more spiritual/affective engagement with scripture and religious learning. Some Muslim creatives understand themselves as capable of bridging this chasm between elite forms of literate knowledge, on the one hand, and the non-specialist world of ordinary believers, on the other.

London-based rapper, Mohammed Yahya, clearly makes this point when discussing the role of popular music in transmitting a religious message to young people:

> you ask a Muslim teenager to attend a lecture by a scholar from Saudi Arabia and unfortunately they often won't because it can be difficult to relate to their reality, however if you ask them to recite a verse from their favourite rap album or the latest track and they'll do that straight away. You know, so many times I've performed at an event and a speaker has spoken for half an hour, and then I'll come and perform a few songs and the speaker afterwards will say, you know what, what I've done in half an hour, you've done it in a song. The message is the same, you know, and you've done it in a way that they, the youth, can digest and relate to. (Mohammed Yahya, musician, February 2011, London)

Yahya is referring to the values, ideas and moral messages that are transmitted colloquially through music. While he does not make any claim to be 'scholarly', Yahya engages with Islamic texts and discourses – as part of his own religious journey – and feels confident enough to find a new way to transmit this knowledge to an audience of young Muslims. This approach – the channelling of individual learning through forms of 'accessible' cultural expression – is typical for many Muslim creatives.

There are also efforts by some to use cultural expression as a platform for scriptural exegesis, relating to both the Qur'an and the Hadith. This can include incorporating scriptural insights into public rhetoric, for example, during public talks, interviews and through social media. This might take the form of sharing a Qur'anic verse, or recounting a particular *hadith*, often with little or no commentary. Or at times making a more direct attempt to apply that wisdom to the practical and moral struggles of everyday life, such as using the example of the Prophet Muhammad to promote the need for patience or understanding in personal relationships. At times scripture can even be incorporated directly into cultural production, as the writer and director, Conor Ibrahiem, explains in relation to his film, *Freesia* (2017):

> I wanted to get in a point about educating women, it was the bit on the porch with Khadija and her dad, I forget what it was now, it's been a while since I wrote it, but the point always was to encompass some of the core values of the Qur'an, to punctuate it with them. You can't make a film about the Qur'an itself, it would go on too long, people would switch off, so you've got to pick your moments. (Conor Ibrahiem, writer and director, July 2018, Keighley)

In this instance, Ibrahiem takes a Qur'anic message, as he understands it, and incorporates it subtly into the dialogue and narrative of the film. During other scenes, the script uses verbatim Qur'anic verses that are dropped in, for example, to iterate the claim that Muslims should be compassionate and loving neighbours. In each of these cases, Ibrahiem argues that he is attempting not just to bring Islamic scripture to a wider audience but also to rebut 'twisted' interpretations of Islam, whether, for example, on gender roles, religious intolerance or violence.

These examples draw attention to the way in which some Muslim creatives transmit their own understanding and interpretation of Islamic scripture and belief through popular culture. It is a form of religious pedagogy that looks directly towards text and tradition, circumnavigating the role of the *'ulama'* as the historic guardians of orthodoxy.

There is also an extent to which Muslim creatives are *mediators* of religious authority and knowledge. By this I mean a more collaborative engagement with existing scholastic networks and discourses. A process of drawing from, curating and filtering the teaching and knowledge of the *'ulama'* – and then expressing this learning through media and popular culture. In this respect Muslim creatives can consider themselves to be students of Islam, sitting at the feet of the *'ulama'*, but then seeking to reflect this pedagogy within their artistic output.

A typical way in which mediation occurs is through the promotion and amplification of specific scholars or intellectual traditions. Sami Yusuf, for example, one of the most prolific and successful Muslim musicians globally, has used his public position over the course of his career to boost the reputation and visibility of particular scholars, including Shaykh Yusuf al-Qaradawi, an Egyptian scholar, and warns against the dangers of religious extremism. Featured by *Emel* magazine in 2004 – at the beginning of his career – Yusuf spoke at length about the scholastic influences derived from his time studying at the Islamic Institute of Da'wa and Research, in London:

> Every day I took lessons in Hanafi Fiqh with Shaykh Talha Bukhari, Arabic lessons with Dr Muhammad Mustafa – who I consider the best Arabic teacher in the world – and with Hasan al-Banna, Tajwid lessons with Ustadh Jamil Rahman and Shaykh Hafidh. Visiting lecturers would arrive every evening to speak on a variety of issues such as 'Aqeeda, Islamic History, Revival and Revivers, Spirituality, Women's Scholarship in Islam, Islam and Health. It was a truly enlightening and definitely a life-changing experience for me. (Sami Yusuf, quoted in *Emel*, March/April 2004)

Yusuf, like many other Muslim creatives, considers himself a student of Islam, drawing from a rich tradition of scholasticism and then channelling it through his music and artistic output. The relationship is mutually beneficial: creatives benefit from the seal of orthodox religious authority, while Islamic scholars are able to tap into the extensive media reach that creatives have, often with large and diverse Muslim audiences.

Of the forty Muslim creatives that I interviewed for this research, twenty-three made a specific point of referring to their relationship with the *'ulama'*. A majority of these referred to specific Islamic scholars, including Sheikh Abdul Hakim Quick, Sheikh Babikir Ahmed, Sheikh Hamza Yusuf, Sheikh Michael Mumisa and Sheikh Abdul Hakim Murad. These scholars are all associated with the 'Traditional Islam' network (see Hamid, 2016): a neo-Sufi tradition that brings together classical Islamic modes of transmitting knowledge – including *isnad* (chain of transmission) and *ijazah* (authorization) – with an approach that applies this tradition to the contemporary context of Muslims in the West. Critically, this tradition refutes the way in which *ijtihad* (interpretation) can be incorrectly used by Muslims to apply their own understanding of scripture in a 'simplistic' way (an approach favoured by Salafi scholars), instead arguing that a deep lineage of classical learning should be brought to bear when considering truths of scripture within the contemporary context. This is significant, because it means that Muslim creatives can partly understand their role as one that includes engaging with and transmitting the specialist training and knowledge of the *'ulama'*.

British Muslim TV is illustrative of this relationship. It regularly provides a platform to scholars from the Traditional Islam network. This includes, for example, Sheikh Hamza Yusuf's popular series, *The Rihla Lectures*, and regular appearances from Sheikh Babikir Ahmed, including during the annual Ramadan Live coverage (the most widely watched series of programming on BMTV). These scholars are provided space and autonomy with which to share their learning and knowledge; yet, by filtering and curating the inclusion of the *'ulama'* – by choosing *which* scholars are given a public platform – BMTV is effectively gatekeeping and mediating religious authority. Islam Channel includes a more 'orthodox' and 'conservative-leaning' selection of scholars, drawn from centres of Sunni learning, such as Al-Azhar University, while Eman Channel, in contrast, while hosting a range of scholars, typically draws from a broad Salafi perspective, such as the international public figure, Mufti Menk, and Sheikh Abdul Basir, the imam of the West Ferry mosque. Whether on an individual or institutional level, then, there is a close relationship between lay

Muslim creatives and the *'ulama'* – a relationship that is characterized varyingly by collaboration, mediation and gatekeeping.

Finally, it is important to acknowledge that, when it comes to matters of religious knowledge, this relationship is informed by the deference that creatives often afford to the advanced training, reputation and specialism of the *'ulama'*. While creatives may well interpret and mediate religious authority, there is without exception a widespread recognition that the *'ulama'* are the final arbiters of religious knowledge. Sukina, from Poetic Pilgrimage, expresses this foundational relationship when discussing the permissibility of female musical performance:

> as women it's just important to keep on and to just be strong in that. When we came into Islam and when we performed, you know, our first three performances were with scholars and people who are learned in Islam, who are respected. So we always came in with blessings of what we were doing. If they're giving us their blessing, then for me that's a sign that it's okay. (Sukina, musician, February 2011, Cardiff)

Of course, there is still a degree of judicious autonomy occurring here. Poetic Pilgrimage were collaborating with scholars that they recognized as authoritative, but there is also an acknowledgement by Sukina that scholastic judgement is a necessary and final arbiter, partly out of deference but also in order to reassure British Muslim audiences that these musical performances are permissible. Other examples of this deference include that shown to scholars during religious programming – with lay Muslim presenters displaying embodied and verbalized signals of respect to 'learned' and 'wise' scholars – and in fictionalized popular culture through the depiction of scholastic characters that possess gravitas and a deep well of privileged learning.

Such deference can also be more direct and 'hands-on'. This includes, for example, Islamic television channels that ask scholars to vet their religious programming – to provide oversight and input into sensitive areas of religious knowledge – as well as musicians and spoken word poets who submit their lyrical content for approval. The *na'at* (Urdu religious poetry) performer, Ameena (not her real name), describes how she submitted a book of *na'at* to two locally respected scholars from Bradford and Birmingham:

> I gave my book draft to two scholars and they both said it's just fine, there's nothing wrong in it, nothing wrong in it. So you can just publish it. . . . They actually looked at the language and the words we use, how we use words for, like, the Prophet. I think the best scholars, they check not only the wording but the

balance as well. The poetry balance. They can check that as well. (Ameena, *na'at* performer, July 2011, Bradford)

Ameena's choice of language in the interview, and her decision to incorporate the suggested changes from local scholars in her book of poetry, is indicative of this deferential approach. She recognizes that not all scholars are equal – some are 'better' than others. Equally, she acknowledges that a specialist seal of religious approval is required to authorize her poetry, particularly in relation to that which is considered sacred (such as in reference to the Prophet Muhammad). It is a finely struck balance between autonomy – choosing which scholars to engage with – and deference towards the learning of not just individual scholars but also the *'ulama'* as an institution.

Teledawah: Pietistic charisma in the media age

The *'ulama'* can be prominent actors within media and cultural spheres – in a sense, they can at times themselves become creatives, performing their scholastic identities within spaces of media and culture. This is most evident within the broadcasting output of Islamic television. To varying degrees, Islamic television stations in the UK regularly feature the *'ulama'* within their programming and are helping to create a new generation of media-savvy Islamic scholars, whereby traditional Islamic authority is recast in an alternative form, with innovative modes of religious communication. Given the often-fierce competition between different schools of thought and legal traditions within Islam, a sophisticated approach to media and culture can enable scholars to extend their individual influence across larger audiences, both nationally and globally.

The involvement of the *'ulama'* in Islamic television varies. Islam Channel relies on significant involvement of the *'ulama'* in the production and broadcasting of its programming. The majority of scheduled programming on Islam Channel – approximately 80 per cent of its output – has been developed in order to educate and better inform viewers about core Islamic practice, devotion and scriptural knowledge. This includes, for example, *Me, Myself and Allah*, *How to Fall in Love with the Qur'an* and *Small Deeds Massive Rewards*. Each of these shows, which are typically broadcast twice daily, are presented by – and produced in collaboration with – an *'alim*. Similarly, the schedule of Eman Channel is dominated by *'ulama'*-led programming, such as *Ramadan Reminders*, *The Greatness of Allah* and *Islam Q and A*. In contrast, British Muslim TV has a smaller selection of programming in this genre, with scheduled shows that include little more than *Ask the Alim* and *Wisdom and Tea* – the remaining bulk of the BMTV schedule is broadly aligned towards the genres of lifestyle, entertainment and historical documentary.

Programming of this kind – which is clearly a type of Islamic popular culture (see Chapter 3) – indicates two important points. First, the growth and development of a subgenre of broadcasting, which has been labelled varyingly as 'teledawah', 'dawah-TV' or 'Islamic teledawah' (all three terms were used by participants). This type of broadcasting performs a distinct religious function. It has a receptive audience, but there are others who argue that it is functionally too narrow, and that Muslims need to develop a wider spectrum of broadcasting content that is culturally rich rather than religiously proscriptive. As television producer, Aziz (not his real name), argues:

> I call it dawah-TV, or Muslim teledawah. It's okay, it does its thing, which is fine. But it can be a bit preachy, to be honest, telling Muslims what to believe and what to do. But we need something different, to have content that really reflects the heritage and lives of Muslims, in the communities that they actually live in. (Aziz, television producer, July 2018, London)

According to Julia Howell (2008a), 'Islamic televangelism' (this is the term used by Howell), which is modelled on the Christian televangelist culture of the United States, is predominantly concerned with articulating and reinforcing notions of Muslim piety – or as Aziz frames it, being 'preachy'. Such efforts can range from the projection of hard boundaries, relating to acceptable practice and devotion, through to the softer manifestation of spiritual intimacy and transformation. It can also arguably range across genres, from formal religious oratory through to chat-show-style debate and casual/informal monologue presentation. The phenomenon of teledawah is broadly conceived and is not well understood. El Naggar, for example, has examined the digital broadcasting of the American comedian Baba Ali, pointing towards the seemingly attractive 'ordinariness' of Ali for Muslim youth (El Naggar, 2017). Howell has examined Sufi expressions of religious immanence in South East Asian teledawah (2008b), while, in sharp contrast, Saleh (2012) has discussed the ways in which Salafi Arab teledawah develops a sense of 'otherness' – that is, the 'othering' of both non-Salafis and the West – and in doing so has created hard boundaries of internal membership. Teledawah in the UK, as I will demonstrate, is focused on Muslim piety, but with nuanced inflections that highlight the diversity of Muslim audiences and their varyingly different religious and spiritual needs.

The second point is that this genre of Islamic broadcasting requires a particular set of competencies from those involved, something which I define here as *pietistic charisma*. In contrast to El Naggar (2017), I would argue that teledawah is not marked by the 'ordinariness' of comedians such as Baba Ali, but rather that teledawah is characterized by a projection of seriousness, devotion and, most importantly, the fixed and weighty authority of classical Islamic learning (i.e. it is stylistically very different to comedians such as Baba Ali). It is precisely the *un-ordinariness* of teledawah that distinguishes it from the wider landscape of lay Muslim cultural production. Rather than generically defining teledawah as an 'any and all' expression of Islamic religiosity through broadcasting (which might include lay Muslim actors or comedians, such as Baba Ali, for example), rather, I conceptualize it as the direct extension of the *'ulama'* into the modern media market, with a distinctive style of pietistic charisma, as a means to communicate and define orthodox Islamic knowledge.

The credibility of teledawah rests on the ability of those involved to project pietistic charisma. As I explain shortly, with reference to two case studies, pietistic charisma is the *performance of Islamic scholasticism*. It is the deployment of specific verbal and visual cues that serve to elevate teledawah *'ulama'* above Muslim lay commentators on matters of specialist religious knowledge. This involves deploying legalistic and scriptural language, coupled with a seeming depth of performed learning – a restrained and understated comportment, matched by crisp and considered speech inflections – and the perception of both spiritual clarity and gravitas. The concept of pietistic charisma problematizes Weber's influential typology of tripartite authority (Weber, 2004) – traditional, rational-legal, charismatic – precisely because pietistic charisma contains elements of all three, in a way that is not so easily divisible. As Spickard argues, Weber conceptualized traditional authority as a form of deadening 'inertia', presuming instead that modernity was being forged through the dynamism of an avowedly superior and rationalized individualism (Spickard, 2017: 77). This was something that Weber believed to be expressed through the bureaucratic institutions of secular Europe (indeed, a specific target of disapproval for Weber was *shari'ah*, which to his mind seemingly lacked the criteria of modern secular law (Asad, 2003)). Teledawah *'ulama'* therefore help to disprove such notions: they combine a complex array of traditional, rational and charismatic authority, which is expressed through a distinctive style of pietistic charisma.

I turn now to an illustrative and comparative discussion of two teledawah programmes: *Ask the Alim* and *Islam Q and A*, broadcast respectively on British Muslim TV and Islam Channel. These are both flagship programmes, with regular daily slots, and are featured prominently in the digital marketing material for each of these television stations. This discussion is based on an analysis of ten episodes of each of these programmes (twenty in total) throughout October and November 2020. The programmes are notable for their similarities and differences. They each fit the mould of teledawah – that is, a direct extension of the *'ulama'* into the modern media market – but their differences suggest that this activity can address divergent needs and audiences. Accordingly, an analysis of their style and content helps to illuminate the nature of the audiences for British Muslim TV and Islam Channel, respectively, as well as to explain the role of Muslim teledawahs in contemporary media.

Ask the Alim and *Islam Q and A* are hosted by an Islamic scholar who responds to questions that are either asked over the phone by viewers or sent through in advance via the messaging service WhatsApp. The *'alim* responds with guidance that draws upon his understanding of *shari'ah*, typically justifying their response through recourse to *fiqh* (Islamic jurisprudence) and by providing a recommended course of action. This role is in many ways identical to that which has been performed by *'ulama'* throughout Islamic history: as jurists and custodians of knowledge, with a duty to guide other Muslims upon request. The distinctiveness of this format, however, can be found in the fact that these programmes are tailored to reach a much wider audience, regardless of the interest that individual viewers might or might not have in any particular question. The programmes are therefore designed to be engaging, with more rounded discussions that, in theory at least, find a connection to the daily lives and experiences of a wider Muslim audience. The expectation is that something can be found for everyone, in the response to every question, notwithstanding often very specific lines of questioning. The programmes therefore reflect the religious needs and world view of their audience and indicate how the programme editors believe that these needs should be met.

One striking difference can be found in the questions that are asked and the make-up of the viewers asking those questions. Here I divide the question topics into three broad areas: devotion, health and family. Questions concerning devotion include, for example, those about breaking *wudu'* (ritual purification), performing *salah* (prayer), correct *niyyah* (intention), the most effective *du'a* (invocation), etc. These questions are about refining correct devotional practice. Questions concerning health often relate to faith healing (e.g. reading the Qur'an to cure diabetes, an Islamic approach to Covid-19, etc.), the Islamic implications of certain medical practices (e.g. a blood sugar prick test breaking *wudu'*) or the permissibility of health-related 'vices' (e.g. smoking and non-alcoholic cocktails).

Questions relating to family typically focus on practical issues concerning marriage, inheritance and divorce (e.g. the validity of *talaq* (repudiation: to utter the phrase for divorce) when intoxicated, access to children during separation, etc.). The frequency of these topics for each programme is summarized in Table 2. These categories cover all of the questions asked during each of these programmes.

Clearly there is a notable trend here, with viewers of *Ask the Alim* expressing a greater interest in topics that relate to social and family issues – with divorce being the most frequent topic of discussion – while the *Islam Q and A* audience largely inquire about ritualistic and devotional practice. The make-up of these audiences perhaps goes some way to explain this. While personal information about the questioners is only occasionally provided by the presenter, verbal ques and the phrasing/context of the question do enable some insight. Questioners on *Ask the Alim* were seemingly always British, with confident and accurate English, and appeared to be younger or middle aged. Those for *Islam Q and A* were typically older, sometimes with heavily accented or broken English, including both British and international callers. In this particular sample, these international callers were from African commonwealth countries, where English is a first or second language, including Tanzania and Nigeria.

Perhaps somewhat aligned to the nature of these audiences, there were a range of presenters on each programme. *Ask the Alim* had two different presenters, Imam Hamzah Hassan, the head of Manchester Central Mosque, and Mufti Yusuf Akudi, the director of the Muslim Family Centre, a UK-based Shari'ah service provider. Both are British-born *'alims* educated in the UK (at a British Darul Uloom and the University of Leeds). In contrast, *Islam Q and A* incorporated a more diverse range of presenters, a far smaller selection of whom were British-born and educated, ranging from Sheikh Dr Saalim Al-Azhari, London-born, with a British medical degree and a postgraduate award from Al-Azhar University, to those from overseas or with a first-generation migrant background, such as Sheikh Suleiman Kibuka, a graduate of Medina University,

Table 2 Question Topics on *Ask the Alim* and *Islam Q and A*

	Number of Questions Asked N (%)	
	***Ask the Alim* (BMTV)**	***Islam Q and A* (Islam Channel)**
Devotion	9 (20%)	42 (77.8%)
Health	10 (22.2%)	8 (14.8%)
Family	26 (57.8%)	4 (7.4%)

and Sheikh Dr Khalid Khan, a retired neurologist and the imam for Lambeth Islamic Cultural Centre.

It is possible to make a number of remarks based on these observations. *Ask the Alim* (British Muslim TV) is tailored for a culturally British audience and reflects many of the everyday social and religious dilemmas faced by Muslims in the UK. The presenters were selected in order to better understand and address these concerns – and their choice of phrasing when responding reflects this approach. While the advice provided by the alim presenters was rooted in *fiqh* and *sunnah*, it took on a greater degree of pastoral responsibility, attempting to align the injunctions of Islamic law with the realities of contemporary family and social life. One particular discussion, about access to children during divorce proceedings, illustrates this claim. Responding to a caller, Mufti Yusuf Akudi provided the following guidance:

> Allah talks about *talaq*, divorce, custody, etc. And the *sunnah* of our Beloved, *salla Allahu 'alayhi wasallam*, also addresses these issues. Unfortunately it's not a very good thing, *talaq*, divorce, but there is a whole *surah*, called *talaq*, divorce, in the Holy Qur'an, as well as talking about how divorce should take place . . . keeping it amicable, keeping it civil, keeping it in the lines of the Qur'an and *sunnah*. So we should be human, be just, be fair, be caring, be loving. At the end of the day, if a husband and wife are not getting along, for whatever reason it is, or if there is no reason. They are like chalk and cheese, as one might say, they don't get along. There's no domestic violence, like the brother has stated, there is no non-molestation order, there are no other issues. Amicably resolving this matter is very important and one should understand that, you know, we ask for our rights and demand our rights, but we don't shoulder our responsibilities. It's the responsibility of the father and the mother to look after the welfare, upkeep, maintenance, wellbeing, education, nurturing of the children, or the child. (Mufti Yusuf Akudi, *Ask the Alim*, 9 October 2020)

The structure and phrasing of this response is typical for *Ask the Alim*. First, Akudi locates his response in the primacy of *sunnah*. He does not provide technical detail but uses scriptural language (e.g. *talaq* and *sura*) to imply a specialist depth of understanding. Akudi then proceeds to speak with a moral and ethical framing that is not specifically 'Islamic', by using the language of 'rights' and 'responsibilities', with reference to UK civil law (e.g. non-molestation and orders), and the English-language idiomatic reference to 'chalk and cheese'. In this sense, Akudi is *performing* a type of Islamic scholasticism for the audience. Rather than dwelling on the intricacies of Islamic law and teaching, he first reminds the audience of his authority to speak on these matters, before then providing an engaging, accessible and culturally sensitive response, framed by wider moral sentiments that address the pastoral and social needs of both the questioner and a wider (British Muslim) audience.

In contrast, the *'ulama'* presenters on *Islam Q and A* typically provide responses that are rooted more in the perceived universality and uncontestable injunctions of Islamic law. Rather than engaging so much in a broad moral reflection, the emphasis is often on the scriptural boundaries of permissible or recommended Islamic religiosity and ritual. This partly reflects not only the diversity of the audience – with both British and international callers – but also the nature of the questioning, which tilts more towards very specific inquiries relating to devotional practice, rather than to social or cultural dilemmas.

An illustrative response followed a question from a first-generation Muslim caller, in Britain, about the principle of *tawassul*, which refers to seeking an intercession from an individual who is close to Allah. The questioner asked if *du'a*s can be made to such individuals. Most interestingly, the caller mentioned the widespread nature of this practice on the subcontinent, most likely referencing the Sufi veneration of *pirs*, which is particularly widespread across Pakistan (Rozehnal, 2016). The response from Sheikh Wasim Guyani was unequivocal:

> As a principle, we understand *tawhid*. And *tawhid* is very simple. That we worship, we only worship Allah. *Iyyaka na'budu wa iyyaka nasta'in*. This first, we recite it so many times in *salah*. It [*al-Fatiha*, the opening *surah* of the Qur'an] is one of the most recited *surah* in the Qur'an and we stick to that understanding. *Iyyaka na'budu wa iyyaka nasta'in*. You alone Allah we worship, and you alone Allah we seek help and assistance . . . so seeking help in terms of *du'a*, or anything that is beyond humanity, we always seek help in Allah first. And then we beg Allah to assist us in terms of whatever problems we go through. . . . So as Muslims, we are not allowed to go through anyone, be they prophets, be they companions, be they righteous scholars, imams of the path, righteous people that recently passed away, or righteous people even of today, we are not allowed to go through them. The only time you are allowed to go through them, is to ask them to make *du'a* for us. (Sheikh Wasim Guyani, *Islam Q and A*, 7 November 2020)

The question and the response are both typical for *Islam Q and A*. Guyani locates his answer very directly in scripture and – as he understands it – in the first principles of Islamic belief. The rhetorical device of scriptural repetition, both in Arabic and English, reinforces the centrality of inviolable Islamic teaching. It also reinforces his authority as a scholar, with unique access and insight to the truth of scripture. He then proceeds to offer clear guidance about the impermissibility of this particular practice. The aim is therefore to provide a universal framework of 'correct' Islamic practice, rather than necessarily reflecting on cultural nuance or a personal/social dilemma. Of course, broader pastoral discussions of this kind do emerge on *Islam Q and A*, but in contrast to *Ask the Alim*, they are less frequent and the emphasis tends to be on the rules of permissible and recommended practice.

Despite these differences, which mostly concern the type of advice given, there are many similarities between the two programmes. The visual backdrop and the delivery have similarities in relation to visual cues and an oratorical style that convey authority and learning. *Ask the Alim* features the *alim* presenter seated in a high-backed leather armchair, in front of a grandfather clock and beside an antique lamp – as if in a cliched professorial study – with a copy of the Qur'an resting on a pedestal to one side. *Islam Q and A* is presented before a backdrop of golden gilded hardback books, similarly with a copy of the Qur'an resting on a pedestal. The visuality of both programmes manages to convey a sense of authority and learning, both 'literary' knowledge and scriptural knowledge. Similarly, presenters often take notes, pause in reflection and contemplation before responding and strike a tone of delivery that is measured, thoughtful and without excessive ornamentation. This style of presentation is, as I have suggested, a type of pietistic charisma: a performance that *expresses and reinforces* the authoritative tradition of Islamic scholasticism and the *'ulama'*. Rather than providing the detail of scholastic knowledge – which might often be inaccessible to a lay audience – pietistic charisma channels performed religious authority through the format of a chat-show-style broadcast, both visually and oratorically.

Teledawah is notable then, as a form of Muslim cultural production, because it extends the influence of the *'ulama'* into contemporary media and is characterized by a unique presentational style. This combination of modern media production and Islamic scholasticism creates a distinctive version of religious authority – pietistic charisma – which helps to project and reinforce the unique significance of the *'ulama'*. As the two case studies indicate, despite a similarity in presentational style, teledawah responds to the different religious and sociocultural needs of diverse audiences. The challenge that contemporary media have posed to the *'ulama'* is the need to develop new competencies and forms of communication, as a means to remain relevant in the face of competition from new sources of religious authority (including from lay Muslim creatives). Teledawah shows that – at least in this limited way – the *'ulama'* are managing to adapt to meet this challenge.

Music and instrumentation: Defining the religiously permissible

The complex landscape of Islamic religious authority – and the role played by the '*ulama*' – is relevant for another area of cultural production: music and the permissibility of instrumentation. This has long been a topic of interest and has been discussed widely in academic writing elsewhere (see al-Faruqi, 1985, 1986; Nelson, 2001; Otterbeck, 2008; Rasmussen, 2010; Shiloah, 1995, 1997). The extent to which this issue has played out amongst Muslims in Britain has not received detailed or sustained attention to date. As I will argue, there are a wide range of views, and, in some respects, music is a bellwether for wider religious, cultural and social attitudes. Broadly speaking, Muslims in Britain are divided on the issue of music and instrumentation, with a spectrum that runs from the complete disapproval of all accompanied music (including that deemed to be religious) through to the everyday consumption of mainstream secular pop music. Muslim musicians are pivotal figures in this debate; they are required to make strategic choices about the nature of their ensemble and repertoire, as to whether certain lyrical content is appropriate, which instruments might be permissible in a specific context (e.g. at an Islamic conference) and if instrumentation is even permitted at all. The '*ulama*' are also central to this debate, because their seal of approval is often sought by musicians and consumers of music. Furthermore, the views taken by individual scholars on music are often (unsurprisingly) linked to their school of thought and a wider religious-political understanding of Islamic practice within the context of the Global West. Religious rulings and authorities are therefore not just constitutive of musical practice amongst Muslims, but music itself is a symbolic marker of the complex relationship that exists between Muslims and the non-Muslim world. This is especially the case in the Muslim-minority West.

Islamic arguments against music can be traced back to Ibn Abi al-Dunya (823–894), who drew on a selection of *hadith* to write a moralistic treatise against music (Shiloah, 1997). In many respects, Ibn Abi al-Dunya provided the template upon which all subsequent critiques of music have resided: that music too often encourages forbidden activities, such as drinking alcohol and promiscuity, and should therefore be considered *haram*. Later arguments within the Wahhabi and Salafi traditions have extended this claim, suggesting that the early Muslim community only practised music in a very limited set of circumstances (such as with war drumming), and this ostensibly because of a concern with the immorality that music incites (see Baig, 2008). Attempts to proscribe music today still occur alongside a concern with public morality, but even those who view music as permissible are concerned with morality as an overriding dimension of cultural practice. As Jonas Otterbeck has observed, religious 'conservatives' take a firm position against all or most forms of music, while 'moderates' typically assess the merits of each individual case:

> If it has slanderous or crude language or if it is sexually exciting (through rhythms or through dance) it is generally haram. Further, if the listening is done to excess it is haram as Islam is against taking things to extremes. But there is a personal dimension to it; if you are not aroused by the songs and you keep your spirituality then there is no problem. (Otterbeck, 2008: 220)

Even the most ardent defenders of music are therefore often engaged in something of an apologia, either dismissing music as a harmless distraction or justifying it on the grounds of religious and moral utility.

Alongside this moral dimension there are additional concerns about the use of instrumentation. For those who adhere to a literalist interpretation of the *sunnah*, attempting to follow the example of the Prophet Muhammad and nothing else, the only acceptable form of instrumentation is a simple frame hand drum (*daff*). This instrument was commonplace amongst the early Muslim community and was used typically at weddings and to accompany performed poetry. This continues to be the favoured instrument in the contemporary *nasheed* genre, sometimes with other equivalent forms of simple percussion.

Parallel to these literalist religious debates are of course alternative teachings and practices relating to Sufi mysticism. Sufism has long emphasized the important role that sound and music can play in encouraging spirituality and a closeness to God – particularly when deployed through specific practices such as *dhikr* (remembrance – often involving chanting). Different sounds have therefore been classified by Sufi scholars and placed into a spiritual hierarchy, such as by al-Maqdisi (thirteenth century), who wrote about forbidden, permitted, estimable and laudable sounds (Shiloah, 1997). Indeed, when referring to the act of *sama* (listening – particularly within a religious context), the early Sufi mystic al-Makki wrote:

> The [singing] voice is an instrument said to carry and communicate meaningful ideas; when the listener perceives the meaning of the message without being distracted by the melody, his *samā* is lawful; otherwise, and when the content expresses physical love, simple desire and simple futilities, the *samā* is pure diversion and must be banished. (al-Makki, *Food of Hearts*, quoted in Shiloah, 1997: 149, emphasis in original)

While Sufism has often been portrayed as inherently sympathetic towards music and the role that it can play for spiritual development, it is apparent here that Sufi teachings can nonetheless emphasize the idea of 'correct' sound and musical practice. This echoes a concern within Islamic religious debates outside of Sufi practice and provides a common theme that can be found within contemporary Muslim debates – that is, the need to assess when and whether music has specific religious merit.

These controversies have a long-running and complex history within Islamic intra-religious debate, as explained by Amnon Shiloah:

> In the interminable debate about the *Sama'*, legalists, theologians, spiritual leaders, custodians of morality in the cities, the *literati* and Sufi leaders all participated. The debate elicited views that varied from complete negation to full admittance of all musical forms and means, even dance. Between these two extremes we can find all possible nuances – some, for instance, tolerate a rudimentary form of cantillation and functional song, but ban all instruments; others permit cantillation and add the frame-drum but without discs, of course forbidding all other instruments and all forms of dance, and so on. (Shiloah, 1995: 31, emphasis in original)

The contestation about music and instrumentation furthermore has greater or less relevance in different parts of the Muslim world. For example, in Egypt, a favourable view of music is, according to Otterbeck, the 'prevailing attitude among scholars in public positions' (Otterbeck, 2004: 13). While I have found that Muslim musicians in Britain generally tend to fall under the aegis of Sufism – whether consciously or more indirectly (see Chapter 7) – a central concern with the religious merit of music remains constant and is certainly consistent with these deeper historical currents of Islamic intra-religious debate. Muslim musicians in Britain frequently discussed the contested nature of music within an Islamic/Muslim context – as did others – with the strong implication that the permissibility of music is very much a live issue in the UK.

Outside the Global Peace and Unity Event in 2010 – an Islamic conference and festival that included live music – I interviewed a protester from the Salafi group, Al-Muhajiroun. After criticizing the conference for gender mixing and promoting secular ideas, he raised the issue of music and instrumentation, not only demonstrating the symbolic importance of this issue but also showing some uncertainty about exactly where the line should be drawn on instrumentation. An anti-Western concern can be read into this equivocation – the *daff* maybe, but certainly not 'decadent' 'Western' pop culture:

> The daff I'm not sure about. I don't know about the daff, but all other types of instruments, pianos, and all of these guitars, all of these are forbidden by Islam. (Protester, GPU, July 2010, London)

Others in Britain, including of course musicians, reject this literalist interpretation, using *ijtihad* (independent reasoning) or scholastic rulings to argue that the Prophet Muhammad and his followers did not actually reject instrumentation; rather, they simply used those instruments that happened to be available at the time (i.e. the *daff*, a widespread instrument on the Arabian Peninsula in the seventh century). This point has been made repeatedly by musicians defending their repertoire, as argued most passionately by the *nasheed* and R&B musician, Usman:

> Some people condemn certain instruments, some people say you're only allowed to play drums, why do they say that? So where do they even get that perception from? They say that the people at the time of the Prophet, when they came, when they celebrated the Prophet migrating, you know, they all had drums, you've probably heard this story, they all had drums they were playing. So basically that's all we're allowed to use, I say, well no, that doesn't really say anything, because at that time the only thing available was drums. You didn't have keyboards, you didn't have a guitar, so no, you can't say that, it's just silly. (Usman, musician, October 2010, Bradford)

Usman's view is typical of those Muslim musicians who are aghast at what they perceive to be outdated and literalist interpretations of Islam. There is, however, a question about how widespread these views actually might be – and by extension how musicians are able to make sense of their music within a wider religious landscape where music can be so fiercely contested.

The hip-hop musician and social activist, Rakin Niass, suggested that Muslims in the UK are more or less evenly divided into two camps: those influenced by Sufi teachings, who accept all styles of music and instrumentation, and those who follow literalist injunctions against musical practice. This is of course a sweeping generalization – my own ethnographic research indicates that there is a spectrum of nuanced opinion, not a binary division – but there is a kernel of truth in this claim. It also replicates a perceived growing division between the supposed two sides of an internal Muslim conflict: liberal/conservative or Sufi/Salafi (see Chapter 7). Faraz Yousufzai, the lead singer for the eclectic Sufi folk-rock group, Silk Road – and also incidentally a presenter on British Muslim TV – suggests that, in reality, Muslims in the UK have more flexible and sometimes contradictory views about music:

the vast majority of Muslims listen to music and they actually don't have any problem with it. They'll listen to music on the radio and they'll listen to music in a Bollywood film, but suddenly sitting in front of a band that's playing meaningful music live, it suddenly becomes haram. It's cognitive dissonance gone crazy. (Faraz, musician, October 2012, Birmingham)

Faraz is indicating that there can be a particular set of concerns relating to the context within which music is performed. This aligns with my own observations: that there is a divergence between public behaviour, particularly when in a religious context (e.g. live performance at an Islamic event) and private consumption (e.g. music through film, television or the radio). The latter is often unquestioned, while the former generates disapproval.

Underpinning this seeming flexibility is a wider world view relating to the mixing of Islam with music – the idea that the sacred should be shielded from secular and potentially profane cultural influences. According to such a view – while one might listen to pop music on the radio while driving the car – religious practice should be kept separate, primary and inviolable. Usman (not the same Usman as just mentioned), the drummer for Aashiq al-Rasul, explained that this was the overwhelming view amongst his parent's generation during the 1970s and 1980s:

Some people believe that you can't mix music and Islam together, that it's not allowed, and I was one of those people . . . I was led to believe this way in terms of my upbringing . . . there weren't the avenues, the creative avenues [to express Islam through music]. (Usman, musician, January 2011, Birmingham)

Despite formative teenage years during which Usman listened to rock and funk for pleasure, for many years he believed that music and Islam should be kept apart. This changed for him during his twenties, and he is now a member of an internationally recognized Sufi musical group, affiliated to the Naqshbandi Sufi order, that uses music to express and celebrate Islam. His journey is typical. The popularity of so-called 'Islamic' (or 'Muslim') music in Britain is a relatively recent phenomenon, dating back little further than the late 1990s, a decade during which *nasheed* artists and Muslim rappers began to take centre stage in an emerging Muslim cultural scene in the UK.

These are partly generational issues – with younger Muslims in Britain more likely to acknowledge the accessible and religiously emotive possibilities of faith-inspired music – but there has undoubtedly been something of a shift in overall, cross-generational opinion since the 1990s. In short, older Muslims are increasingly persuaded that music can and should play a role in their religious lives. Yet there remains an ongoing and fractious debate about the permissibility of instrumentation within religious music. Responses to this vary and are often quite nuanced.

One typical response – which partly explains the success of stripped-down *nasheeds* with little or no instrumentation – is predicated on a process whereby a musician will survey different religious and scholastic voices, on opposing sides of the debate, and then look to adopt a 'middle' position of compromise between the two. Percussion instrumentation and vocal performance are considered by many – both musicians and consumers – as an appropriate 'middle ground' of mainstream Islamic teaching. Amir, a *nasheed* artist – who cites Michael Jackson as a major musical influence – explains how he approaches this contentious issue:

> So I try to keep to the middle ground of things and use vocal and percussion only, that's drum kits of different kinds, Arab drums, Asian drums, Oriental drums. A lot of it, the music that you'd have, like the piano, or your guitar, or your woodwind, is done by myself. Or people who are with me will provide harmonies in the background. So it's quite interesting, if someone listens to it they wouldn't be able to tell the difference, but it's a much fresher and more true sound that the actual instruments . . . there are a few people who come up to me and say, oh you've used those instruments there and I'm like, no I haven't [laughs]. (Amir, *nasheed* artist, January 2011, London)

The aim is to ensure that there are no limits to creative and artistic output, while nonetheless remaining true to ideas of correct Islamic practice. Such music often involves the use of multiple membranophones, different styles of percussion, as well as the imaginative use of synthesized sounds and sound amplification/recording equipment to make the most of the human voice and other permitted sounds.

The overall picture amongst Muslim musicians regarding the use of music remains mixed. Of the forty-four individual musicians whom I looked at for this research (only some of whom that I interviewed), twelve performed with nothing but their own voice, eight used live percussion instrumentation, seventeen used a recorded backing track (but with no live instrumentation) and seven performed with a full and unrestricted repertoire of instrumentation. Running throughout these views tends to be a desire to cleave towards a perceived place of compromise. This can involve distinguishing between 'secular' and 'religious' music (in order to keep the sacred pure from inappropriate musical practice), or in pursuing creative outlets that restrict instrumentation but nonetheless enable rich musical expression.

This attempt at compromise is usually driven by a desire for inclusivity and Muslim unity. Musicians recognize that performing with instrumentation – especially at a religious event – can necessitate the exclusion of some Muslims on religious grounds. If the purpose is to transmit a religious message or to celebrate shared faith, then it is often more effective to forgo instrumentation in order to reach a greater number of fellow believers. Musicians are therefore regularly asked by event organizers to perform without instrumentation, particularly at Islamic conferences, even if such music is a normal part of their repertoire. Several musicians explained with self-deprecating irony that they prepare *acapella* material for a growing number of Islamic events that request for instrumentation to be omitted from the performance. This approach extends to recorded music. Several musicians have produced albums that use only percussion or no instrumentation at all, despite the fact that their normal repertoire might involve a full range of instrumentation. Sami Yusuf, for example, produced two versions of his successful album *My Ummah* – a 'Music Version' and a 'Percussion Version'. Similarly, Amran, from Aashiq al-Rasul, explained their decision to produce a non-instrumental album:

> This is to cater for those people that may be in a dilemma about listening to devotional sounds accompanied with music. We try to support as many communities and beliefs as we possibly can but still stay strong to what we believe in. (Amran, musician, January 2011, Birmingham)

Such compromise represents an attempt to create a common cultural space: a diversity of activist trends and schools of thought, but unified around a shared faith and visions of belonging to a wider *umma*. This serves to cater for diverse religious inclinations, but it also allows musicians to reach out to (new) audiences that might otherwise be wary of listening to their music.

This movement towards voice-only performance is causally linked to the surge in performance poetry amongst younger Muslims. Ayman, the founding member of hip-hop group, *The Planets*, captured this cultural phenomenon rather well:

> What you have now, you have a lot of young Muslims, like early teenagers, who have started writing poetry, for example. Never, like in the nineties, you never came across Muslims writing poetry, but now you can go to an event, some event full of teenagers, it's no club, everyone's just sitting quietly and well behaved. This is like on a Friday or Saturday night, for example . . . Muslims want to be entertained, but they want to express themselves as well. (Ayman, musician, October 2011, London)

I was already familiar with the phenomenon that Ayman was highlighting – poetry performance is a regular feature at Islamic events – yet the definition of such poetry is often stretched so that it more accurately refers to melodic rap and spoken word performance. This is a consequence of the desire that many young Muslims have creatively to express themselves, though within the boundaries of communally negotiated ideas of correct Islamic practice.

There is, then, a complicated range of opinion and attitudes in relation to music and the use of instrumentation. Yet underpinning all of this is a divided spectrum of religious scholarship, within which many musicians and consumers seek to locate themselves. In being cautious about decisively adhering to one polar position or another, individuals strategically locate themselves in a place of religious and practical compromise. This might involve a simple restriction to the use of membranophones, or perhaps through making a distinction between 'secular' and 'Islamic' music. Yet informing this approach, almost always, is a desire to avoid an outlier position, outside of a perceived mainstream, and to carefully tread a path of moderated compromise.

In this chapter I have examined the complicated relationship that exists between religious elites and Muslim creatives, in relation to the carefully negotiated borders of religious knowledge and permissibility. While traditional structures and authorities of religious knowledge remain critically important, Muslim creatives are nonetheless becoming competitors within this diversifying field, whereby individual autonomy and choice are prioritized over unreflective and uncritical hierarchies of Islamic learning and knowledge. In the next chapter I turn away from the realm of Muslim elites, to look at the way in which Muslim creatives project ideas of desensationalized Muslimness and everyday Islam.

5

Ordinary Muslimness

Everyday experience, commodification and spirituality

> *I just wanted to tell a story that had nothing to do with a lot of what you see. I think what compelled me to write is that you don't want to see people talking about terrorism, about Islamophobia, I don't want to see any of that. I just want to see normal interactions where the characters, or some of the characters, happen to be Muslim, like me.*
>
> Taiba, screenwriter, July 2018, Leeds

In this short, heartfelt explanation, Taiba manages to capture a motivation that can be found running across the whole spectrum of Muslim cultural production, from writers and actors to comedians and musicians: a desire to express and explore authentic (Muslim) identities and experiences. As I outlined in the opening chapter, Muslims have not been ignored by media and popular culture – a lack of portrayal is not the issue. Muslims have been repeatedly depicted through film and television, as well as through print and news media, but almost always in a way that is 'othering': whether that be through sensationalization, pathologization or exceptionalism. Narratives might vary, but the overriding sentiment is often the same: Muslims are *not like us*. Beyond these frequent and now rather cliched depictions, there is also a wider issue concerning Muslim self-representation and the institutionalization of Islam in the public sphere. Greater space has been afforded for Muslims to engage in meaningful public debate, but this dynamic is often shaped by state-led assumptions, which privilege Muslim elites from within visible and seemingly representative groups and institutions. These elites are often inspirational role models for many Muslims across the UK – from London mayor, Sadiq Khan, and Baroness Sayeda Warsi to Zara Mohammed (secretary general of the Muslim Council of Britain) and Qari Asim (chair of the Mosque and Imams Advisory Board) – but in their role as advocates these voices tend to understandably construct Muslimness through a framework that is shaped by the politicized and racialized environment of contemporary public debate. Such discourses of Muslimness rarely contain, for example, discussions about love and romantic relationships, or spiritual reflection, or work and home life, or food and entertainment, or any of the other varied emotions, desires and activities that characterize everyday life for everybody, Muslim and non-Muslim alike.

In this chapter, then, I examine how Muslim creatives are able to project ideas of 'everyday' or 'ordinary' Muslimness. Muslims in Britain are highly diverse, and as I will highlight, these narratives and expressions dwell on the deeply personal and highly individualized nature of day-to-day life for Muslims, many of whom are navigating competing pressures and expectations in order to fashion their own interpretation of what it means to be Muslim in contemporary Britain.

The idea of 'everyday' religion was introduced and popularized by Nancy Ammerman, with the intention of shifting the focus of research away from the spaces and places of an institutional religious elite to the commonplace and less observed experiences of 'ordinary' people:

> To start from the everyday is to privilege the experience of nonexperts, the people who do not make a living being religious. . . . Similarly, everyday implies the activity that happens outside organized religious events and institutions. . . . Everyday religion may happen in both private and public life, among both privileged and nonprivileged people. It may have to do with mundane routines, but it may also have to do with crises and special events that punctuate these routines. We are simply looking for the many ways religion may be interwoven with the lives of the people we have been observing. (Ammerman, 2006: 5)

In outlining this agenda, Ammerman is specifically responding to the challenge posed by paradigms of secularization – whereby institutional religion is seen to be declining across the Western world – with a riposte that religion can flourish in everyday and non-institutional spaces. It is also a recognition and an echo of both 'vernacular religion' (Bowman and Valk, 2014) and 'lived religion' (Hall, 1997; Orsi, 2010; McGuire, 2008) – which tend to emphasize the cultural and ethnographic study of religion – whereby personal expressions and narratives are given greater recognition, often in place of orthodox beliefs and clerical worldviews.

Islam is not in institutional decline across the Western world – quite the opposite – but as I have indicated, the privileging of institutionalized Islam and Muslim elites can crowd out the daily lives and struggles of 'ordinary'

Muslims across the UK. In writing about everyday forms of Islam, Nathal M. Dessing et al. refer to this as a form of 'postconfessional religion' – something that is 'much looser, more diverse, less organised' (2016: 2–3). They make a distinction here between a study of strategic/elite Islam, on the one hand, and tactical/lived Islam, on the other. Their aim is not to replace one with the other but to recognize the complementary nature of different frameworks of study. In this sense, it is possible to remark that an Islam of the Global West is subject to a version of secularization, whereby there may be institutional growth and forms of increased confessional religiosity, but that there are countervailing and supplementary processes of privatization, diversification and individualization.

Muslim popular culture aligns with this landscape in complex and interesting ways. As I indicated in the previous chapter, there is a deep and important connection between Islamic religious authorities and Muslim creatives: traditions of learning and orthodoxy can shape Muslim expressions of faith through popular culture. Yet, as I outline in this chapter, Muslim creatives also project identities and experiences that have little to do with conventional or codified forms of religion – that which Taiba, in the opening passage, refers to as 'normal interactions'. I specifically look at these ideas of 'ordinary Muslimness' in this chapter.

All of these ideas and activities are highly specific and individual – that is, they are about personal experiences, activities and feelings, filtered through a particular world view – yet they are also universal, in the sense that they are familiar to anyone and everyone (Muslims and non-Muslims alike). While they might intersect with frameworks and subjectivities of faith – and in doing so inform ideas of Muslimness – they are also modes of activity and feeling that can have little, if anything, to do with 'religion'. Confessional faith might be important for many Muslims, although as the Muslim creatives in this chapter argue, the warp and woof of everyday life is not usually defined by politicized or racialized Muslim identities (important those these might be) but rather by the perennial threads of a shared humanity.

Muslims like us: Projecting 'ordinary Muslimness'

In his autobiography, *The Secret Diary of a British Muslim Aged 13 ¾*, the comedian Tez Ilyas tells the story of growing up in a working-class South Asian community in Blackburn (Ilyas, 2021). Woven together in his memoir are two important narratives: a political and social commentary, which provides insight into the racial and class dynamics of Blackburn, a post-industrial northern town, and the story of Ilyas as a teenager, coming of age and navigating the personal contours of family, friendship, school and sexuality. The structure of the autobiography in this way is deliberate. Ilyas is acknowledging the specificity of his upbringing – his community, faith and ethnicity – and in doing so he works within existing frames of reference, concerning the imposed exceptionalism of British Muslim identity and belonging. Yet he simultaneously seeks to escape the limitations of this framing, writing within the timeless narrative style of *bildungsroman*, with an exploration of universal teenage experiences. The balance is delicate. To address and examine contemporary ideas of Muslimness but not to be utterly defined by them.

This evocative memoir speaks to a common motivation that drives many Muslim creatives, from comedians, such as Ilyas, to musicians, comedians, screenwriters and film-makers. The desire to tell a personal story, or to express a deeply held inner life, or more prosaically to reflect on everyday behaviour, but in doing so to emphasize a common and shared humanity. In some form this view was articulated by almost every participant that I interviewed. It was phrased in a variety of ways: musicians tended to discuss emotion and feeling, film-makers and playwrights referenced narrative arcs, television producers pointed towards themes and representation, comedians reflected on the absurdities of daily life and so on. Yet the underlying message was always the same. A desire to de-exceptionalize Muslimness – to make it *ordinary*.

Some cultural producers argue that this is the fundamental objective of art – to explore universal truths. Speaking about his own love of film, the playwright and screenwriter, Ishy Din, used the *Godfather* trilogy as a device to explain what he hopes to do with his own writing:

> If you watch all three movies it's a beautiful story of the human condition . . . couched in this wonderful world of American gangsters and the mafia. But do you know what really gets you is this journey of this Michael Corleone becoming corrupted by this world that he didn't want anything to do with. So those stories and how can I tell those stories about a human being. Of a human being becoming. Changing. Because if your character's the same at the beginning as it is at the end then really you haven't done your job. And some of the most gratifying sort of things have been when I used to do Q&As for *Snookered,* which was about four Pakistani kids, twenty-somethings from the north. And you'd have middle-aged, White, middle-class men who'd say, 'I get that. It's about friendship isn't it?'. (Ishy, playwright and screenwriter, August 2017, Middlesbrough)

This is the craft of all good storytelling, according to Ishy, to reach for larger themes that resonate beyond context and the specificity of any one time and place. There are both artistic and strategic aspects to this:

> I think what I would encourage people to do is, again, think of bigger universal things to write about, that might be set in the Muslim world . . . I think it becomes quite boring if it's just about an issue. I think it's really difficult to sustain interest in that piece of work, if it's just so narrow. So I'd always encourage people to express themselves universally, within the prism of being a Muslim. (Ishy, playwright and screenwriter, August 2017, Middlesbrough)

There is a critique here of issue-based art and culture, such as that dealing with terrorism, racism or arranged marriage. It can be 'boring', but it can also fail to resonate with larger and more diverse audiences. Accordingly, Ishy, along with others, feels uncomfortable with the labels that are sometimes attached to his work: he is not a 'Muslim' or a 'South Asian' writer, but just a writer, telling universal stories that are, in his words, 'sometimes' about people who 'happen to be Muslim, or happen to be Asian'. The success of his first play, *Snookered*, is attributed, he believes, to the fact that it portrays young South Asian men in a way that emphasizes their everyday humanity, of the friendships, and the bonding rivalries, that just so happen to be forged in a northern snooker hall.

Similar reflections can be found amongst those commissioning and supporting the development of television and film production. Aziz, a producer based in London, with a career spanning national broadcasting and working within the Islamic television market, suggests that minority and Muslim creatives need to avoid becoming 'pigeonholed':

> There are currently lots of avenues for Muslim writers and actors, where they can fit in to the representation agenda that organisations like the BBC have. Where it's all about creating stories about Muslims and Asians, and what not. And I think it's good that these aspiring talents make use of whatever path they can find to success. But there is a danger that they become totally defined by it, as if Muslims can only write stories about being Muslim, stories that are expected to be about Islamophobia, or terrorism, or whatever. Instead we need to be telling more complex stories, about the whole spectrum of human life. Romance stories, adventure stories, about growing old, about characters who are complicated. I think we need characters in cinema and television that happen to be Muslim, but with character arcs that are actually about something else. (Aziz, television producer, July 2018, London)

Partly this is borne from a desire to portray positive Muslim characters and role models on-screen – to counter the persistent negativity and problematization that is attached to Muslimness through broadcast media and cinema (Morey and Yaqin, 2011) – but it is also about wanting to explore a fuller range of intersecting human experience – experiences that transcend religious identity. Discussing the involvement of Muslims in the broadcasting output of the BBC, former commissioning editor for *Religion and Ethics* (with a remit to commission all BBC television programming within this area), Fatima Salaria, argued that during her time at the BBC she was encouraged by the diverse Muslim faces that were emerging 'organically' within Britain's largest public broadcaster. Specifically mentioning Muslim presenters such as Nadiya Hussain, Adnan Sarwar and Mehreen Baig, Salaria argued that these important public voices are not a product of a 'tick box' representation agenda – whereby Muslims are hired by the BBC to address 'Muslim' issues – but that their natural charisma and talent has seen them emerge as programme presenters on a whole range of topics. Their Muslimness might be a visible part of their public role, Salaria argues – and this is certainly important – but it is also often a backdrop to other more important aspects of their broadcasting persona – from Hussain as a chef and cultural critic, to Sarwar as a former solider, to Baig as a beauty and fashion commentator.

Everyday experience: From romantic love to sexual desire

On the whole, Muslim musicians are more likely to express devotional themes through their cultural output – and therefore project an explicitly religious identity – in comparison to those within broadcasting culture. This is partly because music and poetry lend themselves to religious and spiritual performance (Ingalls, Landau and Wagner, 2016). Yet while the musicians that I spoke with would often conceive of themselves as Muslim performers, with a paraliturgical style that complemented religious ritual and feeling, there was also often an emphasis on a fuller range of human experience and emotion, particularly in relation to love (a common theme within music), whether platonic, humanitarian or romantic. Faraz, the lead singer from the folk-rock group Silk Road, suggests that, as an ensemble, they will often perform pop songs addressing themes of romantic love:

> We'll happily sing love songs and all the rest of it, but we'll more often joke with our audience, you know, who's never been in love, as if Muslims can't sing a

love song. I hope it just opens up and blows away a few cultural cobwebs that we really don't need, that have been passed down, particularly from South Asian culture, and people aren't happy with them, they don't like them. (Faraz, musician, October 2012, Birmingham)

Faraz is drawing attention to an important issue here, rejecting the notion that Muslim performers should somehow only project devotional and puritan themes in their music. He is referencing a refrain that is often articulated by younger and middle-aged Muslims: that an older immigrant generation has carried with it a cultural conservatism that denies the legitimacy of romantic love and correspondingly justifies this puritanism through recourse to ideas of Islamic modesty and respectability. For Faraz, there is a disjuncture here between the ordinary lives and experiences of younger generations of Muslims – many of whom have soaked up the 'conventional paradigms of romance' in Western pop music (Bradford, 2003) – with the expectations of an older generation.

Muneera, from the hip-hop duo Poetic Pilgrimage, makes a similar point, arguing that Muslim musicians are helping to synthesize the religious identities of young Muslims with their wider British cultural backgrounds and expectations:

They're trying to be Muslim, they're not sure how to be Muslim, they look at their parents and their parents are maybe Muslim in a particular context, or from a certain culture, so culturally this is how they dress. Or someone converting to Islam, they see an image of Islam and think I've got to be like that. . . . [W]e have no form of culture or outlet, and for anything to exist there needs to be that culture surrounding it. . . . [W]e may not always reflect Islamic themes, but us being Muslim, it is a Muslim perspective, we're talking about love, and we say, you know, Sukina's talking about her husband, I'm talking about what I'm looking for in a husband, we're still reflecting that from a Muslim perspective. (Muneera, musician, February 2011, Cardiff)

For Muneera, like with Faraz, it is the idea of romantic love that strikes a chord during this discussion. A rejection of the notion that there is somehow a clash between this commonplace emotion, on the one hand, and communally enforced ideas of acceptable Muslimness or Islamic behaviour, on the other. For Muneera, these feelings are inseparable from her faith identity – they are fundamental experiences that are woven together with one another.

While musicians might balance these themes alongside their otherwise devotional performance, for others, such as film-makers and comedians, a focus on the soft culture of everyday life is a predominant concern. It is notable that the first British Muslim-produced feature film, *Finding Fatimah*

(Icon, 2017), is a romantic comedy, framed very deliberately as a search for love – not 'just' for a spouse – by the principal protagonist, Shahid. When I discussed it with him in October 2017, the director, Oz Arshad, explained that the film has a 'universal message about finding love' and that the two main characters 'just happen to be Muslim'. While the film provides an insight into the 'Muslim dating scene' – with Shahid connecting to Fatimah through an online Muslim dating platform – and incorporates themes of modesty and spiritual connection, it otherwise plays down expressions of overt religiosity. Instead, the film examines the awkwardness, excitement and comedic elements of a blossoming romance. Similarly with the BBC short drama, *My Jihad* (BBC, 2014), written by Shakeel Ahmed, which explores the developing relationship between 'penniless' Nazir and 'single mother' Fahmida, who meet at a 'Muslim speed dating' event. Tired of fielding questions about his financial success (or lack thereof), Nazir responds to the question, 'how do you expect to support a wife?', with the seemingly novel response: 'with love and goodwill'. As with *Finding Fatimah*, while everyday themes of Muslim and South Asian experience are interwoven throughout the drama (such as cultural expectations about a 'bread-winning' husband), they provide no more than a backdrop – a social and cultural richness – that underlies the principle romantic narrative. The title itself is a deliberately ironic deployment of the term 'jihad', referencing here the struggle for romantic love and self-realization, rather than the connotations of British public debate, within which jihad is most evidently associated with violent terrorism.

Beyond these gentle romantic comedies, television and stand-up Muslim comedians explore more risqué themes relating to sexuality. For example, Sadia Azmat's podcast series, *No Country for Young Women* (BBC, 2018–20), co-hosted with Monty Onanuga, explores a range of issues relating to being 'a women of colour' in the UK, but with a deliberately provocative approach that includes discussing sensitive and intimate issues, often relating to sexual activity, from pornography, dating and sex toys to polygamy, foreplay and pubic hair. While in some respects 'issue based', the podcast series doubly seeks to explode myths about South Asian and Black women, as well as to connect to real and lived experiences of sexuality. So too with Tez Ilyas, whose comedy at times can veer into self-deprecating discussions of sexuality, again, often with reference to British cultural discourses that rarely acknowledge or reflect the sexual realities of Muslims in Britain. In one of his most notable performances, about 'sexy beards', he jokes: 'Why is it that when Alex grows a beard, he's a sexy lumberjack, but when Tez grows a beard, you've got to ask him questions?' Guz

Khan's series, *Man Like Mobeen*, similarly explores sexual and cultural taboos, for example, with an episode that focuses on polygamy and the pornography collection of an elderly South Asian grandfather ('Upper Room', *Man Like Mobeen*, 2017).

Across the diverse and complex field of Muslim cultural production, there is, then, a repeated desire to project ordinary and de-exceptionalized ideas of Muslimness into the cultural imagination of a wider British public. To detach faith identities and practices from the remote realm of politics and social discord – and to instead ground them in the shared everyday spaces that we all inhabit. The examples from this discussion all revolve around ordinary human relationships – friendship, romantic love and sexuality – that are familiar, ubiquitous and, while possibly shaped by confessional religion and ethnic culture, are nonetheless situated beyond it. To use terms that my participants frequently turned towards: these are *universal* human experiences that just *happen* to be felt by people who are Muslim.

The fact that Muslim creatives need to continually emphasize this point – to stake a claim to universal art and culture – is itself indicative of the context within which they are working. They are not ethereal auteurs, but culturally and socially situated actors, responding to the pressures and expectations of societal context.

At the forefront is a need to respond to a social framing and Orientalism that exceptionalizes Muslims in the UK. These writers and comedians, filmmakers and musicians are provocative because of their ordinariness. Muslims are rarely depicted in British popular culture as protagonists who fall in love, navigate friendships or manifest sexual desire. The banality of these narratives is deliberately pitched against the sensationalism that so often dominates the representation of Muslims in popular culture. It is a soft, gentle and deeply humane form of cultural politics. Less a shattering of stereotypes – more of an unwinding. Linked to this, these cultural expressions further problematize the notion of hard and essentialized Muslim identities. They point to the complexity of Muslimness, the daily negotiations and contradictions that Muslims are required to navigate – just like everybody else. This is a riposte to forms of community censure – whether based on religion, class or ethnicity – but also to wider cultural expectations concerning the conformity of 'puritan' and 'conservative' Muslim identities. As I now examine in the next section, these daily negotiations and individualized forms of identity can be made manifest in other ways, including through the hitching together of religion and belief with late modern commodified capitalism.

'Generation M' and the commodification of culture

With the emergence of a new Muslim middle class in the UK – that which Navid Akhtar has labelled 'Global Urban Muslims' (see Chapter 3) – there is an increasingly visible market for consumer products and services that cater specifically for Muslims. In an influential book, *Generation M* (2016), the journalist and author Shelina Janmohamed captures the motivations and lifestyle of this growing demographic. The book considers politics, gender and religious ritual/belief, but it is telling that Janmohamed focuses consistently on the way in which young Muslims have 'embraced' Western commodified culture:

> Generation M love brands. They aspire to assert their identity through the brands that they feel best reflect them. They have no problem with Western brands as long as the values they represent resonate with their Muslim lifestyle aspirations. Brands have been slow to understand and respond to Generation M, whether in their products, their communications or their community engagement. As a result, products, brands, ideas and creations that address that gap are being created by Generation M themselves. (Janmohamed, 2016: 19)

According to Janmohamed, as affluence and digital connectivity continue to shape the lives of (young) Muslims, they are increasingly looking to express their religious identities through everyday consumption and the expressive outlets of commodified culture. As I argue in this section, Muslim cultural production cannot be isolated from these wider economic and cultural trends. Muslim musicians, film-makers, writers, comedians and television professionals are important figures within this new landscape of Muslim commodified culture. By marketing, modelling and portraying particular lifestyles, through the prism of their faith identity (sometimes only very loosely connected to their faith), they can have a pivotal influence on the way in which Muslimness might be manifested within everyday cultural production and consumption.

The expression of Muslim identities through commodified culture is neither settled nor uncomplicated. While it is possible to point towards the recent emergence of a Muslim consumer market – with distinctive products, brands and ideas that are underpinned by seeming 'Muslim values', such as modesty, charity and the centrality of gendered family life – there are political and cultural differences that channel the diversity of Muslims in Britain. In this sense, Muslim commodified culture is a contested space. Muslim cultural production is deeply enmeshed within this emergent commodified culture and spans these diverse tendencies and values. Archetypes range from those cultural producers who have linked themselves to a marketing company and in so doing have become a 'Muslim influencer' – that is, deploying their celebrity status to market brands, commodities and services to Muslim consumers – through to anti-capitalist auteurs who critique the appropriation of Islam by business elites (I discuss examples of these different approaches in the next section). Janmohamed's outlining of Generation M, while compelling and persuasive, should not detract from a recognition that significant ideological differences exist between Muslims in Britain and within this emergent consumer market.

The formation of group identities through commodified consumption is arguably one of the defining features of Western modernity. Arjun Appadurai suggests that consumption, rather than being a form of 'atomized' individualism, is instead 'eminently social, active and correlative' (1990: 54). This is something that Manuel Castells understands in terms relating to social class and economic power, in relation to the uneven distribution of commodities, but also, much like Appadurai, in the way that complex identities can be expressed through collective consumer behaviour (Castells, 1997). Canclini develops these ideas more systematically and argues that consumption is an important site of political and social interaction:

> A more complex theory of the interaction of producers and consumers, senders and receivers, as developed in certain currents of urban anthropology and sociology, shows that consumption is also motivated by an interactive sociopolitical rationality. When we examine, from the perspective of consumer movements and their demands, the proliferation of commodities and brands, of communications and consumer networks, we see the contribution to these processes of the rules and motivations of group distinction. . . . If consumption was once a site of more or less unilateral decisions, it is today a space of interaction where producers and senders no longer simply seduce their audiences; they also have to justify themselves rationally. (Canclini, 2001: 39)

Accordingly, consumption is a social activity through which wider identities are expressed, developed and negotiated. It contains structures of power and interaction, between producers and consumers, but it also enables distinctions to emerge between different types of consumers, as well as allowing pre-existing group identities to be reinforced and articulated through consumption activities. Commodified consumption is therefore another vehicle – and an important one within late modern capitalism – through which social identities and cultural belonging can be manifested. Bourdieu seminally made this claim in relation to class (Bourdieu, 1984), but his ideas have merit when extended elsewhere.

Muslim popular culture and media in the UK can be understood in relation to this theoretical framing: it is a space where ideas of Muslimness can be expressed, as well as one where differences can be illuminated, both inwardly (between Muslims) and in opposition to others (i.e. distinguishing Muslim from non-Muslim consumers).

The Muslim culture industries are themselves a type of commodified consumerism – that is, they *sell* cultural products, performances and celebrity lifestyles to Muslim consumers. Echchaibi argues that Muslim consumer culture is largely motivated by an attempt to distinguish the ethical superiority of Muslim goods and services from the 'meta-narratives of Western modernity . . . such as individualism, secularism, pluralism, and equality' (Echchaibi, 2012: 37). Mecca Cola is often held up as a prime example of this – as a subversion of 'neo-liberal' Coca Cola (Aggarwal et al., 2011) – while Islamic Barbie is seen to oppose popularized ideas of sexuality and the female body (Yaqin, 2007). This is a type of countercultural consumer politics, but one that is seemingly less widespread than it once might have been. While some cultural producers certainly express these combative political and cultural critiques – particularly in Muslim subcultures such as hip-hop and auteur film-making – these critical voices have become less vocal. Indeed, as I discuss in the following section, Janmohamed's picture of an enthusiastic 'embrace' of consumerism by Muslims is closer to the mark. The reworking of Western modernity through Muslim consumer culture therefore typically takes place in ways other than through an anti-capitalist or anti-consumerist politics. As I now argue, instead of challenging liberal marketization and disposable consumer culture, there is more often a gentler social politics that highlights modesty, the empowerment of women, family values and religious/ethnic equality. With the increasing corporatization of Muslim cultural production – with 'Muslim companies' built on a business model linked to the 'Muslim pound' – there is a visible attempt to develop Muslim brands that appeal to Muslim consumers, by hitching together commodified lifestyles with apparent 'Muslim values'.

Commodified culture: Alternative and aspirational

The Deventi Group, formed in 2017 by Sharif Banna, is at the forefront of linking the production of Muslim popular culture and media to wider forms of perceived Muslim consumer culture. Deventi is a large holding group that oversees six different companies: Awakening Music, Claritas Books, Ziryab

Fashion, Black Swan Pictures, Global Muslim Influencers and MiniMuslims. The group is involved in a large array of cultural production, most notably music, but with more recent efforts to expand into film, publishing, fashion, digital content for children and 'brand promotion'. The aim of Deventi is to capitalize on the 'synergetic' overlaps between these areas and to promote the idea of a lifestyle whereby Muslims combine their religious values with a form of comfortable consumerism. This enables brands and products to be marketed to Muslim consumers who are perceived to be unwilling to compromise on certain religious and ethical beliefs. At the heart of this strategy is the utilization of cultural celebrity (of 'influencers') – from musicians through to fashion bloggers – to communicate paid-for advertisements to Muslim audiences on social media platforms.

Of course, production and consumption are two different things. There is no guarantee that the production of certain cultural outputs will actually meet the needs and values of Muslim consumers themselves. But the way in which producers attempt to shape their cultural output, based on their understanding of what this consumer market looks like, is itself significant. It is the attempt to monetize culture and religion, to treat audiences and believers as a consumer market – and in so doing to provide an income to Muslim creatives who might otherwise struggle to make a living from their cultural output. Yet it also helps to project ideas of Muslimness – of shared Muslim identities and behaviours – into the public sphere. The significance of Muslim commodified culture therefore extends beyond economic and business interests to impact upon the social and cultural lives of Muslims in arguably quite profound ways.

The Muslim Influencer Network (MIN), founded in 2017, is illustrative of these developments. Holding what was described by MIN as the 'first Muslim influencers meetup' in August 2017, Shoreditch, London, the guest list for the event demonstrated the way in which Muslim creatives are adopting a secondary role as brand influencers. Notable cultural figures ranged from the fashion model Mariah Idrissi through to the comedian Ali Official and the musician Harris J. Attending alongside these cultural producers and celebrities were a selection of *'ulama'* – also considered 'influencers' – including the (female) scholar, Shaykha Dr Tamara Gray (based in the United States), Shaykh Sulayman Van Ael, a prominent Muslim chaplain serving at the London School of Economics, Imperial College & SOAS, and Shaykh Adam Kelwick, a religious scholar and human rights activist/relief worker in the UK. This mix of cultural celebrity and religious scholasticism is unsurprising given the links that I discussed in the previous chapter, but it does also draw attention to the way in which

MIN projects itself and the influencers that are associated with it: as not just a marketing business but as a vehicle for social and religious change. In this sense religious scholars and cultural producers inhabit this space as equals, both able in their own way to market products, values and ideas to Muslim consumers.

Writing about the aims of MIN, founding co-director, Saiful Islam, argues on a blog post that branding and marketing is directly connected to larger social and cultural issues:

> Like I said, brands **are** also recognising that it's **cool** to have Muslims represent them, and partly to give Muslims an opportunity to speak for themselves. We hope through our venture, and the power of our Influencers including hijabi bloggers to nasheed artists, **we can create a better image of Muslims around the world and reshape the narrative of our faith.** We want to take the fascination (and often terror of Muslims in our post 9/11 era), and turn that into a *true positive. To help people recognise that diversity in marketing, and in the world, is key to the success of societies.* (Islam, 2018, emphasis in original)

Saiful Islam captures here several important themes that emerge in the narratives of cultural producers concerning Muslim consumer culture: diversity, representation and agency. It is a claim that Muslims have different/nuanced consumer needs, that there is an urgency to promote positive and complex ideas of Muslimness and that this is most effectively done by Muslims themselves. As writer and 'hijabi blogger', Zahrah Surooprhjally, argues, writing about the work of Muslim influencers and cultural celebrities:

> We can now shape the narrative of the way Muslims are portrayed. We're not flat characters that the world is unable to empathise with. We're real, genuine, wonderful people with flawed and nuanced personalities, and that's OK. (Surooprajally, 2018)

Muslim cultural production – which aims to connect with the perceived demand of a wider Muslim consumer culture – is therefore a space where collective Muslim needs and concerns are expressed in a way that not only normalizes the everyday experiences of Muslims in the UK – by making them visible and familiar – but also in a way that can reinforce certain tendencies and expectations. I discuss this now using the broad categories of 'alternative' and 'aspirational' to characterize the way in which Muslim cultural production can attempt to align with the perceived values of a wider Muslim consumer market. As I argue, these are complementary categories – so not necessarily in contradiction to one another – and are general tendencies, rather than hard or fixed modes of cultural and consumer behaviour. In other words, they are a rough guide to thinking through the implications and features of emergent Muslim cultural production.

Muslim consumer culture is alternative because it is a distinct sphere of economic activity – with products and brands created specifically for Muslim consumers – and because those involved in this market – from producers through to consumers – cultivate the idea that unique Muslim values and beliefs can be addressed and manifested through commodified consumption. That is, it channels the notion that authentic Muslimness can somehow be better expressed and experienced if only one can consume the correct array of tailored goods. For example, using commodified culture to make a symbolically loaded statement – for example, T-shirts with Islamic slogans or Eid party plates – or in meeting functional religious-cultural needs, from modest fashion and *halal* food through to devotional music and Islamic books. It is alternative, then, because it creates a subcultural consumer market (i.e. specifically for Muslims) and because it expresses values that are seen to stand out in contrast to the perceived failings of mainstream Western consumer culture (e.g. as vulgar and highly sexualized).

While there is often no clear way to measure the demand for such products, the most distinctive part of this alternative Muslim consumer market relates to the specific goods and services that align with religious beliefs and devotional practices. This is a type of religious consumerism. For instance, musicians have long been sensitive to the concerns that some Muslims have with the use of instrumentation. The title track from Sami Yusuf's album, *My Ummah* (2005), had 47,000 views of the 'Percussion Version' and 81,000 views of the 'Music Version' on YouTube (see Chapter 4 for a discussion of these different versions). While these figures are only indicative, they do provide some idea of the different needs of a wider Muslim consumer market. Other musicians have since followed suit, such as Ashiq Al-Rasul, producing versions of their music without instrumentation, in order to better reach sections of a Muslim consumer market where there is a demand for these types of cultural product. Ritualistic and devotional practices are often also seen as important areas for marketing, such as My Ten Nights, a digital provider that allows Muslims to automate their *sadaqa* (charity) donations during the last ten days of Ramadan, including on Laylat al-Qadr (The Night of Power), when the spiritual rewards for such donations are multiplied. The success of My Ten Nights – which is now widely used by Islamic charities across the UK – is partly attributable to the way in which it has worked with Muslim influencers and cultural producers to digitally market the service to Muslims during Ramadan, such as the social media interventions made by Maher Zain (also with Awakening Music), one of the most successful Muslim musicians and influencers in the UK:

> Why should you opt for #MyTenNights? It's the single most efficient platform for disbursing your donations on Laylatul Qadr. Setup now at: salamcharity.org/mytennights. (Maher Zain, Facebook, 24 May 2019)

Similarly, Ramadan provides an annual focus for the promotion of food products – both *halal* and more general food ingredients/appliances that align with perceived 'Muslim' cultural tastes (e.g. Persian spices) – and gifts to family and friends. The Islamic brand consultants, Ogilvy Noor, estimated in their 2018 report, *The Great British Ramadan* (Janmohamed and Miah, 2018), based on a survey of 606 Muslims in Britain, that Muslims in the UK spend an additional £200 million during Ramadan on luxury items, travel bookings and food. While this is one small data set, it does point towards anecdotal evidence that a month of spiritual reflection and communal celebration has also now become a month of mass consumption – one that is fronted by Muslim influencers, celebrities and cultural producers.

While specific goods and services might be seen to meet Muslim devotional and cultural needs, this market is not without ethical dimensions and it contains within it a range of contested values. Cultural production can therefore be used to articulate a form of social politics. While some Muslim creatives are the public face of Muslim consumer brands, others are highly critical of what they perceive to be excessive consumerism and the commodification of Islam. My Ten Nights, for example, has been particularly criticized for automating religious worship (*sadaqa*) and for watering down what should arguably be a personal action to bring one closer to God (Qasim, 2020). The adoption of Muslim marketing campaigns by global consumer brands has also been met with dismay by some. The clothing company Primark (notorious for 'cheap fashion' and environmental damage) ran a highly visible campaign in 2020, entitled #ModestMyWay, during the launch of their 'Modest Collection' clothing range. Again, it utilized a range of Muslim influencers and cultural producers to promote the campaign. While there is no existing research about how Muslim consumers in Britain actually perceive or respond to these marketing campaigns, Marwa (not her real name), an assistant producer in television, provides an insight into how there may at times be some scepticism. Marwa uses Primark as an example to highlight the superficiality of 'Islamic branding', suggesting that it is an attempt to replicate the success that *halal* food certification has achieved in the UK (Fuseini, Hadley and Knowles, 2020):

It's not good really, is it? Modesty is a new brand, the new halal. Sometimes it's just another way of trying to sell stuff. (Marwa, television producer, August 2017, London)

The hip-hop musician, Ayman Raze, is a similar critic of mainstream commodified culture, but he also recognizes the power that it has to shape and express authentic Muslim identities. In 2006 he started his own clothing brand, Tawheed is Unity, with a selection of 'sweatshop-free' T-shirts emblazoned with unique designs, including one with the Arabic slogan, '*Al Maarifah Quwah*' ('Knowledge is Power'). During our interview, in a London café, he explained that young Muslims are developing their 'own culture' – one that is both Islamic and Western – and that cultural products need to be sensitive to this complexity. Discussing the name of the brand, he explained:

The name itself means a lot of things, *tawheed* means the oneness of God, [so] Tawheed is Unity is the belief that through the belief in *tawheed* we can have unity, it's a bit of a hippy sort of, an airy-fairy statement. There's lot of issues between Muslims, lots of different sectarian issues, but the thing we all agree on is *tawheed*, we all agree on *tawheed*. We all agree there's only one creator. And that's what I've tried to focus on. (Ayman Raze, musician, October 2011, London)

Tawheed is Unity Ṭ-shirts therefore attempt to 'make a statement' – to use commodified culture as a means to project 'alternative' religious, social and cultural Muslim identities. One addition to the clothing line included an inversion of the famous 'Just Do It' slogan by the American clothing company Nike, which for many years was seen to be synonymous with cheap factory labour (Stabile, 2000). Ayman's design displays the words 'Just Dua It', utilizing the Islamic concept of supplication as a way to critique excessive Western commodified capitalism.

These critical voices – such as those of Marwa and Ayman – are seemingly in a minority when set against the more powerful, institutional currents that link Muslimness to a commodified Muslim consumer culture. The politically vocal and alternative hip-hop subculture of Ayman and others is less visible than it was even a decade ago. Instead, Muslim creatives are increasingly tied to larger business and corporate interests – such as the Deventi Group – that appeal to the materialistic consumer tastes of a newly emergent Muslim middle class, or Global Urban Muslims, to return to Navid Akhtar's terminology (see Chapter 3).

The linguistic and visual messaging used in marketing campaigns by Deventi, MIN and others is striking. Muslim influencers and cultural producers are portrayed as leading comfortable consumer lifestyles that their audiences can and should aspire to. This consumer culture is 'aspirational', then, because according to this messaging, Muslim values, such as modesty and family, are entirely compatible with the material rewards that Western consumer culture is able to offer. The 2018 Rubicon campaign was indicative of this. Utilizing a range of Muslim creatives and influencers, the campaign sought to portray Rubicon as the drink of choice for a new Muslim middle class: family oriented, modest, abstentious from alcohol and at ease in comfortable, well-appointed households. Another example might be the comedian, Tez Ilyas, who broadcast an entire series of videos dedicated to the games console, Playstation 5, during a time when this expensive and much sought-after product was in short supply due to the Covid-19 pandemic. Or the musician, Harris J, who regularly models the latest fashion items, from leather jackets through to 'modest sportswear' by the clothing brand Adidas.

This is not intended as a critique of these fully justified aspirations for material and consumer comfort – particularly given that approximately 50 per cent of Muslims live in poverty in the UK (Heath, Li and Woerner-Powell, 2018) – but more an observation that the aspirational tastes and lifestyles of a Muslim middle class are increasingly central to the output and public image of Muslim creatives in the UK – and that this aspirational and celebrity lifestyle culture is oriented towards the notion of a growing Muslim consumer market (Janmohamed, 2016), both in terms of 'Islamic' products (such as luxury hajj tour packages) and more general products (such as Rubicon drinks), all of which have bespoke marketing campaigns built up around them to target Muslim consumers. As I now discuss, this has implications for the fostering of Muslim individualism, not just within the framework of late modern commodified capitalism but also in relation to changing religious belief, practice and spiritual 'questing'.

Everyday Islam, individualism and 'old style/new style' religion

In their discussion of 'everyday Islam', and with reference to the ways through which Muslim religious belonging is changing in the minority context of Europe, Dessing et al. (2016) argue that a form of 'postconfessional' faith is becoming dominant for Muslims. Through this reading, hard communal boundaries – those guarded by Muslim elites – are giving way to a more open and less proscribed landscape of Islamic belief and practice, relating, for example, to how Muslims deal with religiously informed issues relating to family, education, health and well-being. Drawing on Michel de Certeau's *The Practice of Everyday Life* (1984), Linda Woodhead (2013) argues that this tension can be understood as one between the strategic (i.e. metadiscourses/institutions of religion that are proscribed by elites in a position of authority) and the tactical (i.e. lay members, occupying micro spaces of religion and practising an individualistic faith 'on the ground').

The discussions so far in this chapter can be seen to align with this model. Whether through expressions of 'ordinary Muslimness' – with an emphasis on subjective experience and a lived reality – or with the projection of a religious and cultural *bricolage*, expressed through the everyday production of commodified culture (from Islamic clothing through to 'Muslim' tastes in music and food) – Muslim creatives promote a dynamic form of religious individualism that lives and breathes beyond the 'old' institutions of Islam in Britain. This does not mean the abandonment of community membership but rather that which Flory and Miller have termed 'expressive communalism', whereby, for believers, 'the individual spiritual quest is mediated through the communities in which they are active and in which they seek membership and a sense of belonging' (2007: 216-17). A shared Muslim religious identity was important to all of the cultural producers that I spoke with – and this was articulated through ideas of membership within the global *umma* and of belonging to a Muslim community in Britain – but there was diversity in how this membership could be understood and enacted. In this sense, for Muslim creatives – as well as arguably for Muslims in Britain more widely – Muslimness is an identity and a set of behaviours that are strongly held, but often loosely and individually defined.

This emphasis on individualism manifested itself in different ways for Muslim creatives. For some – most particularly for converts or for those whose parents were converts – there was a recollection of how their religious upbringing might have given them a unique perspective. For example, the film director and television producer, Ahmed Peerbux, stressed that while he did attend a Deobandi mosque during his childhood years, he did not grow up in any one specific 'community':

> We grew up in a house that I would say, it wasn't so much defined by what you did, but more by what you didn't do. So you didn't eat pork, you didn't eat non-halal meat, but things like fasting it was more laissez faire, you would fast one day but then you might take the next day off, something like that. My mum is a convert. As I say it wasn't like that whole praying five times a day, that kind of thing, when I was growing up at least it wasn't the kind of environment I was brought up in, but at the same time it was profoundly religious. Like we had a

sticker on the door in the living room when we were growing up and it said, 'Did you say your prayers?'. No one prayed five times a day, but we went to the Friday prayers. I'm sure it's the same for a lot of Muslims, I'd imagine, not waking up at *fajr*, but celebrating Eid. (Ahmed, film director and television producer, June 2017, London)

In a different way, Conor Ibrahiem stressed the unusual nature of his religious upbringing, whereby 'religion' did not feature prominently and was often confused with 'cultural issues'. He articulates his later faith as a personal journey and a form of individualistic seeking, rather than as a tradition that had been passed on through familial or community ties:

> My father wasn't particularly religious, so therefore neither was mum. If anything she was more cultural rather than religious. That then gave her the impression that Islam had restrictions in places where it doesn't, as culture and Islam are very closely interwoven, so that you can't always tell one from the next, as to what ruling applies to where. . . . So I took my own journey, rather than my dad taking me there and leaving me there to learn, I couldn't understand the language for one thing, but just do the parrot thing and read. I knew that was the path I was going to be ending up on, so I was naturally more drawn to Islam, but of my own volition rather that someone else's expectation. (Conor, writer and director, July 2018, Keighley)

For the musician, Usman Rehman, who has experimented with different musical styles – from R&B and pop to *nasheed*s and *na'at* – both his religious journey and artistic career have been defined by an attempt to forge his 'own' path:

> My parents split up and I've lived alone for twelve, thirteen, years of my life. I've had no support there, no brothers, no sisters, and I've had no guidance so to speak, to put me on the straight and narrow. So I've done everything my way, my style. I've actually got a lyric as well: 'I do my things, my way, my style, I go crazy, go freestyle'. I just kind of go with my own flow, and that's exactly what I've done. (Usman, musician, November 2011, Bradford)

For these cultural producers – and for many others that I spoke with – their religious and cultural lives have, in their mind, been unique and highly individualistic. This connects to their identity as artists and cultural auteurs, but it also shapes their expectations of and attitude towards their faith. That is, the view that personal autonomy is paramount and that 'tactical' choices about their religious life takes precedence over the 'strategic' institutions of Muslim elites.

The writer, Ishy Din, for example, suggested that his faith is highly personal. He specifically rejected the 'strategic' impositions of religious elites:

> Just within Sunni Islam, there are so many schools of thought, that, 'Oh, it's like this,' but, 'No. It's like this,' and what have you. And they all can't be wrong, and they all can't be right. And really, being Muslim, there are only five pillars to being Muslim. Two of them, you don't really have to, you only need to do charity if you can afford to do it. You only have to perform Hajj if you can afford to do it. So really, there are three things that makes you a Muslim. And then, I just take home the things that make sense to me. And the things that I think don't [make sense], I don't really follow. (Ishy, playwright and screenwriter, August 2017, Middlesbrough)

For Ishy, his own judgement was more important in determining the nature of his belief rather than any external orthodoxy or orthopraxy. Similarly with comedian, Nabil (not his real name), who was sceptical of religious elites who 'preached' the 'true message of Islam':

> I think, I don't know, you just need to make your own decisions about what you believe and what you do. I don't always pray five times a day, I hardly ever do really, but Allah can see into my heart. We get told lots of things, all of the time, by Muslims with really loud voices, but there's too much of that and you have to take your own view a lot of the time. (Nabil, comedian, December 2016, London)

Muhsin Kilby, a photographer, who has worked with musicians and artists across the UK, was more direct in criticizing the influence of proscriptive religious readings. He argued that these 'strategic' voices have a dampening effect on Muslim creativity, by implicitly or explicitly proscribing artistic creativity amongst Muslims – and that Muslims need to be more vocal in critiquing these impositions:

> One of the things I'm kind of concerned about is with young people in this country, Muslims are very often devoid of any kind of cultural stimulation or artistic stimulation, Islam is being presented in a very rigid manner. Like just a set of rules, a do and don't list. (Muhsin, photographer, October 2011, London)

Faraz, from the folk-rock Sufi group, Silk Road, similarly refers to 'cultural' issues, but in a way that drew attention to the seeming 'confusion' (for some) between 'Asian culture' and Islam. His argument was that the false imposition of South Asian cultural expectations, through the censorious dominance of community elites, can either drive Muslims away from Islam or can lead individual Muslims to develop a more personal understanding of their faith:

> People are left with a choice because they have to either accept the culture in its totality or they have to leave it, reject it. And then they leave it and reject it, and some will come back and find their own little niche way of being a Muslim, a practicing Muslim, a more practicing Muslim I guess, but I mean like leading a God-conscious life. (Faraz, musician, October 2012, Birmingham)

Muneera, from the hip-hop duo Poetic Pilgrimage, a convert to Islam with Jamaican heritage, makes a related argument, but almost in reverse, suggesting that there can be a view that converts are required to abandon their cultural background for something that is 'authentically Islamic' (but which is often actually the prioritization of a particular type of South Asian cultural Islam). Instead, Muneera recognizes that there is a synergy between her cultural background and faith, which she proudly celebrates as a distinctive and rich form of Muslimness:

> It's important for us to make sure that we show who we are and what we're about. And we are unapologetically Muslim and at the same time we are unapologetically Caribbean, you know, and a lot of times we find a lot of people convert to Islam, and from whatever cultures and countries or backgrounds, convert to Islam, and sometimes unfortunately a lot of people think that they have to let go of their culture, as if their culture's something that is ugly or that's bad. And there are many elements of Jamaican culture which I don't adhere to ... however, there are many elements of Jamaican culture which are very upright and which in fact remind me so much of Islam. (Muneera, musician, February 2011, Cardiff)

For all of these cultural producers, then, there is a tactical process whereby they navigate the strategic contours of Islam in Britain. Their religious identities and practices are self-determined but are also shaped through critical interaction with wider cultural and religious expectations, including the rejection of certain ideas. That is, in the words of Ishy Din, by only taking 'home the things that make sense to me'.

One way of making sense of this is through Woodhead's typology of 'new style' and 'old style' religion (see Introduction). Through this argument (see Davie, 2014), Woodhead suggests that the contemporary religious landscape in Britain is characterized by a shift from centralized and institutional 'old' religion to a dispersed and highly individualistic form of 'new' religion. Woodhead makes this claim in relation to the decline of hierarchical church-based

Christianity (particularly Anglicanism and to some extent Catholicism). For Muslims in Britain more generally, as I argued in the Introduction, this shift can be registered in relation to the partial move from a traditional mosque-based, often South Asian-leaning, Islam – described as 'cultural Islam' by the Muslim creatives with whom I spoke – to a more diverse and diffuse arrangement where individual Muslims sift through competing authorities, beliefs and practices to create their own distinctive and individually realized understanding of Muslimness. Of course, this should not be overstated; there are still powerful networks of mosque-based Islamic institutions in the UK, but they are facing stiffer competition from (often younger) Muslims, many of whom are unwilling to compromise their personal autonomy through deference to networks of tradition and authority.

A discourse of 'postmodern spirituality'

Everyday spirituality is another way through which a sense of individualism and universalism is expressed by Muslim creatives. I have discussed this at length elsewhere (see Morris, 2016), so I keep my discussion here relatively brief, with the aim to summarize and refresh some of these arguments. Spirituality is a notoriously vague and often contested concept. It has been considered before in relation to the idea of a spiritual marketplace (Roof, 2001), through to the notion of embodied spirituality (Flory and Miller, 2007), including commercial appropriation (Carrette and King, 2004), and most notably with reference to the 'subjective turn' and 'holistic milieu' (Heelas and Woodhead, 2005). Drawn together, these frameworks envisage spirituality as a diverse set of beliefs and practices, which are individualistic and, while centred on personal experience and inner life, can often be channelled through material culture and contemporary consumer capitalism. Ivan Varga provides perhaps one of the most useful definitions of contemporary spirituality:

> The (re)discovery of spirituality re-presents the individual's effort to make conscious his or her 'inner life', that is, his or her personality and moral ideas. Contemporary spirituality therefore expresses several features of postmodern conditions, especially the possibility offered to the individual to shape his or her view of the world. It also makes possible for someone to join a spiritual or religious group that is rooted in a culture different to one's own. (Varga, 2007: 145)

While Varga is highlighting the way in which contemporary spirituality is characterized by certain postmodern conditions – such as the constant reinvention of personal identities and churning forms of group membership (e.g. see Giddens, 1991) – I would add to this by suggesting that 'postmodern spirituality' is also very much a linguistic and conceptual discourse – one that can be shared across otherwise different religious and spiritual traditions. As such, a common language of spirituality can have universalizing tendencies, despite finding root in distinctive religious spaces and traditions.

For Muslim creatives this conceptual and linguistic currency of postmodern spirituality – while still located in an Islamic religious tradition, including a distinctive lineage of Sufi spirituality – is nonetheless often interchangeable with wider discourses relating to inner being and the transcendent. As such, Muslim confessional experiences can be universalized or translated through this shared discourse of spirituality. Muslim creatives express this in a number of ways: (i) through recourse to a language of spirituality, (ii) the conscious desire to 'universalize' Islam for a non-Muslim audience and (iii) an emphasis on the idea of a spiritual/personal quest or journey.

Spirituality and related cognate concepts are themselves frequently used by Muslim creatives when discussing their personal stories, artistic output and individual faith practices/beliefs. Interviews – both conducted by myself and by those in media outlets – are peppered with this type of language. This ranges from the use of the term 'spirituality' itself (with the idea of *being* spiritual), through to the evocation of religiously ecstatic emotion (such as 'love', 'passion' and 'inspiration'), to ideas around inner change and transformation (such as 'journeying', 'questing' and 'changing'). Discussing his 2019 film *Sound of Metal*, Riz Ahmed, for example, applied the concept of spirituality to the professional process of adopting and performing a particular role:

> [It's] about not trying to control the process too much; seeing what comes along and catching each bus and train that comes by as if it's been sent by God to get you there. When you have that sense of surrender, you'll find a sense of flow. Something I'm learning more and more about is that flow, which is such a holy grail for creative endeavours, but also life and spiritual tradition. Let go, let God. Flow is realising it's not something that you do. It's not the way you do something, it's something you get carried away in. (Riz Ahmed, quoted in Greenwood, 2021)

Similarly, Atallah, from Silk Road, when discussing ensemble performance, suggested that a spiritual energy could be felt running through their music-making:

> People have come up to us after the gig and they had been affected spiritually . . . we were playing sometimes and I would feel very spiritually active, I would feel my heart had been affected, and that's a good sign of connecting. (Atallah, musician, October 2012, Birmingham)

For others, spirituality provided a frame of reference to describe an inner faith that is different from and distinct to external confessional beliefs and practices. The comedian, Guz Khan, for example, pointed towards individual religious and spiritual journeying, while also suggesting that this personal experience nonetheless still enabled a form of collective 'Muslim politics':

> A lot of dudes I speak to, the doctrine aspect isn't massive but politically it's a voice for them. I gravitated towards Muhammad Ali and Malcolm X, people following faith who were confident in themselves and found a voice through it. Their spiritual journeys were very influential. (Guz Khan, quoted in Tate, 2019)

These selected examples – and there are many more – all avoid direct or exclusive references to Islam. They instead draw on a frame of reference that is rooted in a more generic and cross-fertilizing form of spiritual language.

An important aspect of this language is the desire to universalize Islam. Not to deny the transcendental truth of confessional Muslim belief – all of the cultural producers linked to this research considered themselves practitioners within the scripturally revealed tradition of Islam – but to use the language of spirituality as a device to translate Islamic beliefs and values for the benefit of a wider non-Muslim audience. For example, Sami Yusuf notably rebranded his entire musical output, from 'Islamic pop' – a label which he believes is necessarily excluding – to 'spiritique'. Discussing the term, Yusuf explained what exactly he means by 'Spiritique':

> It incorporates and utilises Middle Eastern and Western harmonics, underpinned by spirituality. It's all-encompassing, all-inclusive. . . . It will utilise music as a facilitator for spiritual appreciation, regardless of race and religion. (Yusuf, quoted in Tusing, 2010)

The aim, then, is to use the concept of spirituality to transmit and translate beyond the traditional boundaries of Islamic communality.

Similarly with Poetic Pilgrimage and Silk Road, who both took time to explain the meaning behind their lyrics. Discussing 'Land Far Away', a rewritten and reworked version of 'Sata Massangana' by the Jamaican reggae group, The Abyssinians, Sukina, from Poetic Pilgrimage, explained the power of a shared spiritual message within the song:

> The concept of what they're singing about, 'land far away', it was just so universal, you know, like we believe in a land far away, where there's no night, only day. They say, look into the book of life, and that could be a Qur'an, a Bible, a Bhagavad Gita. . . . So kind of the fact that it referred to the scripture, to the book of life, that was wicked. It doesn't conflict with our beliefs, because the Qur'an is the book of life too. (Sukina, musician, February 2011, Cardiff)

When discussing two of their songs – both of which avoided any specific lyrical reference to Islam – Atallah, from Silk Road, explained the inspiration behind each of them:

> There's one song called 'Ask My Heart', and it's the translation of a poem by a great Sufi sheikh about the relationship between his heart and his spirit, in conversation . . . [and another] called 'The Stranger', it's actually based on a Hadith, [the Prophet Muhammad] said that the person in life is like a traveller who stops under a tree for a while, knowing that he's got to go on . . . so this song is all about that, and it's about a person travelling in life. So it is enthused with spiritual overtones. (Atallah, musician, October 2012, Birmingham)

Fellow band member, Ash expanded on Atallah's explanation, suggesting that this lyrical approach was deliberate:

> we don't really want to alienate the majority of audiences. We really want to do something for someone that hasn't got the linkages to the spirituality of Islam, can still take something good from it, and still relate to it on a personal level. (Ash, musician, October 2012, Birmingham)

For Muslim creatives, then, the language and framing of spirituality – rather than confessional Islam – can provide an outlet to connect with diverse audiences.

Finally, another visible feature of postmodern spirituality could be found in the emphasis that Muslim creatives often place on the idea of journeying or questing – that is, of travelling along a spiritual and deeply personal path. Reflecting on personal religious change is not unusual and is to be expected in interviews where individuals are asked to discuss their background, upbringing and religious lives. What was striking was the way in which these narratives were placed within the framework of a 'spiritual journey'. For example, as with hip-hop musician and Muslim convert, Mohammed Yahya, who reflected on his movement from Pentecostal Christianity, to Rastafarianism, and finally to Islam. A 'journey' that he stated is reflected through his music:

> my music is always a reflection of me, how I am as a person, so I try to, without wanting to, whatever I'm feeling inside, whatever my personal experience are,

you'll be able to hear that through the music. (Mohammed, musician, February 2011, London)

Or the writer and director, Conor Ibrahiem, and the musician Quest Rah, who both discussed the journey that they have been on, from non-practicing Muslim backgrounds through to a period of religious and spiritual transformation. The metaphor of journeying can similarly be enmeshed in the artistic output of cultural producers, such as with Ahmed Peerbux and Sean Hanif Whyte's film, *Blessed Are the Strangers* (2016), which recounts the 'journey' of a convert community in Norwich, from 'White hippies' following the Sufi author Ian Dallas through to the welcoming and involvement of Black converts from London in the 1980s. The film is beautifully and sometimes ethereally shot – with a spiritual aesthetic that includes, for example, hazy black and white footage of practitioners in contemplative silence, or shots of them gazing in rapture at the breaking of dawn – and incorporates visible themes of change and transformation – suggesting the idea of a community that is repeatedly trying to 'find itself'. Or one can look at musical examples, as with Poetic Pilgrimage, whose lyrics frequently evoke themes of travelling, searching and journeying. In each of these cases, the aim is not to conceal or downplay a visible Muslim identity but to place this confessional experience within a broader framework of personal change and questing – a framework that will have wider and more universal resonance.

Of course, not all cultural producers adopt this approach. For example, teledawah 'ulama' and *nasheed* artists are typically oriented towards well-defined Muslim audiences and place a far greater emphasis on exclusive forms of Islamic language, devotion and piety. Generic spirituality therefore tends to be less evident for those working in these definably and distinctively 'Islamic' cultural spheres. But for those Muslim creatives who are looking outward, with an eye to larger audiences, 'spirituality' can provide a framework that allows for those connections to be made. It also suggests that the wider so-called 'Spiritual Revolution' (see Heelas and Woodhead, 2005) – whereby faith and belief is arguable defined now by the 'subjective turn' – is registering as a feature of religious and cultural change for Muslims in Britain. That rather than being isolated from the wider landscape of religious change within the UK, Muslims are very much connected to these deeper shifts in faith and belief.

Taking the points within this chapter together – in relation to ordinary Muslimness, consumer culture and spirituality – there is a sense in which Muslim creatives are helping to promote highly individualized ideas of everyday Muslim practice, belief and culture. This challenges the tendency that can exist in media and popular culture to essentialize Muslim identities, whereby pathologized and sensationalized ideas of Muslimness are constructed for wider public consumption. In the next chapter I examine these tensions within the context of professional career trajectories for Muslim creatives in the culture industries. I consider the different strategies that Muslim creatives adopt to define and locate their work, and how this might enable stereotypes to be challenged and Muslim creativity to be nurtured within the culture industries.

6

Escaping the 'Muslim trap'

Typecasting and the search for creative freedom

> *I describe myself as a Muslim writer not because my faith informs my work, but more because that's how other people see me here, in this country ... I'm going to a meeting, the rare meetings I have now, and they'll go, 'So where are you from?' 'Oh. Manchester.' 'No. No. No. I mean, where are your parents from? Where are your parents from? No. Where are they from, originally? ... and their grandparents?' ... You identify yourself as being from here. And they don't want that because they don't really like it, or they want a kind of exoticism, or they want to fit you in a box and go, oh, yeah ... I didn't want to be that pet in the corner that would just rubber stamp, would go, 'There, there, you're absolutely right,' which is a common trap for most talent to fall into, for BAME talent to fall into, especially Muslim talent, as I've learned.*
>
> Faisal, screenwriter and producer, October 2017, Manchester

Muslim creatives face a weight of expectation – 'a Muslim trap' – whereby they are either excluded from the public sphere or, following demands for greater representation and inclusion, are only admitted within a narrow scope of preconceived or assumed 'Muslimness'. As I recount in this chapter, Muslim creatives face barriers throughout their careers, including pervasive Islamophobia in the creative industries. Yet they also find that strategic routes through this morass can involve shouldering a visible Muslim identity, which can be equally restricting. As Faisal argues: 'they want a kind of exoticism, or they want to fit you in a box.' Thus, if 'Whiteness' is a *tabula rasa*, upon which the imagination can roam freely, Muslimness is at times a millstone around the neck of creatives, etched with preconceptions and expectations. The dilemma is acute. Muslim creatives point towards the exclusion that they face within the culture industries – an exclusion that is only just now becoming systematically evidenced in academic literature (Khan et al., 2021) – but a demand for greater representation can in itself shape directions of creativity, with the implication that this representation must necessarily involve 'Muslim creatives' telling 'Muslim stories'. In this chapter, then, I examine the career trajectories and cultural positioning of Muslim creatives, considering the different strategies that are adopted to develop and ultimately disseminate their creative output.

Muslim creatives are in some respects faced with an important choice: to build their career within the Muslim culture industry (or the 'Muslim cultural field' – see Introduction) or to direct their efforts towards mainstream British audiences and institutions. While there is some crossover, for the most part the Muslim culture industry in the UK is a distinct field of subcultural activity, with its own niche features, audiences, funding models and network of mostly Muslim professionals. Mainstream broadcasting, performance and music production are different, with unique barriers that Muslim creatives must overcome in their struggle to reach larger and diverse audiences. There is therefore a dual framework of Muslim creativity. The Muslim culture industry is oriented towards devotional output and community mobilization, while mainstream cultural production gravitates towards secular themes of political, social and cultural commentary. The challenges faced in each are different. The Muslim culture industry is more inclusive of Muslim creativity, but it faces financial constraints and at times a lack of accountability and transparency. Mainstream cultural organizations (particularly public service broadcasters), in contrast, often have deep pockets and a depth of expertise to nurture Muslim creativity, but widespread Islamophobia and preconceived ideas about 'Muslim culture' are also inhibitive of creative freedom.

These dilemmas point towards a more fundamental issue for Muslims in Britain. Nasar Meer's concept of 'Muslim consciousness' is instructive here. Drawing heavily on the work of W. E. B. Du Bois, Meer argues that Muslims face a challenge in attempting to develop and define authentic forms of Muslim consciousness, 'specifically the movement from a self-consciousness *in* itself to the transformative potential of a self-consciousness *for* itself: from one's historically *ascribed* identity to one's politically *self-constructed* identity' (Meer, 2010: 53–4, emphasis in original). This tension, in a Du Boisian formulation, creates a 'double consciousness' for Muslims in Britain: on the one hand, shaped by the perceptions of wider society (whether by internalizing these views or reacting to them), while on the other seeking to legitimately project authentic, transgressive and plural identities into the public sphere.

This conceptualization of double consciousness is useful when considering Muslim creativity. First, there is a sense in which Muslim creatives can either look 'inward', towards the fostering of religious devotion and community mobilization, or 'outward', in responding to, and at times, if not always, challenging forms of social censure. The point should not be overdone, but these tendencies are reflected somewhat in the dual framework of Muslim versus mainstream cultural industries – that is, inward/outward. Yet, paradoxically, while seemingly different from one another, both these approaches can entail the envisioning of Muslim consciousness in Britain through the filter of non-Muslim views: that is, of Muslims as a closed and problematic religious minority, rather than as active members of a civic and cultural polity. Whether or not non-Muslim prejudice is accepted by Muslims themselves – and of course most reject these crude characterizations – the point is that Muslims are either required to respond to these views or that they create a context and a framing through which even authentic self-knowledge is understood. Second, double consciousness highlights the gap between Muslim self-knowledge – of authentic understandings of the self – and wider views about Muslims. This disjuncture is constantly changing – as outlined in Chapters 1 and 2 – but it still bears down heavily on any expression of Muslim creativity, particularly for those working in the mainstream culture industries – that is, through the need to somehow bridge or dissolve this 'gap'. Through both of these points, then, there is a sense that wider and sometimes prejudicial views or framings about Muslims can be internalized, if not necessarily accepted, by Muslims themselves.

Double consciousness therefore represents the 'Muslim trap' within which creatives can become ensnared. A binary choice or set of directions, fundamentally shaped by the context of minority/majority relations. Meer not only recognizes this binary but also points towards a path beyond Du Bois, towards a 'synthesised Muslim consciousness', which will enable Muslims to 'eschew the peculiar sensation that they are "a problem", and instead allow them to see their "strivings" incorporated into mainstream society and politics in a way that would herald reciprocity and mutual respect' (Meer, 2010: 204). In relation to media and popular culture, this must surely involve Muslim creatives being able to develop and share stories that are no longer framed or restricted by narrow perceptions of what Muslimness should or should not entail. Where to be 'Muslim' can mean many different things – not necessarily burdened by ethnic tropes, or discourses of national belonging, or presumed beliefs and practices of devotion. And to delink the expectation that a 'Muslim creative' must necessarily have a story to tell – and *only* this story to tell – about 'being Muslim'.

In this chapter, then, I examine the alternating struggle and fortunes of Muslim creatives within different cultural and industry contexts. My aim is to consider the way in which Muslim creatives locate and define their work, to reflect on their professional experiences and development, and in doing so to consider how Muslim creativity can be nurtured, and how it might continue to flourish.

The Muslim music scene

The idea of a 'Muslim' or 'Islamic' music culture in Britain is something that has been of critical interest to musicians for nearly two decades, since the emerging public visibility of Muslim musicians producing self-consciously 'Muslim' or 'Islamic' music in the early 2000s. For musicians, Awakening Music has provided a distinct home for such music since it was founded in 2000. Building on the success of the first album that it released – Sami Yusuf's *Al-Mu'allim* (2003) – Awakening Music has since become a principle advocate for the contemporary *nasheed* genre (see Chapter 2). Over the last two decades it has identified, signed and then promoted artists who perform in this devotional and soulful style of music. A particular strength of Awakening Music can be found in the reach that it has with global Muslim audiences. This includes the ability to market music and organize performance venues for Awakening musicians in key regional markets, including North Africa, Turkey, the Balkans and Southeast Asia. Awakening Music therefore provides a structured route and institutional framework for musicians who seek to reach these larger audiences. However, a critique often levelled against Awakening Music is that it has developed a business model based on a small number of hyper-successful musicians and that it promotes a safe – and consequently 'bland' – style of devotional music. As Imran (not his real name), a folk-rock singer from London, argues:

> The biggest beast out there is definitely Awakening. But it's all a bit samey, a bit bland at times. I think it does well with people who want to listen to something uplifting and Islamic, but it isn't experimenting with different sounds or genres. It just plays it safe and rakes in the cash. (Imran, musician, July 2017, London)

For the last decade Awakening Music has relied primarily on the success of two artists, Maher Zain and Mesut Kurtis, both of whom have significant international appeal. There has been some attempt to foster and develop emerging musicians, but the most notable of these, Harris J, subsequently left Awakening Music to join Virgin EMI, where his style has shifted towards something that is less overtly 'Islamic' and resembles mainstream pop music, with backing pop beats and a mixture of rap and soulful singing, albeit with his Muslim identity remaining a part of his public image. Similarly with Sami Yusuf, who left Awakening Music (then known as Awakening Records), in 2008, partly due to disagreements about the direction of the label, but also borne from a desire to distribute his music more widely. After short spells at several record labels, including Sony Music Malaysia, Yusuf eventually founded his own recording company, Andante Records, which partnered with the independent distributor Fairwood Music (notable for releasing music by pop musicians such as David Bowie and U2). The result is that Yusuf retains creative control over the production of his own music, while maximizing the potential for distribution. Following the split with Awakening Music, Yusuf criticized the label for exploiting his music in search for a 'quick HARAM pound' (Yusuf, 2009, emphasis in original).

Muslim hip-hop artists have typically lacked the institutional framework provided by an organization like Awakening Music and have tended to release their music in a grassroots fashion – that is, either through self-release or by means of an independent/boutique label and distributor. For a time, there was a certain degree of excitement and cache concerning the idea of 'Muslim hip-hop'. This was partly generated by Muslim media outlets and products, from films such as *New Muslim Cool* (2009), which explored the Muslim hip-hop scene in the United States, through to magazine and web coverage, including the dedicated Muslim hip-hop magazine, *Platform*, launched in 2006 (before it quickly ceased production), and MuslimHipHop.com, founded in 2004. The mid- to late 2000s was therefore a critical time during which there was an expectation that 'Muslim hip-hop' might become a subgenre that would foster a new generation of Muslim musicians. At the time this involved a number of initiatives, including the creation of independent performance spaces and record labels for 'alternative music'. This included the 'Rebel Muzik' hip-hop night, held monthly in London during 2009, and the 'I Am Malcolm X' tour (see Chapter 2), held in 2009 through a partnership between the Radical Middle Way and Crescent Moon Media (an independent record label founded by the Muslim hip-hop group Mecca2Medina). Critically, these initiatives gave Muslim hip-hop artists a degree of public visibility at the time – a visibility that extended to coverage in mainstream news outlets, such as *The Independent* and *The Guardian* – and allowed them to connect with wider Muslim audiences in the United Kingdom and the United States.

Ultimately, though, this critical mass faded away and Muslim musicians became sceptical about the notion of a 'Muslim hip-hop' scene. Quest Rah, for example, argued that he has tried to avoid the label:

> For a group like Mecca2Medina, who when you switch on their record you can identify it, I'd say you can call that Muslim hip hop, right? For me, what the term means is a Muslim person doing hip hop, which isn't restricted to something Islamic, something that's gonna isolate people. That's what I've always tried to do, I've tried to do something which is more universal, but I'm a Muslim that's doing hip hop and that to me is what the term means. (Quest Rah, musician, October 2011, London)

Similarly with Ayman Raze, from The Planets:

> We're just making music and we happen to be Muslim as well, we don't put ourselves in that bracket where we're Islamic rappers or Muslim artists and rappers. Others may want to do otherwise, but we've never approached it that way . . . So if there's an interview with a Muslim radio station or a Muslim magazine and they mention it, then I'll talk about it, but we don't use it as a selling point. (Ayman, musician, October 2011, London)

These views reflect the wider trend amongst Muslims who produce and perform hip-hop, from Mohammed Yahya and Poetic Pilgrimage to Quest Rah and The Planets. Certainly not the downplaying or concealment of their religious identity but rather the shying away from an overt 'labelling'. As Sukina Noor, from Poetic Pilgrimage, emphasized: 'We're not trying to Islamicize hip hop, we're not necessarily trying to make a Muslim point of view in the music.'

The 'Muslim music scene' has therefore changed somewhat over the last two decades. It is perhaps more appropriate now to reference the idea of a *nasheed* industry', which has a focus on a particular style of uplifting and 'safe' devotional music. This addresses the practical religious and cultural needs of some Muslim music consumers. More experimental and transgressive styles of music – and I include not only hip-hop within this formulation but also the pop experimentation of musicians like Sami Yusuf and Harris J – are instead gravitating towards the mainstream music industry. This is not dissimilar to broadcasting culture, where a growing division is emerging between television and film produced by Muslims for Muslims and those who are looking to bring Muslim subjectivities and stories to a wider cultural audience.

Muslim broadcasters: Financial constraints and the nurturing of creativity

Muslim-run broadcasters, such as Islam Channel and British Muslim TV, as well as streaming services, such as Alchemiya, can in some respects provide a natural home for Muslim creatives working across television and film. Yet issues concerning funding, support, internal politics and the creative output of these broadcasters are an area of concern and debate. The industry grapples with a challenging financial model, with broadcasters typically eking through, mostly relying on advertising revenue (free-to-air broadcasters) or with subscriptions (streaming services). Both are limited and potentially unreliable sources of income. In short, the Muslim broadcasting industry lacks serious money. Various strategies are adopted to generate revenue, such as partnering with advertisers or more actively aligning with well-funded Islamic charities. Yet there is a lack of investment in costly creative endeavours, most notably dramatic production, and in areas that receive less viewing attention (such as the arts and long-form documentary). This difficult financial context underpins Muslim cultural production in film and television – it is a model that is in many respects replicated for small broadcasters elsewhere in the industry (Peitz and Valletti, 2008). As I will show, this has implications for the opportunities available to Muslim creatives – in relation to their experiences as employees and freelancers – and it undercuts the diversity and richness of Muslim popular culture. As several of the creatives interviewed for this research claimed – and this is based entirely on their view as insiders in the industry – parts of the Islamic/Muslim television industry (and Muslim film production) are in some respects suffering from slow and constrained growth due to the absence of a sustainable and independent business model for creative development.

I spoke 'off the record' with several current and former employees at both Islam Channel and British Muslim TV. Junior professionals, starting or developing a career, were understandably cautious about anything other than an informal conversation. Their comments were often positive, but in many instances they could also be highly critical. There was a general acknowledgement that these broadcasters provide a route for young Muslim graduates into the world of media, both on-screen and in research/production – a route that might not readily be available in the highly competitive industry of mainstream broadcasting (e.g. with the BBC). Yet, particularly in the case of Islam Channel, there was a frustration that the broadcaster could at times be uninterested in nurturing and supporting emerging talent. Phrases such as 'toxic', 'favouritism', 'unprofessional', 'racist' and 'internal politics' were used by some to describe the internal working environment at Islam Channel. Both Islam Channel and British Muslim TV make use of unpaid internships, which is a standard starting route into media for graduates hungry for relevant work experience. While this experience was positive for some, others found the work monotonous and exploitative. More encouraging stories highlighted the range of work experience, from camera operation and research through to on-screen presenting/reporting, while others criticized the long hours, unreasonable expectations, lack of internal opportunities/training and the seeming whims of overbearing managers. The overall narrative was that Muslim/Islamic broadcasters provide a route into the professional world of media, but that they can lack internal structures of support and accountability, which are needed to properly nurture new talent. This was a source of grievance for some that I spoke with. All participants – including those with negative and positive experiences – argued passionately that Muslim-run organizations have a duty to create a critical mass of new generational talent.

Muslim creatives who have worked with Islam Channel and British Muslim TV as freelancers/collaborators had similarly mixed views about the role of the broadcasters. Again, there was sometimes a hesitation about speaking in a non-anonymized or recorded capacity, with a worry that this might jeopardize future opportunities. Kamran (not his real name), for example, recounted having brought several ideas for programming to both Islam Channel and British Muslim TV. Stating that the broadcasters could 'blow hot and cold' – that is, expressing an engaged interest in a programming pitch, which would then subsequently evaporate for unidentifiable reasons – he suggested that the broadcasters had a limited interest in original programming and were typically looking for 'cheap' and guaranteed programming 'hits' (such as reality TV and, in the case of Islam Channel, devotional programming). Kamran suggested that there was a general underappreciation of the arts and in-depth documentaries, which were perceived as being too highbrow and less likely to attract viewers and, consequently, much needed revenue via advertising. He recognized the pressures that both of the broadcasters are under to find a funding model that works but felt that this arrangement was stifling creative opportunities. He described this as a 'lack of maturity' in the 'Islamic television sector' compared to mainstream television broadcasting (including public broadcasters, but also broadcasters in the private sector). Samira (not her real name) discussed a similar experience with Islam Channel. After having developed a *nasheed/na'at* reality television programme – which was filmed, produced and ready to air – the programme was then rejected by Islam Channel because, in Samira's words, they 'wanted more money' from her. That is, at the last minute they sought to renegotiate payment for the programme in a way that was not in Samira's favour, as part of the deal to finance and broadcast the programme. While Samira has subsequently worked on other projects with Islam Channel, her experience at the time was one of disappointment. She argued that 'they're running a channel in the name of Islam but they haven't even got basic morals and principles if they can't keep their word' (Samira, television producer, October 2016, Bradford). Oz Arshad, the director of the feature film, *Finding Fatimah*, in contrast suggested that he felt supported by British Muslim TV, which funded the film, and that he was largely given creative control. His only caveat was the suggestion that BMTV required the film to be a romantic comedy about Muslim dating, to appeal to large audiences and, crucially, to align with BMTV founder Adeem Younis's primary and highly lucrative business venture, SingleMuslim.com. He did however suggest that this arrangement was reasonable – after all, they were funding the film – and that BMTV had to consider income generation and the commercial appeal of any film venture.

These stories are ultimately selective and are only from a small sample of freelance television and film creatives. They do however point towards the tension that can exist between creatives, who can feel that their output is constrained, and Islamic television stations, which face commercial/financial pressures to produce a particular and perhaps narrow range of programming.

In connection to these comments, a lack of cultural and media independence was raised by participants in relation to the two biggest Muslim broadcasters, both of whom are funded by affiliated non-profit organizations. Islam Channel derives a sizeable income from The Dawah Project, which was established in 2007 (by Mohamed Ali Harrath, also the founder of Islam Channel), with the aim of raising donations to produce religious programming for Islam Channel. Similarly, BMTV is reliant on the non-profit Penny Appeal, established in 2009 (by Adeem Younis, also the founder of BMTV), with significant revenue flowing to BMTV through the form of advertising and sponsored programming. While there is nothing wrong with this arrangement – it is transparent and perfectly legitimate – it does point towards the underlying issue that neither broadcaster is able to generate necessary revenue through a standard commercial model. Islamic broadcasting in the UK, in this respect, can be considered an extension of the Islamic non-profit sector – British Muslims are paying for broadcasting output, but through indirect means (i.e. donations). Several of my respondents commented on this, referring to BMTV in slightly derogatory terms as 'Penny Appeal TV'. There was a suggestion that programming could be skewed towards charity appeals and, especially in the case of Islam Channel, towards devotional programming. Muslim creatives were at times critical of this model, suggesting that it constrained broadcasting output – partly because there is limited funding for the creation of new and untested programming but also because the aims and objectives of the affiliated charities have a disproportionate impact on the production of television content. This was seen to limit the creative opportunities available for television production and to shut out a wider assortment of Muslim creatives working in areas such as the arts and long-form documentary.

While still in an early phase of development, some respondents highlighted the positive development of a subscription model by streaming service, Alchemiya. As Kamran suggested:

> Alchemiya is a really, really good thing. It shows that British Muslims are willing to pay for good, high-quality content. I think it will do well, because there's a hunger for this kind of thing. It has everything, comedy, drama, documentaries, and they're all very high quality. (Kamran, documentary producer, June 2017, Manchester)

Alchemiya does not directly produce programming – it is a platform for existing content about the Muslim world – but it was highlighted by Muslim creatives as a positive development that will help to bring their content directly to paying Muslim consumers. Notably, Alchemiya is not constrained by the same live scheduling issues that underpin Islam Channel and BMTV, so it is able to include lengthy documentary and dramatic film productions within its growing streaming catalogue. If successful, this would create a viable funding model for Muslim creatives, many of whom are now able to develop programming on an independent basis (i.e. through their own production company), but with a degree of confidence that they will then be able to distribute this content to a (paying) Muslim consumer market. Ahmed Peerbux and Sean Hanif Whyte's film, *Blessed Are the Strangers* (2016), is illustrative of this phenomenon. The film was funded through a combination of small grants, personal financing and individual donations, but, apart from a limited number of in-person screenings and a direct purchase option through the film's website, Peerbux and Whyte were unable to monetize it with a reliable revenue stream, or indeed distribute it to a larger audience. The film was, however, eventually picked up by Alchemiya, following its partnership with Amazon Prime – a funding stream that will help Peerbux and Whyte (and producers like them) to invest in future projects. The phenomenon of streaming – currently spearheaded by Alchemiya – should help to significantly diversify, deepen and enrich the landscape of Muslim cultural production in the UK.

Breaking through: Muslim creatives and mainstream broadcasting

While Muslim creatives acknowledged the role and importance of the Islamic television sector – in that it provides a space for devotion and intercommunity debate – most expressed a desire to work in the mainstream broadcasting sector. A typical career trajectory – for writers, producers and actors – involves some involvement, at some point, with the institutions of public service broadcasting. This has not always been an easy or satisfactory relationship, but it is through awards, workshops and grants – most often from the BBC and Channel 4 – that Muslim writers and actors have been able to find a start with their career. Participants with longer careers, dating back to the 1990s and 2000s, tend to be more critical of these media networks and institutions, while those in an earlier and more recent stage of their career, spanning perhaps only the last few years or decade, spoke more favourably. There has been something of a shift in public service broadcasting over the last decade, especially since the appointment of the BBC's comedy director, Shane Allen, in 2012, which led to the British Muslim Comedy series in 2015 (more on this shortly). Channel 4, the other large, publicly funded broadcaster in the UK, has made similar, if less extensive, attempts to draw in Muslim creatives. Efforts to address diversity and inclusion over the last decade have therefore borne some fruit.

Muslim creatives always have a narrative about how they first became involved in television and/or film. For Muslim writers, these narratives were usually linked to writing competitions, awards and workshops run by public service broadcasters and publicly funded networks in the culture industries. Taiba, for example, explains that after watching a live performance of a BBC programme – and finding the depiction of an Asian family problematic, thinking, 'I could do something better than this' – she submitted a two-page script to a competition run by the London School of Writers Festival. This led to a training course, followed by script feedback, and then another course, run this time by New Writers North, with another script submission, which was then longlisted for the Northern Writers Awards in 2018. These successes paved the way for Taiba's subsequent involvement in New Writing North's talent development programme. These organizations – all of which are publicly funded and based at higher education institutions in the UK – have provided a structured route through which Taiba's writing talent has become recognized, and then further developed.

Alongside these courses and awards, Taiba also attended a course taught by Shakeel Ahmed, through the charity, Inspiring Grace. Shakeel was the writer for the BBC short drama series, *My Jihad* (2014), which was developed as part of the Original Drama Shorts scheme run by BBC Drama, BBC Three and BBC iPlayer. Shakeel submitted his script in 2013, as part of this scheme, where it was subsequently picked up and developed into a short drama series. He now uses his experience in writing and production as material for workshops aimed at encouraging and developing writing talent for Muslims in Britain, such as Taiba. Ishy Din had a similar start after submitting a radio play script to a competition run by Radio 5 Live. Again, this was picked up by the BBC and developed further. Encouragement from the BBC led to various writing courses and a blossoming career in radio, television and theatre. Like Shakeel, Ishy now uses this experience as the basis for workshops and mentoring activities with aspiring writers from under-represented backgrounds in the North of England.

Faisal entered the screenwriting industry in the 2000s and in some respects had a more difficult experience than Taiba, Shakeel or Ishy. A documentary that Faisal wrote, while at university, about young Muslims celebrating Ramadan, was selected as part of a writing competition organized by Channel 4. This has led to a twenty-year career as a writer, researcher and film producer. During this time, however, with a growing reputation as a 'Muslim' writer, he recalls numerous occasions when producers and programme commissioners were looking to validate their preconceptions, which were coloured by links between Muslims and terrorism/radicalization:

> They wouldn't even want me to write. What they were looking for me to say was, oh yeah, you're absolutely right. And my experience in this world [as a Muslim] shows that you're on the right track . . . And so when these guys would find out about me, these producers . . . then they would call me down. But it would never be as a writer. It would always be as a rubber stamp. (Faisal, screenwriter and producer, October 2017, Manchester)

After turning down various opportunities and writing commissions, Faisal achieved something of a breakthrough with filmmaker Chris Morris, who brought him in as an associate producer for the black comedy, *Four Lions* (2010), which satirized the phenomenon of 'home-grown' terrorism in the UK. As Faisal states, Chris Morris 'approached it like a journalist. And he just basically, he was just devouring everything. He didn't take anything at face value. He wasn't afraid to meet people and he wasn't afraid to have his preconceptions challenged.' Despite this success, Faisal continued to face challenges in the UK media market, including with disappointing experiences at the BBC. He subsequently decided to move his career to Hollywood, in the United States, where 'I'm being seen as the writer who basically wants to do all kinds of stuff'. He has since worked on wide-ranging productions, including the high-profile 2019 documentary, *Leaving Neverland*, about the abuse claims made against Michael Jackson.

Conor Ibrahiem took a more traditional educational route into television and film, after graduating from college with a qualification in the performing arts, in the early 2000s. Initially as an actor, Conor gained experience with speaking parts on the northern soap series, *Emmerdale*. Like Faisal, he too became subject to a dominant media context that arose following the London bombings in July 2007. As he said, 'it's eased off a bit now, but certainly the amount of auditions I went to for terrorists, I've lost count.' Disheartened and pressured by an environment of repeated typecasting, Conor was inspired by the work of Luqman Ali, at the Khayaal Theatre Company, and established his own production/theatre company, Arakan Creative, in Bradford, with the aim of telling authentic Muslim stories. Funding has been difficult, as he explains:

> I've never had a wage properly, as in from the Arts Council or anything like that. I've applied four times and have got four rejections, fine, they've got their reasons . . . I came to realise later, through an off the record conversation with a member of the Arts Council, sorry you're not getting the funding because the word 'Islamic' is in there. (Conor, writer and director, July 2018, Keighley)

Arakan produced a number of small plays before receiving a grant from the Joseph Rowntree Foundation Charitable Trust to develop a trilogy of outputs that would present, in a creative form, the findings from research about racial injustice and Islamophobia. The result was a theatre production, the film *Freesia* (2017), and a series of interfaith comic books, entitled *ABX: The Abrahamix* (2021), about a Muslim, Jewish and Christian trio of superheroes.

The most sustained effort at bringing Muslim voices to the small screen has been through the British Muslim Comedy series, screened in 2015, on BBC Three and BBC iPlayer. The series was conceived in 2013, by BBC Director of Comedy, Shane Allen, and was a conscious attempt to diversify comedy on the BBC through the commissioning of productions by Muslim comedians. It initially began with five comedy shorts, each around five minutes in length, which were written and performed by British Muslim comedians. The series was able to draw on an existing grassroots network of Muslim comedians, including Tez Ilyas, Prince Abdi, Sadia Azmat, Guz Khan and Asim and Sadia Chaudhry. It is notable that these comedians had all been performing for several years, developing their material at comedy clubs, Islamic/Muslim conferences and festivals (including the Edinburgh Fringe Festival). The comedy industry in Britain is typically a precarious environment to work within, with comedians hunting for work and for opportunities to perform, but it is also a varied and diverse industry, with multiple performance venues and spaces (including online spaces, for example, YouTube), many of which have emerged alongside the growing interest in stand-up comedy over the last two decades (Mills and Horton, 2016). Muslim comedians were able to access this industry because these performance spaces, while precarious and competitive, are nonetheless relatively accessible for new and emerging acts. A grassroots Muslim comedy scene had therefore already been given space to develop, before the BBC made a deliberate effort to bring it to a larger, national audience.

Since 2015, Muslim comedians have been commissioned to produce extended comedy programming, such as *Man Like Mobeen* (2017) and *Muzlamic* (2019), both of which screened on BBC Three. Most importantly, the phenomenon of Muslim comedy on the BBC enables Muslim comedians to have a 'speaking position' (Toynbee, 2000), in the sense that they write and perform their own material, with a sense of authorship, rather than as appropriated voices, or as a veneer of 'diversity'. The new wave of Muslim comedy therefore stands as a counternarrative to widespread perceptions of Muslims (Miles, 2015), in stark contrast to previous offerings, such as *Citizen Khan* (2012–16), which have tended to reproduce Muslim stereotypes (e.g. the buffoonish 'community leader') rather than to problematize them (Ahmed, 2013; Huq, 2013).

The Muslim trap: Navigating expectations in mainstream broadcasting

An almost existential decision facing Muslim creatives working within mainstream broadcasting and film is the extent to which they actually want to portray themselves as 'Muslim' artists, writers, producers, and performers – or whether they should avoid such labelling entirely. Responses to this dilemma are understandably complex, and most creatives have an ambivalent and nuanced response to this open and ongoing question. There is a desire to project authentic Muslim stories and experiences, but there is also a danger that Muslim creatives can be used in a tokenistic way, or that their work becomes viewed solely through the lens of religion and race. There are opportunities in projecting oneself as visibly and creatively 'Muslim', but it can also create an invisible trap of expectation, within which creatives might become forever ensnared.

Ishy Din, for example, discussed how he has walked this tightrope, both acknowledging the opportunities that 'writing about Brown people' can provide and trying to avoid being forced into a narrow creative space. Reflecting on conversations during his early writing career – following the production of his first radio play for the BBC – Ishy reflected on the decisions that he needed to make about the trajectory of his developing career:

> Generally, I get offered a lot of gigs for Brown people, with Brown people in, which I'm cool with. Many years ago, when I first started, I said to this old-hand radio producer, quite arrogant and I said, 'I don't just want to be a writer that writes about Brown people. I want to be a writer that's just a really good writer that writes about everybody.' And he said, 'That's fantastic, but you know over there, there's like ten thousand White writers going to write about White people.' Not necessarily White people, but, 'And over here, there's three Asian writers. So why do you want to go and join that group with ten thousand people in it, where your odds of getting a gig are ten thousand to one, instead of joining this group here, where your odds are four to one?' And I thought, 'Hmm.' . . . I come from quite a niche world, that there's not many people who come from that environment in doing what I do. So why not exploit that, and it's a world that I know intimately well. So I can bring a certain authenticity to it that perhaps others couldn't. (Ishy, playwright and screenwriter, August 2017, Middlesbrough)

Yet he also warns about the dangers that such an approach presents, suggesting that there is a need to project his writing beyond the artistic cantons of race and religion:

> There is, I think, on one level, there is this need to say, 'I'm a Muslim artist. And I write about Muslims.' But on another level, I think you're simply doing yourself a disservice. Because you put yourself in a corner. And then, you're not giving your work the greatest chance of success, of giving it the best opportunity to run its course. Because you've shut off a number of avenues to yourself because you've become so pigeonholed. (Ishy, playwright and screenwriter, August 2017, Middlesbrough)

Faisal Quershi had a more outspoken and critical view of the way in which 'Muslim' or 'Asian' writers could be narrowly confined to certain roles. Following his work on *Four Lions* (2010), Faisal was increasingly identified as a 'Muslim writer' who was seen to offer 'authenticity' for the pre-existing agenda of television and film producers:

> I used to get a lot of calls from drama producers. And they would go, 'Oh. We've got this – I want to do a show about extremism.' Because the reason is this, that because I believe it's because of . . . and it would be foreign policy, sexual

repression, kind of just like people talking shit in mosques and stuff. And what they really wanted was a Brown person to come in and say, 'Oh, yeah. You're absolutely right.' And so they were basically, they just wanted someone they could [use for their] preconceptions. I met a few of these guys. And I just didn't like them. (Faisal, screenwriter and producer, October 2017, Manchester)

Ahmed Peerbux, reflecting on some of the job opportunities that he has been offered, recounted a similarly bruising experience. He contextualizes his response with reference to a controversial documentary, *What British Muslims Really Want* (Channel Four, 2016), presented by Trevor Phillips, which was criticized at the time for being 'biased, misleading and totally inflammatory' (Haque, 2016):

I went to one interview . . . and they were finishing up the Trevor Phillips documentary . . . and then when I got there, there was just disdain, I wouldn't say disdainful of Islam, but they were actually quite disdainful of Muslims. The people interviewing me, the producer, I remember her saying to me, oh God it's such a miserable religion isn't it . . . and they wanted me as their kind of, they wanted their Muslim to go in there and speak to other Muslims, you know, you're a Muslim can you go in there and be all 'Muslim'. And they essentially wanted me to cast some nutters, that was it. I mean, they didn't say it exactly like that, but what they wanted was a bunch of nutters. You know can you go and find some shouty, beardy extremists, basically. (Ahmed, film director and television producer, June 2017, London)

Others are more relaxed about being labelled or identified as a Muslim creative. The actor and comedian, Nabil, who has worked in small roles for the BBC but also performed independently on the comedy circuit, argues that his Muslimness is an important part of his performance and public persona:

My performances and jokes are always a reflection of me, of who I am, if you know what I mean. And I'm Muslim. I want to cut through all of the rubbish out there and try to present something more meaningful, rather than all these preconceptions and Islamophobic views that exist. I think that's something positive that I can do. (Nabil, actor and comedian, December 2016, London)

Similarly, Taiba argues that the public visibility of Muslims – particularly Muslim women – is something that she hopes to bring to wider audiences in mainstream broadcasting:

I wanted to bring those characters to life . . . I wanted to write them as characters, and Muslim women, because you don't often see what they want you to see there. So that's what I'd like to happen. (Taiba, screenwriter, July 2018, Leeds)

These voices reflect some of the diversity and nuanced awareness amongst Muslim creatives concerning the expectations and opportunities provided by adopting a visible Muslim identity in their work and professional lives. The 'diversity and inclusion' agenda within mainstream broadcasting and media has provided a route through for otherwise neglected Muslim creativity, but there are institutional and cultural pressures that can impose a weight of expectation, potentially stifling authentic and creative freedom.

The Riz Test: Developing a counternarrative

As I have outlined, Muslim creatives face a number of pressures throughout their professional journey. Widespread expectations in mainstream broadcasting and film production impose a double burden of representation, whereby Muslim creatives are, on the one hand, expected to produce 'authentic' Muslim culture, while also, on the other hand, simultaneously expected to align with audience preconceptions and the agenda of those working within the media and culture industries. There is a strong desire amongst creatives to move beyond these limitations and to subvert typecasting – which is widespread for all 'minority' creatives (Friedman and O'Brien, 2017) – but this spectre of prejudice does also provide an overarching framework that cannot help but shape the work of Muslim creatives. Even when providing alternative stories and narratives, there is an inevitability to the fact that Muslim creatives are sucked into a defensive position, whereby their work is characterized by the need to critique or subvert these stereotypes.

These concerns were brought to public attention following a 2017 speech delivered by Riz Ahmed to the House of Commons (Ahmed, 2017). Ahmed linked Muslim experiences of hate crime, Islamophobia and feelings of national belonging to the way in which Muslims are misrepresented and negatively portrayed through popular culture. As Ahmed said in his speech, 'What people are looking for is a message that they belong. Every time you see yourself it's a message that you matter, that you're part of the national story.' Taking inspiration from this speech, academic, Sadia Habib, and technology writer, Shaf Choudry, launched the 'Riz Test'. Based on the Bechdel Test (Bouchat, 2019) which examines the portrayal of women in popular culture, the Riz Test provides a similar set of criteria against which representations of Muslims can be assessed:

The Riz Test

If the film/show stars at least one character who is identifiably Muslim (by ethnicity, language or clothing) – is the character . . .

1. Talking about, the victim of, or the perpetrator of terrorism?
2. Presented as irrationally angry?
3. Presented as superstitious, culturally backwards or anti-modern?
4. Presented as a threat to a Western way of life?
5. If the character is male, is he presented as misogynistic? Of if female, is she presented as oppressed by her male counterparts?

If the answer for *any* of the above is *Yes*, then the film/TV show *fails* the test.

This failure of representation has been well documented in academic writing (see Morey and Yaqin, 2011), but the intervention of Riz Ahmed and the subsequent development of the Riz Test is notable for two reasons. First, it is significant that Ahmed – the first (and only) Oscar-nominated and highly visible Muslim actor in the UK – feels compelled to change an industry within which he has thrived. There are clear dimensions of power and influence at work here, in the same way that gender inequalities within television and film have only gradually been challenged following the emergence of women in senior positions willing to speak out against gender inequalities, both on- and off-screen (Perkins and Schreiber, 2019). Second, Ahmed is engaged in a broader commentary, whereby he links the representation of Muslims through media and popular culture to wider social issues concerning Muslim experiences of belonging and Islamophobia. Through this reading, then, Riz Ahmed is adopting the mantle of secular Muslim leadership, becoming a spokesperson for not just struggling and overlooked Muslim creatives but also for Muslims in Britain and North America more widely. His argument is simple enough: the negative depiction of Muslims causes social harm, and these depictions will not change unless Muslims are actively involved in the production of media and popular culture. As with previous accounts in this chapter, Muslim creatives face barriers to effective inclusion and recognition. Ahmed has taken a leadership role in this capacity, working in 2021 with the Pillars Fund to create a funding scheme – the Pillars Artists Fellowship – to provide grants, mentoring and support to Muslim writers, directors and producers. This initiative, while in a very early phase, at least indicates the extent to which this issue is finally taking centre stage after decades of considerable neglect.

Pathways to change: Recognition, production and funding

When asked about the support that they required and the change they would like to see happen, Muslim television and film creatives made a number of comments and suggestions.

Recognition

There was a desire for Muslims to be formally recognized as an under-represented group in the media and culture industries. High-profile initiatives – such as the BBC's *Diversity and Inclusion Strategy* (2015–20 and 2021–3) – fail to make any mention of religion as a category. During our interview, Fatima Salaria – a Muslim, and at the time the commissioning editor for Religious Programming at the BBC – suggested that change was occurring at the BBC 'organically' and that Muslims were gradually becoming more widely represented in BBC staffing (although there is no established monitoring process). Muslim creatives for the most part reject this gradualism and instead called for a formal and structured approach, with publicly funded broadcasters actively and transparently promoting Muslim inclusion. As one participant said: 'If Muslims are 5% of the population, then they should be 5% of the BBC, ITV, and all of the big broadcasters.' There was a general distrust of professional culture in broadcasting organizations and production companies, which was seen to be White, middle class and quietly prejudicial towards Muslims as a group.

Production

A concern with the internal culture and practices of commissioning, recruitment and production was repeatedly raised. A common experience concerned the views held by non-Muslim commissioners and casting directors, many of whom were perceived to express simplistic or anti-Muslim sentiments. There were repeated examples of overt Islamophobia being expressed by producers, commissioners and casting directors. Suggestions for change included appointing Muslim consultants to be involved in all aspects of production, particularly around recruitment, commissioning and script development. This was seen to be an effective way to avoid poor casting decisions and to avoid the expression of Islamophobic tropes in broadcasting and film content. There was also a call for structured mentoring and training programmes, in order to nurture Muslim talent, and to provide a clear route for Muslims looking to advance their careers in the media and cultural industries. The collaboration that Muslim creatives have had with industry professionals, in a mentoring or educational capacity, was highlighted as particularly valuable over the course of their careers. While participants valued the opportunities that they had been given – and were thankful for schemes run by the BBC, Channel 4 scriptwriting networks and so on – they felt that not enough was being done to reach out to young, and especially working-class Muslims outside of London, many of whom might lack requisite levels of social capital and/or suffer from a geographic disadvantage. It was argued strongly that greater support is needed for Muslims to overcome these intersectional barriers.

Funding

Independent producers and film-makers particularly highlighted the need for funding and revenue streams that would promote Muslim talent and the telling of Muslim stories. Suggestions included grants and award schemes that would invest in Muslim-written scripts and production ideas. These schemes could fund initial production costs – with the possibility of a financial return once a production has been distributed/sold – or could provide funding to develop new ideas and mentor Muslim creatives at the outset of their career. Overall, there was a recognition that financial barriers to entry can be significant and that Muslim creatives often just need an opportunity to 'prove their worth'. There was a feeling that broadcasters and public bodies should provide these funding opportunities, but that more also needs to be done by the 'Muslim community' itself, with a particular role to be played by Muslim philanthropists and Islamic foundations.

Muslim comedians: Subverting and shattering Islamophobia in Britain

As I have argued throughout this chapter, Muslim creatives are attempting to transform the exclusionary structures of media and popular culture in the UK. Greater representation and inclusion is seen as a way in which to challenge and subvert Islamophobic prejudice and to provide Muslims with a cultural stake and a sense of belonging in Britain. Much of this effort is therefore about transformation through representation. Yet Muslim comedians are addressing the issue more directly, by explicitly and consistently attempting to subvert and ultimately shatter Islamophobic tropes. Comedy is well suited for such an endeavour. First, Muslim comedians themselves have achieved more mainstream recognition than any other group of Muslim creatives in the UK (with the singular exception of Riz Ahmed, who of course himself is publicly critical of widespread Islamophobia). Having been given a platform, Muslim comedians, such as Tez Ilyas and Sadia Azmat (both discussed shortly), are using it to effectively dissect and rebuke one of the most pervasive forms of discrimination in contemporary Britain. Second, as a genre, comedy has essential qualities that lend itself to such critique. Classical theories about humour suggest that there are three primary reasons why comedy can impart a social effect: (i) superiority, where we laugh at those who are inferior (including our past selves); (ii) relief, whereby tension is dissipated through shared laughter; and (iii) incongruity, through which a flawed concept or idea is juxtaposed for comedic effect against actual reality (Martin and Ford, 2018). Muslim comedians utilize all three of these approaches to powerfully challenge the myths of Islamophobia – humour can create an extreme position, parody or stereotype, which is then subsequently defused and undone through shared laughter. In a study of Muslim comedians in the United States, Zimbardo makes exactly this claim – drawing on Stuart Hall's remark about making stereotypes 'uninhabitable' (Hall, 1997) – suggesting: 'Humorous strategies are powerful in the capacity to "unfix" dominant meanings through subversive satire and parody, and to affix new meanings that destabilize the underlying assumptions of the stereotype' (Zimbardo, 2014: 62). Both in the United States, and also in the United Kingdom, Muslim comedians adopt a number of comedic strategies in order to create this instability, and, in so doing, to work against the assumptions of Islamophobic prejudice.

This fundamental ambition at the heart of Muslim comedy cannot be overstated. Every single Muslim comedian whom I examined and interviewed over the course of this research was engaged in a recognizable effort to undermine these pervasive stereotypes. Indeed, many of them looked aghast at previous attempts to depict Muslims through comedy, with *Citizen Khan* often singularly identified as responsible for reinforcing damaging stereotypes (Ahmed, 2013; Huq, 2013). The caricatures evoked by *Citizen Khan* – such as the patriarchal father and the duplicitous/sexualized daughter (Abbas, 2013) – are raised by Muslim comedians as exactly the kind of stereotypes that they aim to challenge and ultimately upend. They do this by conjuring absurd caricatures of both Muslim and non-Muslim positionality, simultaneously mocking each and every essentialized identity – deftly switching between two different ways of seeing – until the gap, the tension, falls apart beneath the weight of the ridiculous.

Take the stand-up routine of Sadia Azmat, during her performances for the BBC and at the Edinburgh Fringe Festival. Her jokes often hinge upon the ways in which she is perceived as a South Asian, Muslim and female comedian. She draws an absurd (and simultaneously not-so-absurd) picture of her experience. Stereotypes of Muslim conservatism and cultural discombobulation are brought into contact with similarly stereotypical conjurations of non-Muslim prejudice. Sketching, for example, her ethnically caricatured parent's failure to understand the purpose of a holiday (a long-standing stereotype of an older South Asian generation). This is held up alongside the supposed reaction of White holidaymakers at Butlins (an alcohol-fuelled UK seaside resort), were Sadia 'Al Qaeda' Azmat to arrive for a holiday break (which she declines to take, quipping, 'Even racists deserve a holiday'). Or Tez Ilyas, during his BBC podcast series, TEZ Talks (BBC, 2016–19), who begins the series by explaining Islam and Muslim experience to a non-Muslim audience, whom he jokingly hopes to convert. Similarly, the humour relies on sketching absurd scenes, such as trying to identify those nebulous British values to which Muslims are expected to conform (including, according to Ilyas, 'queuing', 'buy one, get one free' and 'speaking English loudly and slowly to foreigners when abroad'). This is held up, in the same sketch, alongside the comedic lengths that Ilyas has enacted in order to 'remain halal' while out for the evening with alcohol-drinking, non-Muslim, friends. Another example can be found with the BBC series, *Muslamic* (2019), written and performed by Ali Official and Aatif Nawaz. The show relies heavily on observational sketches, such as the lengths that Muslim holidaymakers are required to go through in order reassure a deeply uncomfortable border guard, performing/feigning an official neutrality, despite being engaged in acts of racial profiling. Or the two Muslim office workers, competing for the accolades of their White co-workers, with a series of increasingly frenetic claims to 'prove' their 'Whiteness' (e.g. 'I collect stamps', 'I wear socks with Velcro straps', 'I shaved my friend's eyebrows off and puked on his face for banter', 'Well, I call my mum and dad by their first names').

These illustrative cases are just a selection from a wide array of output by Muslim comedians. They are illustrative because they highlight a consistent theme, whereby stereotypical ideas of Muslimness and Whiteness are brought together in sharp relief. The point is that these stereotypes – Muslimness and Whiteness – do not exist independently from one another; they are products of cultural interlocution, of the tension and misapprehension that can exist in Britain between non-Muslims and the Muslim 'Other'. The Du Boisian concept of double consciousness is apt here. Muslim comedians fundamentally recognize this gap – that is, the uncomfortable difference between Muslim self-knowledge and the imposed framing of non-Muslim prejudice – and they inhabit the space in-between, contorting the boundaries, before the absurdity of this social and cultural divide collapses inward. In a discussion of Muslim comedy in the United States, Mucahit Bilici writes:

> As arbiters of a cultural encounter and as field guides to a contact zone, these stand-up comedians are situated in a unique position. Able to 'leap' from one side to the other, they practice simultaneously the two ways of seeing things. This position is often a tragic one, where a person belongs to both worlds and neither. The comic stands uneasily on the fault line, yet by standing there he becomes a sort of stitch that holds together the two sides of the cultural rift. (Bilici, 2010: 196)

Applied to Muslim comedy in the UK, this is partly true. But rather than a 'tragic' instance of 'not belonging' to either world, I would argue that Muslim comedians instead narrow the gap and sense of difference. By extending these polar positions into the realm of absurdity – and, in so doing, destroying the credibility and reality of these extreme positions – the message,to Muslims and non-Muslims, is an incredulous: 'come on, we're not *really* like this, are we?'

In conclusion, Muslim creatives face a number of challenges relating to their place, positionality and the labelling of their work and public selves within the culture industries. While there are certainly opportunities stemming from a visible Muslim or ethnic cultural identity, this can be outweighed by the pressures and expectations that are at times associated with this labelling. There is furthermore a strong belief that Muslims are damagingly under-represented and that this can undermine the creation of more authentic and complex Muslim stories across the media and popular culture. The response from Muslim creatives is to plot a strategic course through this landscape, at times not only challenging dominant tropes but also attempting to take advantage of the spaces that do exist for visibly Muslim cultural professionals. I turn now in the next chapter to look at the transnational dimensions of the culture industries and to consider the way in which Muslim creatives are able to traverse 'global' Muslim subcultures and networks.

7

Transnational nomads

The Muslim Atlantic and 'global Muslim culture'

I think becoming a Muslim has helped broaden my perspective of the world, politics, different cultures and so on. Before I converted to Islam, I didn't know what was going on in Palestine. If someone had told me what was going on in Palestine I would have felt for the people in Palestine. If someone told me about anyone that's going through oppression, I would have related to that. But being a Muslim encouraged me to search harder, read more and become more concerned with the state of the whole of humanity.

Mohammed, Musician, February 2011, London

In the spring of 2009, the British hip-hop duo, Poetic Pilgrimage, embarked upon a tour across the United States. The trip was organized and sponsored by the Brooklyn-based events and production company, Nomadic Wax, which specializes in promoting West African and Caribbean culture through film and music. It was a modest success, exposing Poetic Pilgrimage to hip-hop audiences across America. Following the tour, they began working on a track and accompanying music video, *Silence Is Consent*, which was released in January 2011 (shortly before the so-called Arab Spring). Written and performed with Mohammed Yahya, the sharp lyrics lambast authoritarian governments across the Muslim world, from the military dictatorship of Mubarak through to the House of Saud, for failing to uphold humanitarian and Islamic values. They furthermore level a critique against political leaders in Europe and North America, accusing them of tacit complicity in supporting these very same governments. Poetic Pilgrimage are in a sense themselves 'nomadic' – with wandering and transnational lives that can elude easy definition – simultaneously British, Jamaican, African, Black and Muslim, yet never satisfactorily or singularly contained by any one of these labels. Their sense of belonging and identification – their loyalties, critiques and positioning – is always contextual, shifting and difficult to define. In this sense they are exemplar figures of an Islam of the Global West. They navigate and inhabit transnational networks that crisscross the Atlantic and globalized Western culture. Yet they also turn their gaze towards the diverse and sometimes fractured landscape of a sometimes vaguely understood but rhetorically powerful idea of global Islam (i.e. diasporic Islam and the *umma*). Poetic Pilgrimage are not alone: Muslim creatives, almost without exception, lead 'nomadic' and distinctly transnational lives.

In this chapter I examine two important dimensions of Muslim creativity and transnationalism: the 'Muslim Atlantic' and wider ideas of 'global Muslim culture' and a global Muslim community (the *umma*). In selecting these foci, I do not intend to downplay or silence other transnational links, particularly those of ethnic diaspora. However, academic research has tended to gravitate towards the ongoing historical dominance of diasporic South Asian culture in the UK (e.g. see Werbner, 2004; Murthy, 2010; Bolognani, 2011; Kim, 2014; Hodgson, 2016). In this literature – and in the field of British Muslim studies more widely – ethnicity and diasporic culture tends to understandably predominate as an area of study. If I had chosen to pursue a similar line of inquiry, this chapter might have examined, for example, Riz Ahmed's 2020 film, *Mogul Mowgli*, which evokes familial memories of Indian partition; or Aashiq al-Rasul's use of Qawwali-based sound; or the playful evocation of 'desi culture' through the comedic performances of Ali Official, Aatif Nawaz and Guz Khan. These postcolonial links and imaginations are, of course, long-standing and formative, but the blossoming alacrity of Muslim creative expansion has also been accompanied by the deepening of other, less examined, transnational connections. Given the future prospects of such links, they form the basis of this chapter.

Muslim links across the Atlantic are perhaps the most fascinating and, until recently, one of the most overlooked dimensions of Muslim transnationalism. In a seminal series of reports, *The Muslim Atlantic* project has started to map and theorize these connections (DeHanas and Mandaville, 2019). Drawing on the celebrated work of Paul Gilroy – who proposed the notion of The Black Atlantic (Gilroy, 1993) – the Muslim Atlantic similarly theorizes the idea of a hybrid space, whereby transatlantic links between Muslims are creatively woven together with new and interesting outcomes. Summarizing this claim, Daniel DeHanas and Peter Mandaville argue:

> Paul Gilroy's work emphasises how the Atlantic is neither American, nor British, nor Caribbean, nor African but something built from and existing in the midst

of all of these. In the same way, looking through a Muslim Atlantic lens places our focus on the spaces in between. As we see how Muslims draw from – and also question and critique – various conversations and cultural influences from across the Atlantic, we become more aware of the dynamic, hybrid, and constantly re-contextualised nature of contemporary Islam. (DeHanas and Mandaville, 2020)

At the time of writing, this research agenda is in an early phase, but it has begun to identify key areas of interest in relation to a Muslim Atlantic. These include, for Muslims across North America and Britain, the shared pressures of securitization and Islamophobia, new networks of English-language Islamic scholarship, the growth of neo-Sufism and the struggle for racial and gendered emancipation (see DeHanas, Khan and Mandaville, 2020). Yet standing clearly in the foreground, just as it did in the work of Gilroy, is the role of cultural experimentation and innovation. That is to say, while the Muslim Atlantic contains important dimensions of religious, social and political change, much of this is bound together and expressed through shared discourses of English-language media and popular culture. As I argue within this chapter, the Muslim Atlantic is a critical space within which Muslim creatives disseminate their work, develop new social connections and express their cultural and religious sensibilities. This ranges from the tentative emergence of a Muslim transatlantic culture industry through to the articulation of 'Muslim' style and subculture and the channelling of different schools of thought through transatlantic culture. While we should be cautious of oversimplification, these developments mirror wider social formations concerning so-called 'Western Islam' (Duderija and Rane, 2019), which is arguably becoming an identifiable region, or socio-religious bloc, within the wider landscape of the Muslim world. Or perhaps more accurately, the Muslim Atlantic represents the cultural expression (institutionally and stylistically) of an Islam of the Global West: that is, the globalization, by Muslims, of Western ideals and diverse cultures.

In the same vein, then, the relationship that Muslim creatives have with 'global Islam' is of critical significance. Muslim creatives are influential cultural leaders – their perspective matters – and it helps to inform the relationship that Muslims in the UK and North America have with the wider Muslim world. As Mohammed Yahya outlines in the opening passage, converting to Islam, for him, served to forge bonds of loyalty and connection that are informed by this sense of belonging to a global Muslim community – to the *umma*. A fraternity that, in his view, is unfettered by borders and boundaries. Yet, despite this discourse of Muslim universalism, Mohammed himself has a unique set of overlapping identities that are grounded, located and often very specific: for example, as an active member of the Afrocentric Tijaniyyah Sufi order, as a musician with strong connections to hip-hop culture in the United States and as a Black Muslim in Britain. Ideas of community and belonging are therefore always contextual, complex and socially constructed – they cut across competing and complementary ideas of local, national and transnational group membership. That being said, ideas of Muslim unity and collective membership, however they might be understood, are absolutely central within the discourses that are deployed by Muslim creatives in relation to global Islam.

As a concept of community, the *umma* has been theorized in different ways. John Bowen, for example, offers three categories of Muslim transnationalism: cross-border migration, transnational religious institutions and globalized Islamic discourse. For Bowen, each of these areas contributes to a belief that there is an 'an Islamic community transcending specific boundaries and borders' (Bowen, 2004: 882). Through this reading, the *umma* is an *idea* that operates across multiple forms of Muslim transnationalism, rather than an actual, socially grounded 'community'. Mandaville provides a similar typology, with the addition of a fourth category – that is, political and religious mobilization around the notion of 'universal Islam' (Mandaville, 2009). This view suggests that there are specific supranational discursive spaces through which ideas of global Muslim unity are generated (e.g. international forums, symbolic leadership, globally significant events). Bowen and Mandaville are both proposing that plural conceptions of a global Muslim community – the *umma* – circulate within the diverse ecumene of the Muslim world. This collective unity might be a utopian idea, rather than a reality, but it nonetheless has real power. In some respects, the *umma* is theoretically analogous to Benedict Anderson's proposal that national communities are *always* 'imagined' – that is, that they are too large to be 'real' but are rather evoked and made manifest through cultural symbolism and shared media (Anderson, 1983). Ideas of Muslim unity and community can therefore be key drivers of Muslim consciousness, particularly when they are bound together and expressed by shared instances of media and culture. As I argue, Muslim creatives are interlocutors within this discursive realm. By evoking ideas of global Muslim unity and community, their cultural production helps to sustain and shape ideas of *ummatic* consciousness. This includes a belief that Muslims should understand themselves as not just a global religious community but also as a transnational cultural group, with shared interests, tastes and spaces of consumption that transcend national and local culture. Muslim creatives can often also be more sharply political, whereby cultural production is used to mobilize Muslims around notions of collective struggle.

A transatlantic culture industry

The last two decades have seen the emergence of institutions, businesses and networks that promote cultural and media exchange between Muslims across the Atlantic – a commercial and cultural exchange that has the critical mass required to be tentatively described as a Muslim transatlantic culture industry. It incorporates a reservoir of shared cultural content, common styles and genres, and also a shared business and broadcasting model designed to appeal to Muslim audiences. Traditional broadcasters and content developers have been central to this, but new streaming services are accelerating the trend. In the United States, there has been a general failure to develop a broadcaster that addresses the needs of North American Muslims, following the closure of Bridge TV, which was launched in 2004 but ceased operations in 2012 (following the unrelated imprisonment of the owner for murder). Following a failed campaign to save Bridge TV, Muslim Americans have been dependent on international broadcasters, such as Peace TV, and, from the UK, Islam Channel and British Muslim TV – all of which have a small North American viewership (Malik, 2016). Muslim production companies have continued to operate in the United States, such as the Islamic Broadcasting Network, founded in 2001, to produce bespoke content about Muslims in North America; however, the primary outlet for distribution by North American-based production companies has been through international broadcasters. This gap in the North American television market has only recently been filled, with Muslim Network TV, launched in 2020 by the Sound Vision Foundation (SVF), based in Chicago, which has deliberately looked to replicate the business and consumer model of Islamic television in the UK. Speaking to Canadian magazine, *IQRA*, the vice president of SVF, Taha Ghayyur, outlines an aspiration to match the broadcasting success that Muslims have achieved in the UK:

> We have studied how the Muslims in the UK have greatly benefited with the presence of a Muslim television in their communities . . . 24/7 television has played a critical role in the development of Muslim voice, public relations, and representation in the British society. On the other hand, the US and Canadian Muslims do not have a Muslim channel or significant professionally run media

outlets. The vacuum has been barely filled by a plethora of ethnic TV and radio shows and newspapers. (IQRA, 2020)

Critically, then, broadcasters in the UK and North America rely on a shared business model, and they have a related set of aims: that is, free-to-air television, funded through advertising revenue and donations from Islamic charities/foundations, with a linked religious or social/political agenda. Programming is similarly aligned, including news broadcasts from an internationalist Muslim perspective, religious pedagogy and cultural shows and children's television.

Muslim streaming services are similarly developing a common model of cultural production and distribution. The two largest and most significant – Muslims Kids TV and Alchemiya – both appeal to markets across the UK and North America. Muslim Kids TV is based in Canada and since launching in 2014 it has pursued an energetic marketing campaign across North America and the UK, which it describes as its 'core subscriber market'. While it does not release subscriber figures, based on annual revenue reporting it is possible to draw a conservative estimate of at least half a million subscribers worldwide. The growth of Muslim Kids TV is astonishing – with a self-reported 400 per cent increase in subscribers between 2019 and 2020 (Cochrane, 2021). Additional revenue and viewers are being generated by Muslim Kids TV through the sale of programming to the streaming service Netflix, and with links also being made to Amazon Prime. Alchemiya has undertaken a similar journey since its founding in 2015, from a small start-up with around 5,000 subscribers to, according to its founder Navid Akhtar, a current ambition for between 70,000 and 100,000. While based in the UK, Alchemiya launched its flagship collaboration with global streaming service, Amazon Prime, in the United States first, before rolling the service out across the UK and Europe. Amazon Prime subscribers in these regions can now purchase Alchemiya as an additional package alongside their primary Amazon subscription.

A transatlantic-based Muslim broadcasting and streaming industry has therefore emerged with relative rapidity over the last ten to fifteen years, with particularly strong growth over the last five years. There are several important implications stemming from the development of this new culture industry.

First, streaming services, in particular, disseminate a wide range of English-language content about Islam and the Muslim world. Much of this content addresses the lives and shared concerns of Muslims in both North America and Britain, which in doing so further reinforces and illuminates the commonalities that exist between Muslims across the North Atlantic. Taken together, then, these streaming services are creating a pool of shared content, for those broadly within an Islam of the Global West, that is analogous with Hartley's model of 'suburban media consumption' (Hartley, 1996) – that is, content consumed in diverse and highly individualistic ways, while also expressing and reinforcing a shared and specific set of values and interests. This is no different to other forms of diasporic and international television (e.g. al-Jazeera English or CNN), which can reach a diverse international audience, yet still identifiably emanate from a particular cultural, regional or national perspective (Karim, 2003). For example, in May 2018, Alchemiya had a total of fifty-three films listed on its streaming platform. Eleven of these related to Islam in Britain, while another eleven were concerned with Muslims in the United States (most of which were grouped together within a dedicated 'Islam in America' section). These films varyingly examined the social and cultural histories and experiences of Muslims on both sides of the Atlantic but drew out similar themes concerning, for instance, the overcoming of racism and the attempt to lead spiritually rich lives within a secular context. Muslim Kids TV, in comparison, is concerned with the accessible (i.e. entertaining) transmission of Islamic history, belief and practice, as well as with secular educational content (e.g. science, literacy and mathematics). This English-language content is less culturally embedded (i.e. often, if not always, less about North America or Britain specifically) and is more often about a particular interpretation of universalized Islamic faith, a shared Muslim heritage and the educational nurturing of children. *Team Noon*, for example, is an animated series that explores modern science through the prism of scientific revelations in the Qur'an. *Orphans Tale*, another animated series, recounts the fictional journey of two orphaned Syrian children attempting to find a home with the First Nation people of Canada. The growth in popularity of this content reflects the concern amongst some Muslim parents, on both sides of the Atlantic, with the relative educational success of their children and the inculturation of Islamic norms amongst otherwise largely secular societies (Scourfield et al., 2013). It also makes clear the strong desire to connect children with a wider Islamic heritage and to global Muslim concerns. It does all of this by utilizing a programming format that is now commonplace across children's educational television in North America and Britain – norms that are rooted in the pioneering success of *Sesame Street* – whereby allegorical narratives and relatable characters are interwoven with problem solving, literacy and cultural/social skills (Fisch, 2014).

Second, this new transatlantic culture industry draws upon and promotes a shared network of Muslim public figures, creatives and celebrities. This ranges from Muslim political commentators, journalists and religious leaders through to comedians, actors and musicians. The importance of individual Muslim personalities and celebrities in the public sphere should not be underestimated. As Barry argues:

> The celebrity endorser influences not only what we buy, but our body image, our career aspirations and even our politics. Celebrity culture is ideologically bound up with the condition of global capitalism in which, as Richard Dyer puts it, 'individuals are seen to determine society'. Whether this is read as being a world of 'triumphant individualism', or an alienated society in which individuals are 'battered by the anonymity of society', the individual remains 'separate, irreducible and unique' (Dyer, 1987: 87). Our behaviour appears to be guided, then, not by social institutions or doctrines, but by the example of individuals who are seen as both like and magically unlike ourselves. (Barry, 2008: 251)

It is notable, then, that on both sides of the Northern Atlantic there exists a common roster of Muslim personalities, many of whom are promoted and projected for consumption by overlapping British and North American Muslim audiences. This includes, for example, religious scholars and leaders, such as Californian Hamza Yusuf, whose Rihla lectures have been a dedicated part of British Muslim TV programming; musicians, such as Canadian Dawud Wharnsby, a regular performer on *nasheed* shows across both sides of the Atlantic; British actor Riz Ahmed, the first Muslim actor to be nominated for an Oscar, as well as an icon for Muslims across the region; and the list continues. The critical point, following Barry (2008), is that in the contemporary context of 'celebrity culture' and 'global capitalism', *personalities matter*. They shape the values and perspectives of those who look to them for inspiration. Anderson (1983) made the argument that 'imagined communities' are generated through a shared language and set of cultural institutions, but in the era of global consumer capitalism it is equally true that a shared celebrity culture enacts a similar binding function. In this way, then, the Muslim transatlantic culture industry has a common dramatis personae that strengthens the links between Muslims across the Atlantic.

Third, as the transatlantic Muslim culture industry continues to grow, it is achieving greater penetration across international consumer markets. It is telling that Alchemiya is often described as the 'Muslim Netflix', and that Michael Milo, founder of Muslim Kids TV, has stated an ambition to become the 'Disney of the Muslim world' (Cochrane, 2021) – both Netflix and Disney are globally pervasive cultural institutions and are emblematic of American and Western soft power (Limov, 2020). To use Netflix and Disney as symbols of aspiration and a cultural reference point is emblematic of the rootedness of Muslim creative culture in North American and European entertainment industry norms. Furthermore, established Muslim broadcasters, most particularly Islam Channel, have always maintained a strong appeal to international audiences, especially in regions where English is a primary or secondary language. Meanwhile, Alchemiya and Muslim Kids TV have both in recent years developed a marketing strategy to appeal to sizeable Muslim markets in West Africa, South East Asia, the Middle East and North Africa. Muslim Kids TV has seen a 350 per cent increase in subscribers figures in media markets such as Nigeria, Turkey, Malaysia, Indonesia and India (Cochrane, 2021). Meanwhile, Alchemiya completed a deal in 2018 with Axiata, one of Asia's largest telecommunications operators, to bring the streaming service to audiences across the region. It has a self-declared strategy to build a significant and lasting presence within these international markets. Similar patterns are evident in the music industry, with Awakening Music promoting a roster of musicians to international Muslim markets, particularly Malaysia and Turkey, where Awakening musicians, such as Mesut Kurtis, have become notable cultural figures. While this growth is some way removed from the establishment of genuine competition with existing non-English-language media providers (which still predominate in these markets) this phenomenon points towards an interesting trend. Migrant Muslim communities across North America and the UK have largely (if not entirely) been passive recipients of ideas flowing outward from the historic hubs of global Islam, whether in Asia or across the Arab-speaking world. The growth of a transatlantic Muslim culture industry perhaps marks the point at which Muslims in the Global West begin to 'speak back'. Given that media institutions in Muslim-majority societies are at times criticized for their close ties to national governments and a narrow definition of Islamic norms – such as the broadcaster Eramuslim, in Indonesia – it is significant that streaming services, like Alchemiya, are explicitly offering cultural output that celebrates values of diversity, pluralism and interfaith dialogue – values which are framed as being rooted in Islamic teaching and historical precedent, yet which further represent the expression, by Muslims, of ideas that emanate from the Global West. Furthermore, international expansion sharpens the class lines that exist between Muslims, with English-language, transatlantic Muslim culture particularly appealing to a demographic of mobile, middle-class Muslims, with transnational lives, who can attach their faith identities more closely to one another than they might necessarily to a version of Islam framed by national culture. As Castells has argued, identities are more often now shaped through transnational networks, rather than within geographic locales (Castells, 1997). This therefore represents a new layer of global Muslim complexity, one whereby Muslims in the Global West, through an emergent transatlantic culture industry, wield greater influence and convey values that are more in alignment with the democratic and liberal norms that have shaped their lives and experiences in North America and Europe.

Muslim style and subculture

While the transatlantic culture industry provides a network of shared institutions and a pool of English-language content, Muslim creatives are also informed and influenced by commonalities of style and cultural form. Creatives are not just producers; they are also consumers: their work is shaped by a deep embedding in the stylistic and cultural contexts from which they have emerged. That is, from a broadly Anglocentric transatlantic realm of media and popular culture. Muslim creatives in Britain consume and draw upon not just familiar British cultural staples but also North American film, television, music and comedy. Some of these influences are of course globally pervasive – such as the cinematic output of Hollywood, which reaches far beyond the transatlantic – but I am making an argument here for a degree of depth and innate cultural familiarity, which can then be found animating the artistic output of Muslim creatives. While international and diasporic culture remains important for some (and I discuss this later), many are oriented in large part by the heliotropic attraction of Hollywood blockbusters, prime-time transatlantic television and Western pop music. These connections are significant because 'style' is freighted with underpinning ideological and social assumptions – that is, *form* involves a set of choices that have symbolic meaning; it is not simply a vehicle for ideas. In his seminal work about subculture, Dick Hebdige argues that style is comprised of meaningful signs, which serve to appropriate and convey social reality. These signs are, according to Hebdige:

> shrouded in a 'common sense' which simultaneously validates and mystifies them. . . . All aspects of culture possess a semiotic value, and the most taken-for-granted phenomena can function as signs: as elements in communication systems governed by semantic rules and codes which are not themselves directly apprehended in experience. These signs are, then, as opaque as the social

relations which produce them and which they re-present. In other words, there is an ideological dimension to every signification. (Hebdige, 1979: 13)

Leaving aside for a moment Hebdige's broader argument concerning youth subculture – which is mostly predicated on a Marxist and class-based economism – the main point here is that any analysis of culture must consider the broader semantic significance of style. Style involves the use of particular symbols that are loaded with cultural meaning – whether a particular genre of music, or a form of comedy performance, or the visual and narrative structure of film – and such choices connect in a significant way to broader social realities and themes.

Muslim creatives both reproduce and refashion transatlantic forms of cultural style. At times this can involve drawing heavily on popular styles of culture, for example, with Muslim comedians replicating a post-1980s genre of alternative comedy (Friedman, 2014), from the stand-up routine of Bill Hicks through to the satire of *South Park* and the observational comedy of *The Office*. In other ways, Muslim creatives can also syncretically combine forms of style, such as Poetic Pilgrimage and their mixing of hip-hop, spoken word and reggae, or Silk Road, with a sound reminiscent of a post-2000s indie folk genre (such as Mumford & Sons), combined with classical Indian music and the poetic intonations of Rumi. There is an experimentation with style, then, but perhaps more importantly, Muslim creatives also demonstrate a native familiarity with, and total absorption in, the cultural landscape of a dominant English-language transatlantic culture. It belongs to them, just as much as it does to anyone else.

This point becomes salient when set against the general backdrop of the way in which Muslims are typically presented in the public sphere. Research has consistently shown that 'cultural difference' is a significant trope in the representation of Muslims in news and cultural media in the Western world (e.g. Moore, Mason and Lewis, 2008; Sian, Law and Sayyid, 2012; Poole and Richardson, 2010). As I argued in Chapter 1, these images and representations reinforce a belief amongst a wider public that Muslims are culturally different, that they are 'foreign' and 'ethnic' and that such differences are loaded with threatening cultural values. As Knott, Poole and Taira argue, following their survey of new media across the UK:

> In general, in coverage of cultural differences, Islam was problematized, homogenized, essentialized and deemed obstructive. Whilst some of the coverage highlighted discrimination and diversity issues, overall, 'difference' was the central thread. Why this emphasis on difference? Important in maintaining power and superiority, differences that were once encouraged and preserved

within multiculturalism are now to be feared as the need for integration and cultural protectionism is stressed. (Knott, Poole and Taira, 2016: 89)

Through this reading, the consumption and expression of culture has become a field of conflict. Knott, Poole and Taira draw attention to one illustrative example, with Sony, in 2008, temporarily withdrawing a game that featured a soundtrack with Qur'anic samples, following comments from unknown Muslim complainants. As they suggest, across the media spectrum, Muslims in general were framed as 'censorious' and 'demanding', and as 'hardliners' rejecting a 'cute' musical accompaniment.

Returning to Hebdige, subculture is theorized as the appropriation of dominant cultural symbols and styles, which are then rearticulated to present oppositional meanings. Hebdige focuses almost exclusively on the countercultural working-class youth movements of the 1960s and 1970s, but his claim – predicated on Stuart Hall's theory of encoding/decoding (see Hall, 2003) – is that these excluded youth movements, sensationalized in news media as 'folk devils', were able to repackage cultural style and thrust it back as a series of 'symbolic challenges' (Hebdige, 1979: 96). Such challenges were ultimately seized by consumer capitalism and 'sold back' to these very same youth movements – and therefore lost their radical and outsider status – but Hebdige highlights the ongoing dialectical tussle, within the symbol-rich realm of popular culture, that exists between subcultural groups and dominant national/global cultures.

A similar dynamic can be observed in relation to what might be described – to use Hebdige's terminology – as a Muslim transatlantic 'subculture' and the engagement of Muslim creatives with wider forms of mainstream popular culture. Rather than being culturally different, Muslim creatives are cultural natives: consuming, reproducing and experimenting with cultural forms that are familiarly banal to a North American and British public. This is itself a symbolically and socially significant act. A claiming of a shared culture. Rather than being 'censorious' and 'demanding', Muslim creatives publicly show themselves to be at ease, as voracious consumers and creators of Western popular culture. During our interview, I asked Muslim creatives about their cultural influences growing up. The answers varied, with a number of different interests, as one would expect, but they all described what might be described as commonplace and totally unremarkable experiences during their formative childhood era. There are many examples, but Ahmed provided a good, illustrative account of his particular background:

So for example, growing up I remember, *Ace Ventura: When Nature Calls*, [this] would be on a lot. Like nineties comedies, *Something About Mary*, a little bit later, like *Me, Myself and Irene*, so a lot of comedy, I was really into my comedy. I remember looking at my . . . old books from reception and year one – my mum kept everything – and I was writing in my diary in year one that I'd watched *Terminator 2* . . . I was exposed to that kind of stuff from fairly early on [by my parents]. Yeah, comedy was one of the things that I was really interested in, I wasn't into horror and any of that kind of stuff. Then growing up, through university, I was really into, in the sixth form, *The Office, Brass Eye*, I really, really loved *Extras, Max and Paddies Road to Nowhere*, in 2004, so I was in Year 10, *Phoenix Nights* before that, *Harry Enfield*. So I would say a lot of comedy stuff. *Sean of the Dead, Hot Fuzz*, the third one, *The Worlds End*, it was rubbish actually. So a lot of comedy, my Dad was really into Westerns, so we watched a lot of Westerns growing up. (Ahmed, film director and television producer, June 2017, London)

Ahmed's ability, without any prior thought, to reel off a long list of British and American comedy indicates his deep embedding in this cultural scene. As Born (2000) has argued, in relation to television production, the consumption and inculturation of 'external' cultural discourses and knowledge has a reflexive influence on cultural production. It is almost so intuitively obvious that it hardly needs stating at all: the cultural products that producers consume, particularly during their formative childhood years, have a decisive impact upon later cultural production. They provide a deep well of symbols, ideas, and forms – of cultural styles and values – from which cultural producers draw upon throughout their career, both consciously, and more often unconsciously, recreating these very same cultural discourses. They do not maintain or fashion an alternative 'culture of difference' for an 'alienated' Muslim public in Britain. Rather, Muslim creatives are able to draw upon the Anglo-American pop culture within which they and their Muslim peers have been immersed throughout their lives. Yet, this also does not mean that Muslim creatives reproduce these cultural resources uncritically, or that, *pace* Hebdige, they fail to issue a 'symbolic challenge'. Indeed, Muslim creatives are judicious and critically engaged when it comes to the production of transatlantic culture.

This critical engagement can include gravitating towards cultural forms that channel the social values to which they most strongly identify, or in critiquing and seeking to change perceived failures in popular culture. Poetic Pilgrimage, for example, while citing a range of musical styles, particularly identify the neo-soul movement in America – including artists such as Lauryn Hill, Jill Scott and

Erykah Badu – as a key influence. As Sukina explains, recognizing parallels with her own identity as a Black Muslim women in the UK:

> The women of this movement were so dignified and gracious in how they carried themselves as women. They were like, you know, they covered their hair and they dressed very modestly and, they had strong, Afrocentric tendencies. (Sukina, musician, February 2011, Cardiff)

Sukina – a convert to Islam with Jamaican roots – is looking across the Atlantic and finding inspiration in popular forms of African American culture for her own sense of Muslimness, which is then carried back across into the music and the public image of Poetic Pilgrimage. Or, as Nabil suggests about comedy:

> Allah Made Me Funny are great, they've really shown that Muslims belong in the stand-up and situational comedy scene. But I love all kinds of comedy, stuff like *South Park*, which I grew up with, and like *Friends*, everyone likes *Friends*. A lot of these programmes were very funny, but they were always too White, if you know what I mean, and *South Park* upset a lot of Muslims, even if it was very funny as well. So we need more comedy like this, but with Muslim voices thrown in to the mix. (Nabil, actor and comedian, December 2016, London)

Sukina and Nabil, each in their own way, articulate a common theme that can be found amongst the views of Muslim creatives. A rootedness in transatlantic popular culture, drawing from North American and British cultural output, with a recognition that there have been failures of racial/religious inclusion and a lack of sensitivity towards Muslim audiences.

Transatlantic Muslim culture grapples with this ambivalence. Muslim creatives not only claim popular styles of culture as their own, but they also advocate for change by utilizing these styles of culture to advance a counter discourse. For example, the BBC series *Muslamic* (2019) enacts a form of situational comedy that is very much a continuation of a genre popularized in Britain by comedians such as Ricky Gervais and Peter Kay. Muslim stand-up comedians, such as Tez Ilyas, are continuing a lineage of countercultural comedy that stretches from the satirist Bill Hicks (United States) through to the cerebral Stewart Lee (Britain). Yet all of these comedians weave in a Muslim perspective – their perspective – that modifies the style, typically by avoiding the use of coarse language to 'shock' the audience, and in regularly expressing important political themes relevant for Muslims, such as racial profiling and social stereotyping, thematic content that parallels globally successful Black comedians, such as Chris Rock and Dave Chappelle. Transatlantic Muslim culture is therefore not so much a different genre, but, following Hebdige's conceptualization of subculture, it is the appropriation of style in order to subvert and challenge an existing social order – that is, a social order within which Muslims face sustained Islamophobic pressure from the state and a wider public.

Transatlantic activism and schools of thought

Muslim cultural production has also become a vehicle for forms of Islamic activism and intra-religious dispute, some of which contain a transatlantic dimension. DeHanas and Mandaville (2020) argue that neo-traditional Sufism is one of the most prominent Islamic religious networks visible within the transatlantic space. By this, they are referring to networks and institutions that have built up around a particular set of North American and British scholars (most notably, Skeikh Hamza Yusuf (United States) and Skeikh Abdal Hakim Murad (UK)). Neo-traditional Sufism is typically understood as the bringing together of Sufi practice with claims to a deep lineage of authenticated Islamic learning: as Sheikh Hamza Yusuf states: 'ours is a tradition based on *isnad* – sound, authentic, reliable transmission of sacred knowledge' (Hamza Yusuf, quoted in Hamid, 2016: 68). Moreover, neo-traditional Sufism is seen to appeal to largely middle-class and educated Muslims in the Global West, with a desire to respond to the challenges of Western modernity. However, there are other traditions that seek to appeal to Muslims on both sides of the Atlantic, including more 'conservative' or 'isolationist' trends (see later in the text). This is perhaps surprising given that the majority of Muslims in Britain are often an unacknowledged attachment to different schools of thought/Islamic traditions, or indeed none at all. As Sophie Gilliat-Ray argues:

> not all British Muslims actively identity with a particular school of thought, and the question of which organisations or individuals should 'represent' them in the public sphere can seem very remote from daily lived experience. Their own 'self-representation' and personal development within family life, within educational and employment settings, or within local religious institutions is, for many, a much more immediately pressing consideration. Just how this is playing out in the rapidly moving context of early twenty-first-century Britain is not always easy to establish. (Gilliat-Ray, 2010: 111)

Yet Muslim creatives – as activists and social elites – are more likely to be self-consciously involved in the streams and currents of intra-Muslim religious politics, and, as I argue, this tendency is replicated in the institutional structures of Muslim cultural practice across the Atlantic. From 'Sufi music' through to 'Salafi TV' (misnomers that need careful handling – see later in the text) culture provides an accessible medium through which to transmit competing Islamic orthodoxies and orthopraxis. Indeed, as energetic innovators, Islamic religious activists in the West have progressed from the print boom of the 1990s through to the adoption of broadcast and streaming media in the 2000s and 2010s.

There are various typologies that have been used to analyse different schools of thought within global Islam. John Esposito understands such divisions as a manifestation of different reactions to Western modernity and sociopolitical change within Muslim societies, identifying traditions that include conservative, neo-traditionalist, Islamic reformist and secularist (Esposito, 1999). Tariq Ramadan provides further nuance to this matrix, with six categories: Scholastic Traditionalism, Salafi Literalism, Salafi Reformism, Salafi Political Reformism, Liberal Reformism and Sufism (Ramadan, 2004). These can be summarized as follows:

Scholastic Traditionalism refers to schools of thought within Islam that maintain a strict adherence to one of the four schools of Sunni, or two schools of Shi'a, jurisprudence. Ijtihad (independent reasoning) is perceived to be of lesser importance. Adherents focus on piety, dress and personal acts of devotion.

Salafi Literalism is a tradition that aims to strictly follow the example of the *Salaf* (the 'ancestors') – by which is meant the first three generations of Muslims. They place great emphasis on the Qur'an and a smaller set of 'authentic' *hadith* (recorded statements or examples of the Prophet Muhammad) and typically reject any interpretation of these texts, which are instead understood in a more literal sense. They are isolationist communities, which seek to practice a 'pure' form of Islam and to protect themselves from Western influence.

Salafi Reformism looks back to the example of the *Salaf*, but followers argue that some interpretation (*Ijtihad*) is necessary in a changing world. They are furthermore often politically and socially engaged, with many Salafi Reformist organizations calling for pan-Islamic unity while simultaneously working within the culture and structures of Western democracies.

Salafi Political Reformism combines a literalist interpretation of Islamic sources with a desire to enact radical political change. Adherents take a strong and more oppositional stance against the Western world, oppose efforts to integrate Muslims into Western societies and often have a hostile position against governments in Muslim-majority countries (with nation states perceived to be a Western innovation), instead calling for a new caliphate defined by Islamic rule.

Liberal Reformism is influenced by secularization, with the suggestion that the Qur'an and *hadith* are not sufficient for Muslims to understand, and make sense of their place in, a changing world. Liberal Reformists emphasize assimilation within, and engagement with, Western cultures and societies.

Sufism places great emphasis on an inward spiritual life and a closeness to God, with mystical practices that aim for spiritual purification, such as *dhikr* ('remembrance' – such as the chanting of phrases or prayers). Sufis look not only to the authority of the Qur'an and *hadith* but also an historic lineage of Sufi scholars and orders. They can be socially and politically engaged, but at times also to some extent isolationist and inward looking.

While illuminating, the fine-grained typologies of Esposito and Ramadan can be problematic, never quite capturing the distinct position of specific groups and individuals. This is particularly pertinent with 'Salafis', who at times reject the actual label of 'Salafi', despite simultaneously declaring their strict adherence to the examples laid down by the *Salaf* (Inge, 2016). The work of Sadek Hamid is particular useful here, then, using that which he describes as 'participation orientations' (Hamid, 2016: 13). According to Hamid's schema, which folds the typologies of Esposito and Ramadan into a broader set of categories, 'Conservative Isolationists' focus on a rigid religious identity, with hard boundaries of inclusion, and with institutions that seek to maintain group cohesion and practice – so-called 'Salafi' groups are a typical example of this inclination. In contrast, 'Integrationist' groups – such as the Islamic Society of Britain – focus on a constructive and active involvement with wider society. A third approach includes those groups that are both isolationist and confrontational, such as Hizb ut-Tahrir, Al-Muhajiroun and certain political Salafi trends.

Unpacking these traditions and locating them in specific instances of cultural production can often be tricky. This is particularly so because Muslim creatives themselves often use a very broad language and set of labels. For example, in reference to more literalist/conservative schools of thought, a variety of terms were used by Muslim creatives: 'Salafi', 'conservative', 'dogmatic Islam' and 'Wahhabism' (a reformist tradition from Saudi Arabia, usually understood as Salafi). Similarly for liberal/Sufi traditions: 'Sufi', 'spiritually inclined', 'open-minded', 'tolerant'. These terms often act as placeholders for the broader participation orientations that have been outlined by Hamid (2016) – that is, between 'Conservative Isolationists' (which can include Salafi traditions) and 'Integrationists' (not just Sufis but also liberal reformers and secularists). Muslim creatives typically fall within the second category – Integrationists – precisely because they see cultural production as an important way to express themselves to not just Muslims but also to a wider public. There are however also examples of 'Conservative Isolationist' cultural production, such as the broadcaster, Eman Channel, which aims to create 'Islamically permissible' media content for distinct and 'isolated' Muslim enclaves in the West.

We should be careful then about too often linking any form of cultural expression to a specific school of thought. At times these links are most certainly explicit and meant in a specific sense – as I show with the affiliation that some creatives have to Sufism – but these connections can also often be vague and only loosely understood. With this caveat in place, I do however think it is possible to make some observations about the inclusion of different schools of thought in transatlantic cultural production. The cultural expression of these networks and traditions, I argue, are 'transatlantic' precisely because they are flourishing in a distinctive and common way across North America and Britain, with links across the Atlantic, not just in the Anglophone world but also including West African Sufi influences that can be found for some Black Muslims in the United States and the United Kingdom.

Sufism in particular has found a powerful voice through the production of music. Sufism is itself a contested and at times hazy tradition. Ron Geaves has provided a typology of Sufism in the UK that identifies four areas of Sufi association, ranging from active membership of a *tariqa* through to subtle traces of Sufi thought and practice (Geaves, 2000). Of the twenty-two musicians interviewed during this research, nineteen self-identified as Sufi, with different locations along the spectrum provided by Geaves (twelve were members of a *tariqa*, seven identified with Sufism and expressed some level of knowledge/ engagement with Sufi practice). In addition to the individual affiliation and spiritual inclination of these musicians, there are also organizational and structural dimensions of Sufism that impact upon music production – most notably through the Tijaniyyah and Naqshbandi-Haqqani Sufi orders.

The Tijaniyyah order, a Sufi *tariqa* based in Senegal, has increasingly appealed to Black Muslims on both sides of the Atlantic since the 1970s. While open to all, the order has strong Afrocentric tendencies and often carries with it a political as well as a spiritual outlook. In the UK it is located most prominently in London, with an unmarked holy site located at St Thomas' Hospital, where Ibrahim Niass (d. 1975), an influential leader of the order, died in 1975. One London-based musician explained (with pride and a note of wry humour) that Tijaniyyah members are known to pray at this sacred site, often literally in the corridors of the hospital. In the United States, the Tijaniyyah order can be found predominantly active amongst African American communities in New York, Chicago and Detroit (Taha-Cisse, 2007).

In Britain, the United States and in Senegal itself, Tijaniyyah Sufi practice has become associated with hip-hop. In Senegal, for example, musicians such as Aïda Faye and Maxi Krezy are attached to Tijaniyyah (Ogunnaike, 2018), in the United States, Daddy Bibson, and in the United Kingdom several well-known Muslim musicians are associated members of the order, including Rakin Niass (from Mecca2Medina), Mohammed Yahya and Poetic Pilgrimage. In the UK, these musicians are in regular and direct contact with the religious leaders of the Tijaniyyah order, based in Senegal, and are actively contributing to a Tijaniyyah network in London. Regular *dhikr* circles, meditation sessions and other forms of spiritual practice take place on a weekly basis at homes and private spaces across the city. These musicians have become powerful advocates for a particular form of West African Afrocentric Sufism that serves to both enchant hip-hop music, to drive the organizational growth of Tijaniyyah, and in so doing to help shape a Black Muslim diaspora across the Atlantic (LeVine and Otterbeck, 2021). It provides a powerful cultural counterweight to the Nation of Islam, which has otherwise often appealed to Black Muslims through the effective use of hip-hop culture (Livingston, 1998).

Another important Sufi tradition, the Naqshbandi-Haqqani order – founded in Cyprus by Nazim Al-Haqqani (d. 2014), but a modern offshoot of the historical Naqshbandi tradition (Damrel, 2006) – is the exemplar of a particular brand of neo-traditional Sufism in the West. With a significant presence online and physically across North America (the United States and Canada) and the UK, the Naqshbandi-Haqqani order engages in energetic forms of *da'wah* – including annual national tours by noted Naqshbandi sheikhs and the involvement of lay members (especially musicians) in religious-cultural events – to challenge the perceived spiritual deficiencies of a materialistic and consumerist society, and perceived Muslim ignorance of *shari'ah*. The fastest-growing Sufi tradition in the Western world, the Naqshbandi-Haqqani order has found itself in regular dispute and scholastic conflict with 'Conservative Isolationist' groups in North America and Britain. The order has a strong presence in London, especially since the opening of the Centre for Spirituality and Cultural Advancement (CSCA) in February 2010, and it maintains strong links to Muslim networks clustered around the School of Oriental and African Studies. The CSCA launched the Rabbani Project (a spiritual and artistic collective) in 2012 and began promoting the Ladies of Light music tour (consisting entirely of female Sufi performers, both musical and poetic). The Rabbani Project subsequently released an album, *Eternity: Music for the Soul* (2012), featuring a range of musicians from both the UK and North America, including London-based musicians Pearls of Islam and Rakin Niass. In total, five of the musicians that I interviewed for this research had ties to the Naqshbandi-Haqqani tradition, either as *murid*s (followers) or with looser social, cultural and religious ties.

Stylistically and semantically, then, there is overlap between all of these musicians (those in both Tijanniyah and Naqshbandi-Haqqani, but also other non-affiliated Sufi musicians), all of whom, through their music and poetry, draw on a shared Sufi aesthetic. This includes references to not just the Qur'an and *ḥadith* but also to Sufi poetry, beliefs and symbolism. Given the important public status of musicians amongst Muslims in Britain and North America, at the very least music acts as a vehicle to help drive the growth of Sufism in the West. This includes superstars such as Sami Yusuf, who, as a good example of the sometime problem of labelling, is not a member of a Sufi order but has argued that 'Sufism represents the inner spiritual dimension of the faith. Without it, the faith is incomplete' (Yusuf, 2016). Yet, in addition, this, and at times broadly defined Sufism – with its emphasis on spiritual feeling and chains of scriptural knowledge – acts as a counter to austere and reformist 'Conservative Isolationist' traditions, which have also achieved notable success on both sides of the Atlantic.

Eman Channel reflects this conservative strand in the television market. The stated aim of Eman Channel is to create an alternative hub of media and culture for Muslims in the West, while staying 'within Islamic principles' – a code, in some respects, for a 'literalist' or 'conservative' interpretation of Islam. Eman Channel draws almost exclusively from a broad spectrum of English-speaking conservative speakers, public figures and scholars, from across Britain and North America, including Salafi figures, such as Wasim Kempson, through to conservative Muslim public figures, such as Abdur Rahmeen Green. Drawing on Ramadan (2004), the general slant of programming tilts towards what might be described as 'Salafi Reformism' – anchored in the often-exclusive primacy of the Qur'an and *sunnah* but oriented towards the sociopolitical challenges of the day. These views are reflected in the nature of programming on Eman Channel, which is predominantly geared towards the devotional and scriptural (recitation, remembrance, Qur'anic exegesis, etc.) and lifestyle shows with a conservative element. The *Nasheed Show* is a good example of the latter – it has exclusively voice-only or simple percussion *nasheed* artists from the UK and

North America, such as Dawhud Wharnsby and Boonaa Muhammad (both are Canadian), and actor/musician/poet, Muslim Belal (Britain). For some, this is a telling indicator of 'Salafi influence', whereby musical performance can be seen as a symbolic marker of religious affiliation and orientation:

> I think behind [the growth of voice-only performance] is actually a Saudi-influenced, Wahhabi, Salafi influence, who want to spread a message that music is bad, but then the way they kind of do it now is by having more events with no music. It's always been there anyway, but I think, you know, at the moment they do more and more events. They've always been there but I think they were much quieter, but now they're kind of getting hands-on. (Rakin, musician, London)

Rakin's claim – that a Saudi-backed version of conservative Salafi Islam has been transposed into the sphere of cultural production – is echoed by other Muslim creatives who see themselves in opposition to 'dogmatic' and 'literalist' forms of conservative Islam. Whether these examples of cultural proscription should be described as 'Salafi', or not, is perhaps an open question, but they certainly do fall within the broad framework of Hamid's 'Conservative Isolationist' categorization (Hamid, 2016).

The most obvious oppositional counter to Eman Channel can be found with British Muslim TV, which expresses what might broadly be described as a 'Liberal Reformist' perspective (see Ramadan, 2004). This includes the prominence of figures such as Sufi neo-traditionalist, American, Hamza Yusuf, the Deobandi-trained, British, Ibrahim Mogra, Sufi scholar, Sheikh Ahmed Babikir, and Munir Ahmed, the former president of the reform-minded Islamic Society of Britain. In contrast to Eman Channel, British Muslim TV provides a wider slate of programming that emphasizes plural positions within Islam and a more overt effort to emphasize the 'cultural ease' of Muslims within Britain. The BMTV music programme – *Faith Inspired Music* – includes a range of Muslim-produced music, much of which incorporates instrumentation, such as Sami Yusuf and Zain Bhikka. It therefore places itself on the opposite side of this symbolic point of conflict between the two sides of an 'Integrationist' and 'Conservative Isolationist' cultural and religious debate. Islam Channel resides somewhere within the middle of this spectrum. It is positioned as non-sectarian and ecumenical, with speakers and presenters from a range of perspectives, although broadly it expresses a Scholastic Traditionalism outlook (see Ramadan, 2004) that is rooted in a normative, conservative-leaning school of Islamic thought, often within the Hanafi school of law.

Muslim creatives and global Islam

While intra-religious debates might at times be fraught, particularly within the fields of music and Islamic television (see previous section and the discussion on the permissibility of music in Chapter 4), there are Muslim creatives who seek to avoid becoming embroiled in these internal debates. Ishy, like several other interviewees, expressed a concern with 'Saudi-led, Wahabi-led, Salafi-led' forms of 'dogmatic Islam', but he also attempted to remove himself from intra-religious struggle, with an emphasis instead on pluralism and wanting to avoid internal Muslim strife:

> Any belief system needs to be humanitarianism. Love for your fellow human being, for your community, for society, for the environment. And if you don't have that, well, then it's just show, isn't it? It's just an act that you're putting on for the world, to say, 'Oh, look at that guy with his beard and he's going to the mosque five times a day. He must be righteous.' But if you don't start from a point of love and humanity, I personally feel, well, the rest of it is a waste of time. So it puts me in good stead. Like I say I'm quite chilled out about it. I don't care. I'm quite happy for people to believe whatever they want to believe, however they want to believe it. Good on you. I don't necessarily agree with them, but that's their choice, isn't it? (Ishy, playwright and screenwriter, August 2017, Middlesbrough)

Ishy is articulating a view held by many Muslim creatives – that there is a fellowship of human feeling and belonging that transcends individual difference and belief. This includes an openness to heterodox Islamic traditions. Ishy, for example, stresses that to be Muslim one only needs to practice the 'five pillars of Islam'. Other creatives articulate it slightly differently, but with a similar emphasis, such as hip-hop musician, Ayman, who remarks on the foundational Islamic concept of *tawhid* (the oneness of God, but, for Ayman, also the global unity of Muslims). For many Muslim creatives, then, notwithstanding their own personal spiritual and religious inclinations, intra-religious struggle is perceived to be problematic and potentially a threat to the more important need for Muslims to find common cause beneath a shared faith.

This notion of a shared faith – and of belonging to the *umma* – is a striking theme that can be found cutting across the whole spectrum of Muslim popular culture and media. It is manifested in varying ways, but, at root, it expresses a sense of global Muslim fellowship, connection and collective responsibility. As I argued earlier, the *umma*, as a concept, has been theorized in different ways. For

Bowen (2004), it is a symbolic idea that can be loaded with divergent and even contradictory values – from the celebration of Muslim pluralism and tolerance through to statist and exclusionary Islamic theocracy. For Mandaville (2009), the *umma* is a transnational/global discursive space – a fertile nexus for Muslim elites, of global cities, digital networking and intellectual ferment. Through these readings, the *umma* is therefore an abstract idea and a process of global exchange – an idea *and* a reality, an ambition *and* an 'imagined' community. For Muslim creatives, specifically, it is an important frame within which international affairs, cultural association and moral responsibility can be understood.

Muslim popular culture and media in Britain is predominantly oriented towards a burgeoning English-language transatlantic culture industry, but there is also an important strand of cultural expression that celebrates and draws upon the international diversity of 'global Muslim culture'. Aziz captures this cultural agenda when discussing the priorities that he believes Islamic broadcasters and other Muslim cultural institutions need to adopt:

> There's so much out there in the Muslim world. Some people are doing it, but it's not enough. We need to be celebrating Palestinian hip hop, and Iraqi film, and Turkish television, and bringing this kind of content to global audiences. Muslim culture is so rich, in so many corners of the world, and we need to share it as much as we can. (Aziz, television producer, July 2018, London)

Aziz is touching here upon an underlying belief, amongst some Muslim creatives, that globally there exists a diverse yet shared 'Muslim culture'. Muslim fellowship is not simply generated through tenants of faith and belief but through a collective reservoir of cultural symbolism, mythology and narrative. In this sense, Palestinian music might be 'Palestinian', Iraqi film 'Iraqi' and Turkish television 'Turkish' – but they are all also 'Muslim'. They belong, from this perspective, to all Muslims. Of course, this ignores the fact that these cultural outputs might be secular in content, or rooted in specific national cultures, but it is nonetheless a view that perceives the bonds connecting Muslims to be not just religious, social and political but also cultural.

With their large catalogue of 'on-demand' material, streaming services are an obvious place to make non-English-language content readily available for audiences. Alchemiya is at the forefront of this agenda, with the stated aim to celebrate the 'rich heritage of Muslim culture'. While much of Alchemiya's content gravitates towards British and North American, English-language production, it also visibly promotes 'global Muslim culture' as part of this package. For example, of the fifty-three films listed on Alchemiya in May

2018, twelve of these were in a non-English language, most notably Arabic and Turkish, but also Swedish, French and Italian. The founder of Alchemiya, Navid Akhtar, frames this agenda with communitarian language, appealing for individual viewers to become a part of 'our community' – that is, Global Urban Muslims. The marketing language deployed by Alchemiya is deliberate, with the evocation of a 'Muslim world' and 'global Muslim audiences'. Unbound by national broadcasting restrictions – with the ability to distribute content to any subscriber with an internet connection – Alchemiya blurs the boundaries between Muslim audiences that once might have been solely located in national cultural and media contexts. There is a strong class element to this offer – Alchemiya is targeting educated and culturally mobile Muslim audiences, not a mass viewership – but it evokes, and in so doing helps to create, the notion of 'global Muslim culture'.

Similarly, rival streaming services and other digital content providers are helping to bring shared content to diverse Muslim audiences. The Turkish drama *Diriliş: Ertuğrul* (2014–19) has become symbolic for an emergent global Muslim culture. Set in the thirteenth century, the series is an historical retelling of the events surrounding the life of Ertugrul, the father of Osman I, the founder of the Ottoman Empire. While funded by Turkish state television, the series became a global phenomenon, distributed by Netflix in seventy-two countries, and with more than 1.5 billion views on YouTube. The series constructs a narrative of Muslim heroism and agency that draws upon a range of contemporary themes concerning, for example, gender, piety and leadership. Responses have been varied, from a ban in neighbouring states, such as Egypt and Saudi Arabia – where senior clerics issued fatwas concerned with Turkish soft power – through to widespread praise and fandom amongst Muslim audiences across the world. Anecdotally, the series has been a phenomenon in Britain (as it has elsewhere), with Muslim audiences devouring this Turkish-language drama, and with widespread coverage across Muslim print and digital media. As Nabil remarked, when asked about his viewing habits:

> Like everybody, I've totally binge-watched *Ertugrul*. Can't get enough of it. It's like *Game of Thrones* for the Muslim world. It's a bit silly at times, but it shows Muslims in a positive light, as heroes and powerful figures. So that's been a regular watch for me . . . for a few years now. (Nabil, actor and comedian, December 2016, London)

Nabil is constructing here a sense of Muslim cultural polity that exists alongside, and as a complementary analogue to, 'Western culture', with *Ertugrul* considered alongside *Game of Thrones* (2011–19). It does not matter that *Ertugrul* expresses strong elements of Turkish/Ottoman culture and history, because it resonates with Muslim audiences, by constructing reimagined ideas of Muslim prominence and power for a contemporary global context. The comparison between these two series is telling, given that Game of Thrones, while entirely fictional, is a reimagined and archetypal reworking of fifteenth-century Europe (Larrington, 2017), with similar themes that relate to gender, politics, religion and war.

The historical reimagining of Muslims is not confined to television, but it also finds an outlet in other forms. For example, *nasheed* artists at times touch upon ideas of shared Muslim history. There are examples of historical themes within the work of several *nasheed* performers – such as Sami Yusuf, Aashiq al-Rasul, SHAAM and Labbayk Nasheeds – but Amir Awan exemplifies this very well with 'Battle of Uhud', a retelling of the clash between early Muslims and Meccans at the foot of Mount Uhud (625 CE). The song has a key moral framework, referencing the notion of Muslim duty for the 'greater good' and the consequences for failing to uphold this trust 'they did not obey, they just walked away, these heedless few lost us victory that day' (Awan, 2009). It is a fascinating song that channels contemporary themes of Muslim suffering, communality and sacrifice through the prism of an imagined Islamic past.

Similarly with the theatre production, *Dara* . . . which tells the story of the Mughal emperor, Shah Jehan (b.1592/d.1666) and a dynastic struggle enacted by his two sons in their vying to succeed him. The play explores themes of orthodoxy and pluralism, with the eldest son (and heir apparent) – Dara Shikoh – defeated in battle and executed by his younger brother, Aurangzeb, who subsequently reigns with a focus on explicit Muslim piety and a lack of tolerance for other faith traditions. The production was a partnership between the National Theatre (UK) and the theatre company, Ajoka (Pakistan), brought together by the online platform, *Samosa* (which seeks to celebrate South Asian and Muslim art and culture in Britain). The founder of *Samosa*, Anwar Akhtar, remarked about the play: 'This idea that there is one overarching, overbearing school of Islam is not the reality and crucially this play explores this multiplicity of the history of Islam . . . Dara does what all great history plays do which is entertain, educate and inform us about our past but also our present.' (Akhtar, quoted in Ellis-Petersen, 2015).

While historical, the play therefore channels contemporary themes, drawing attention to the diverse and contested nature of Islamic thought and practice. Both of these examples – 'Battle of Uhud' and *Dara* – use historical reimaging to speak to a present-day global community of Muslims.

Alongside the imaging of global Muslim culture, Muslim creatives additionally recognize their sense of political and social responsibility towards Muslim struggles elsewhere. Through this understanding, the media and cultural prominence of Muslim creatives becomes a vehicle through which they can advocate for oppressed Muslim groups around the world. Almost without exception, Muslim creatives articulate strongly held views about international affairs, most often in flashpoints of Muslim concern, such as the Rohingya and the Uyghurs, and in Palestine, Yemen, Kashmir and Sudan, but also more widely relating to Muslim experiences of poverty and state violence (including from Western securitization policies). This political agenda was expressed by Muslim creatives as a need not only to encourage Muslim solidarity – to foster collective resistance through the bonds that exist between the 'brothers and sisters' of Islam – but also to promote universal values of humanitarianism. These values might be promoted and celebrated by Western governments, so the argument goes, but they are inconsistently applied to Muslims, who are seen to lack protection and concern from self-righteous and hypocritical governments in the Western world (particularly Britain and the United States). This is therefore not about rejecting Western democratic and humanitarian norms but about ensuring that they are applied fairly to Muslim societies across the world.

'Umar, for example, frames the Palestinian conflict in this way, touching upon the idea of not only a 'Muslim perspective' but also the humanitarian plight faced by the Palestinian people:

> Well, as a Muslim, I see from a Muslim point of view and the Palestinian issue is very important to me . . . I mean, the Palestinian case is not just related to Palestinians, it's not just related to Muslims, it's related to anyone who has a heart, anyone who says that they're a humanitarian person, because we see the massacres that happen in Palestine. . . . And then I think to myself that doing my music actually plays my part, and I play my part in trying to raise awareness because I think that's the most important thing. A lot of people are ignorant towards the cause. . . . With my music I try to lead the way . . . you find that it relates back to a lot of Muslims and how a lot of Muslims feel about their brothers and sisters being occupied, and that's why they see they need to do something about it. ('Umar, musician, December 2010, London)

Similarly, Sami Yusuf evokes strong humanitarian themes within his music. In his most successful album, *My Ummah* (2005), Yusuf directly addresses Muslims as a collective group, calling for action on issues such as Palestine and state violence against Muslims in Chechnya. One song, for example, takes a symbol of Palestinian resistance – hurling stones – and connects it to the ritual of *ramy al-jamarāt* (the stoning of the Devil) during the Hajj – a practice that is symbolic for the struggle to overcome temptation and, in this case, the specific temptation to ignore the difficulties faced by Palestinians. The tenor of Yusuf's lyrics throughout the album makes it abundantly clear that 'we' – the *umma* – including 'you' the listener – have a religious and humanitarian obligation to act. Yusuf broadens this obligation to encompass humanitarian issues that exist beyond Muslim-majority societies. Examples of this include a music video, filmed on location in Port-au-Prince, Haiti, with the aim of raising money for the victims of natural disasters (this was shortly after the devastating 2010 earthquake in Haiti). In lyrical terms, Yusuf chastises the supposed indifference that Muslims might feel towards humanitarian causes in non-Muslim contexts. In 'Make a Prayer', Sami Yusuf signals the open and universal values of Islam, imploring the *umma* to draw on their religious values and beliefs to support non-Muslims in challenging and tragic circumstances.

These discourses – of global Islam/the *umma* and humanitarianism – are not just directed against the failures of Western governments but are furthermore used by Muslim creatives to critique perceived failings within the Muslim world. In this way, approbation is particularly reserved for authoritarian governments that fail to uphold Islamic values and beliefs – governments that are supposedly 'Islamic' but that fail to support the humanitarian causes of Muslims around the world. For example, in their 2011 track, *Silence Is Consent*, Poetic Pilgrimage and Mohammed Yahya launch a critique against selected Arab leaders – including Muammar Gaddafi and Hosni Mubarak – for their unwillingness to prevent humanitarian crimes against Muslims. Beyond international affairs, they also identify social and moral failures, especially against women: 'For women killed, from Somalia to Bahrain, in Saudi Arabia and Iran the treatments the same, this shame you bring upon my *umma*' (Poetic Pilgrimage and Mohammed Yahya, 2011). The decision to use the possessive pronoun – 'my *umma*' – reminds the listener that these three London-based rappers, as members of a global Muslim community, have a moral imperative that requires them to step away from their own national context and to critique the failings of governments and societies across the Muslim world. Similarly, with Tez Ilyas, who in a 2020 speech at a rally in London, organized to oppose military action against Iran, spoke out against the failings of authoritarian Middle Eastern states, calling on the UK government to avoid military action and to instead apply 'sustained diplomatic pressure on countries like Iran, Saudi Arabia, Syria'. His speech challenged Western interventionism but simultaneously highlighted those governments in the Muslim world that fail to uphold humanitarian and Islamic values.

In conclusion, Muslim creatives are uniquely located within various transnational networks and subcultures. This informs creative aspects of their work – aligning them with both transatlantic and global Muslim audiences – but it also shapes their understanding of international politics. Most significantly it suggests that, while national and ethnic diasporic links remain important, there is a reorientation taking place whereby Muslim creatives – and Muslims in Britain more broadly – are finding a new, distinctive and outspoken place within the landscape of global Islam and, in a related way, an Islam of the Global West.

Conclusion

Muslim creatives, future narratives

I opened this book by arguing that there is an inherent danger in 'naming' Islam: that any attempt to identify or discuss 'Muslim popular culture' carries with it the risk and perhaps inevitability of over-exposure and exceptionalism. This tension has been an underlying and at times uncomfortable theme across these pages, not just throughout my discussion but also relating to the way in which Muslim creatives themselves conceive of their work, their identities and their public role. How can one seek to express ideas of 'authentic' Muslimness and to achieve greater levels of Muslim inclusion within the creative industries, without also shackling creatives to the expectation that Muslims should (and can only) produce visibly 'Muslim culture'? This conceptual and structural dilemma contains within it a latent Orientalism, whereby 'Muslimness' is not defined *for itself* – as possessing agency and mutability – but *in itself* – as a distorted and static image, shaped and framed by deep-seated cultural expectations concerning the 'legitimate' place of Muslims in the public sphere. The sad irony is that even when resisting and demolishing these expectations, Muslim creatives are nonetheless often trapped by the need to respond, which inevitably prioritizes their role as faith advocates over other aspects of their personal and artistic story. Given the pervasive nature of Islamophobia within Britain and other Muslim-minority contexts, this is a role that Muslim creatives largely adopt with gusto, but it does also place problematic limits on creative freedom. As Riz Ahmed has argued, there is a 'promised land' out there somewhere – perhaps always elusive in the near future – whereby creative output is no longer tied to the ethnicity or religion of individual cultural producers.

This picture is further complicated by the desire that Muslim creatives have to transmit their faith, in some form, through cultural production. This is an impulse that springs from the conviction, amongst cultural producers, that their religious sensibilities – including Islamic values, beliefs and everyday Muslim practices – cannot be delinked from the creative process. While Muslim creatives might express reservations about the straightjacketing of cultural creativity, or the expectation that they somehow become religious raconteurs, neither do they wish to deny the living, breathing presence of Islam within their artistic vision. This can take many forms, as I have shown, from a gentle and affective spirituality, through to political and social commentary, or the performance of devotion and the exposition of Islamic pedagogy. Critically, it can also entail a certain degree of code-switching, with a language and conceptual framing that can be adjusted to accommodate different audiences and different cultural contexts – Muslim and non-Muslim, religious and non-religious, spiritual and political.

There is also the matter of professional survival and success within the fiercely competitive cultural industries. For Muslim creatives, there is something of a dual system: a Muslim cultural economy, on the one hand, and mainstream cultural institutions and audiences, on the other. There can be enormous benefits in developing bespoke institutions and networks, as well as in building a unique and targeted Muslim audience – the undoubted success of Sami Yusuf is a testament to this approach. These institutional resources – such as the streaming service Alchemiya – can provide support, finance, capital and a platform for the dissemination of artistic work. They can also generate creative hubs that bring artists together in the mutual development of creative techniques and practices. But this can be limiting: an affiliation with niche Muslim institutions, networks and communities can inhibit access to new and more diverse audiences. There are no examples in this research, for example, of a crossover from Islamic television to mainstream public service broadcasting. Of the musicians discussed, Harris J is alone in having moved from an Islamic recording company to a mainstream music label (from Awakening Music to Virgin EMI). Those creatives that have found success in mainstream cultural contexts have largely done so by articulating their Muslimness as a form of soft cultural and societal association (e.g. Tez Ilyas), rather than as an explicit performance of Islamic belief and practice itself. Whether this is a product of Islamophobia in mainstream cultural circles, as some Muslim creatives argue, or whether it merely reflects the secularized nature of the British public sphere, whereby there is often little room for explicit confessional belief, the end result is the same: the circumscription of 'legitimate' Muslim cultural expression.

The challenges facing Muslim creatives are therefore myriad but entirely interconnected. Should they adopt specific labels or frameworks to describe their work – whether 'Muslim' or 'Islamic'? Should they develop a bespoke subculture and set of cultural institutions, or should they push for wider inclusion within the mainstream cultural industries? Should they use cultural expression to address contemporary social anxieties, or does this in itself reinforce their perceived exceptionalism? There is no one answer to these dilemmas. At the very least, Muslim creatives demonstrate a complex agility: there is a simultaneous and not necessarily paradoxical desire by creatives to reinforce Muslim communal identity – and to express universal human stories – while also bringing Islamic religiosity and specific Muslim experiences to play within wider social and cultural conversations.

I will go as far to suggest that this is an historical inflection point: the increasing agency and cultural visibility of Muslims will undoubtedly play a decisive role in shaping the future of Muslim Britain. There are three interconnected trends and speculative projections that I believe will underpin this future. These relate in turn to how Muslimness is understood and expressed, the racialization of Muslims in public debate and that which I describe here as the 'weak' secularization of Islam in Britain.

Muslimness: An identity strongly held, but loosely realized

Depictions of Muslims in popular culture have often relied upon one-dimensional caricatures and stereotypes of Muslimness, whereby there is often not just an emphasis on hypervisibility (in relation to apparel, language, devotional practice, etc.) but also a predominant focus on religiosity at the expense of all other qualities. Even when setting aside obviously problematic tropes relating to terrorism and radicalism, popular culture depictions have typically been hitched together with the framing of a mosque-based, working-class, socially conservative and ethnically South Asian Muslim 'community' in Britain. This image – both evoked and reinforced by popular culture – no doubt serves to inform public and political attitudes towards Muslims. Creatives partly upend this perception by providing rich and diverse expressions of Muslimness. Whether through spiritual and devotional music, subversive comedy, reality television or socially grounded film, Muslim creatives showcase the complexity, contextuality and changing nature of Muslim life in Britain. These artistic stories capture the intersectionality of different Muslim social identities – including ethnicity, gender and class – but, equally, they can delink Muslim stories from areas of overt social, cultural and political concern, with narratives that touch upon the universality of shared human fellowship and experience. Despite these differences, and at the same time, Muslim creatives express a powerful and shared sense of collective identity – even if 'Muslimness' itself is diverse and broadly conceptualized beneath the socially and politically operative category of *being* a 'British Muslim'.

This conceptualization will most likely continue, with an increasing array of everyday, individualistic and diverse Muslim practices and beliefs thriving beneath a shared sense of collective and socially charged Muslim identity in the UK. This mirrors wider changes for Muslims in Britain. Muslims have never been a homogenous community within the UK – there are too many different ethnic, cultural and geographical groups, each shaped by multiple and sometimes very different experiences of migration, settlement and (for a small number) conversion to Islam. This diversity has continued to flourish (Gilliat-Ray, 2010), yet it has also run alongside a parallel attempt by Muslims to assert the socially and politically powerful idea of being 'British Muslim' (Morris, 2018) – with ideas of shared struggle, communal responsibility and loyalty and a shared history – even if British Muslimness itself can be a contested idea or understood in different ways. Muslim creatives exemplify this. They can express Muslimness in ways that are different to one another – for example, ranging from politically and socially charged comedians, to spiritually expressive musicians, to pedagogical teledawah presenters. Yet each is nonetheless bound together by the shared understanding that they are asserting and contributing to a collective Muslim identity in the public sphere. In this sense, while Muslimness might be understood by creatives in ever more diverse ways, these expressions will no doubt continue to be bracketed by the social and political label of 'British Muslim'.

The (problematic) racialization of Muslims in Britain

One of the striking implications concerning Muslim visibility and inclusion in the culture industries is a natural recourse to the racialized language of Muslimness. For Muslim creatives this was certainly not necessarily an assumption that Muslimness equates to a South Asian ethnic identity – although this does circulate more widely within the UK, for Muslims and non-Muslims alike – but rather that discussions about cultural representation were critically informed by long-running debates concerning minority ethnic representation within popular culture. There is an inevitable parallel here with the role of the Black Arts Movement (BAM) in the United States and the United Kingdom, which helped to propel visible Black identities into the public realm. Strategically, Muslim cultural producers are faced with the same dilemma that shaped those active in BAM: to strive for independent institutions, networks and a distinctive aesthetic, or to seek access to a cultural mainstream. BAM enabled thriving independent spaces for Black culture, but it also gravitated significantly towards the latter option – a halfway house, both within and apart from mainstream culture – and in doing so it has helped to ensure that a Black cultural identity remains a distinguishing and politically active label for individual artists and performers. There is a similar force at work for Muslim creatives. While many desire to be set free from the restraints of an overdetermined religious identity – to explore the limits of their artistic imagination – there is a countervailing pressure that emphasizes the need for 'Muslim' inclusion, 'Muslim' cultural institutions and authentic 'Muslim' stories. The result perhaps will be analogous to that achieved by BAM: a powerful and cohesive cultural force that binds together Black/Muslim communities and imaginaries, yet also existing as a distinctive subculture that is partly, yet not entirely, included within a wider cultural mainstream. This implies that British Muslim identities will become operatively closer in form to racial identities, as opposed to other forms of public religion, such as Christianity or Buddhism, for example, which tend in the UK to be backstage identities that lack the same sense of acute visibility in popular culture. For example, just as Elayne Oliphant (2021) has shown with Catholic France, Christianity has a deep-seated yet 'banal' place within the cultural and institutional imaginary of the UK, needing little in the way of explicit effort to convey the historically and socially inscribed power of Christian Britain. Buddhism, meanwhile, is often largely quietistic, making few demands for public recognition, and with a large number of White converts who already see their identity as established within British society (Bluck, 2012). Muslims, in contrast, face the dual challenge of reconciling specific demands and anxieties (e.g. concerning schooling, Islamophobia, etc.) with the growing demographic and social presence of Muslims in Britain. This trend, as it continues, will help to ensure that Muslimness remains a socially charged public identity, providing not only opportunities for Muslim creatives – in terms of funding, recognition and bespoke networks and institutions – but also limitations that arise from a demand to 'represent' community religious interests and concerns.

The 'weak' secularization of Islam in Britain

There are also questions about the impact that Muslim cultural production will have on wider Islamic belief and practice in the UK. The emphasis that Muslim creatives place upon a public and vocal Muslim identity will no doubt help to foster stronger feelings of religiosity, but the strident individualism and at times heterodox faith practices of creatives will also perhaps fuel greater diversity amongst Muslims in Britain. While the traditional religious authorities of the 'ulama' and a mosque-based religious culture remain potent, Muslim creatives belong to a new generation of public figures that demonstrate alternative and diverse ways of practicing Islam and expressing their faith identity. This perhaps represents a form of 'weak' secularization. Not the diminishing of faith identities, nor a decline in the social significance of Islam, but a pluralizing process that fragments previously dominant traditions and practices. This raises challenging questions for those organizations that seek to represent Muslims in the public sphere – such as the Muslim Council of Britain – which have long been perceived to have strong roots in a particular tradition of scholastic and conservative Islam. While there has never been a singular form of Islam in Britain, this rising tide of new lay public figures, including Muslim creatives, will ensure that any claim to religious homogeneity is untenable. Correspondingly, while Muslims in Britain will no doubt continue to enact a form of strategic essentialism – that is, seeking action on issues of shared concern, particularly around social and political settlement – beneath the surface it might be expected that Islamic beliefs and practices become more contested, diverse and increasingly individualistic. The result will be that historic religious elites and institutions find their public status weakened. This will be analogous to Christianity – in the sense that Christian institutions have seen their social position diminished in the post-war period (Bruce, 2017) – but also strikingly different in the way that Muslim religiosity will remain active and socially formative (so unlike Christianity in Britain, which has seen a secularizing decline across almost all forms of practice and belief).

These are speculative projections, nothing more, but there is no doubt that Muslim cultural production will play an ever-increasing role in the ongoing story of Britain. Not just in relation to Muslims in Britain but also as a unique and important strand in the warp and woof of the national consciousness. An open question does remain, however, following Peter Morey and Amina Yaqin (2011), about the extent to which Muslim creatives are able to 'escape the frame' of a deep-rooted Orientalism in British culture. At least for the foreseeable future, resistance to this framing – alongside attempts to carve out distinctive spaces for Muslim expression and Islamic devotion – will provide an impetus for the continued and extraordinary cultural experimentation of Muslims in Britain.

References

Abbas, T. (2013), '"Last of the dinosaurs": Citizen Khan as Institutionalisation of Pakistani Stereotypes in British Television Comedy', *South Asian Popular Culture*, 11 (1): 85–90.

Abu-Lughod, L. (1993), *Writing Women's Worlds: Bedouin Stories*, Oakland: University of California Press.

Ackfeldt, A. (2012), '"Imma march" toward Ka'ba": Islam in Swedish Hip Hop', *Contemporary Islam*, 6 (3): 283–96.

Aggarwal, P., K. Knudsen and A. Maamoun (2011), 'Branding as Ideological Symbols: The Cola Wars', *Journal of Business Case Studies*, 5 (2): 27–34.

Ahmed, A. (2013), 'Faith in Comedy: Representations of Muslim Identity in British Comedy', *South Asian Popular Culture*, 11 (1): 91–6.

Ahmed, R. (2016), 'Airports and Auditions', in N. Shukla (ed.), *The Good Immigrant*, 159–68, London: Unbound.

Ahmed, R. (2017), 'Channel 4 Diversity Speech 2017 @ House of Commons', https://www.facebook.com/watch/?v=10154393155118997.

Ahmed, T. S. (2005), 'Reading Between the Lines - Muslims and the Media', in T. Abbas (ed.), *Muslim Britain: Communities Under Pressure*, 109–26, London: Zed Books.

Aidi, H. (2004), '"Verily, there is only one hip-hop Umma": Islam, Cultural Protest and Urban Marginality', *Socialism and Democracy*, 18 (2): 107–26.

Akhtar, N. (2012), 'The Rise of the Affluent Muslim Traveller', *BBC News*, 20 August.

Akhtar, N. (2014), 'Casting Islam - UK Television and the Muslim Narrative', 2014 Public Lecture Series, Centre for the Study of Islam in the UK, Cardiff University, 11 March.

al Faruqi, L. I. (1985), *Islam and Art*, Islamabad: National Hijra Council.

al Faruqi, L. I. and I. R. al Faruqi (1986), *The Cultural Atlas of Islam*, New York: MacMillan.

Alim, H. S. (2005), 'A New Research Agenda: Exploring the Transglobal Hip Hop Umma', in M. Cooke and B. B. Lawrence (eds), *Muslim Networks: From Hajj to Hip Hop*, 264–74, Chapel Hill: The University of North Carolina Press.

Allen, C. (2010), *Islamophobia*, London: Routledge.

Ally, M. (1979), *The Growth and Organisation of the Muslim Community in Britain*, Birmingham: Selly Oak Colleges, CSIC.

Alsultany, E. (2012), 'Protesting Muslim Americans as Patriotic Americans: The All-American Muslim Controversy', *Journal of Mass Media Ethics*, 27 (2): 145–8.

Amin, H. (2019), 'British Muslims Navigating Between Individualism and Traditional Authority', *Religions*, 10 (6): 354.

Ammerman, N. T., ed. (2006), *Everyday Religion: Observing Modern Religious Lives*, Oxford: Oxford University Press.

Anderson, B. (1983), *Imagined Communities*, London: Verso.

Anderson, J. (2008), 'Towards an Integrated Second-Language Pedagogy for Foreign and Community/Heritage Languages in Multilingual Britain', *Language Learning Journal*, 36 (1): 79–89.

Anderson, J. W. (2003), 'The Internet and Islam's New Interpreters', in D. F. Eickelman and J. W. Anderson (eds), *New Media in the Muslim World: The Emerging Public Sphere*, 45–60, Bloomington: Indiana University Press.

Ansari, H. (2004), *The Infidel Within*, London: C. Hurst & Co. (Publishers) Ltd.

Anwar, M. (1979), *Myth of Return: Pakistanis in Britain*, London: Heinemann Educational Books.

Appadurai, A. (1990), 'Disjuncture and Difference in the Global Cultural Economy', *Theory, Culture & Society*, 7 (2–3): 295–310.

Appadurai, A. (1996), *Modernity at Large: Cultural Dimensions of Globalization*, Minnesota: University of Minnesota Press.

Appiah, K. (1998), 'Cosmopolitan Patriots', in P. Cheah and B. Robbins (eds), *Cosmopolitics: Thinking and Feeling Beyond the Nation*, 91–114, Minneapolis: University of Minneapolis Press.

Archer, L. (2009), 'Race, "face" and Masculinity: The Identities and Local Geographies of Muslim Boys', in P. Hopkins and R. Gale (eds), *Muslims in Britain: Race, Place and Identities*, 74–91, Edinburgh: Edinburgh University Press.

Archibugi, D. (1995), *Cosmopolitan Democracy: An Agenda for a New World Order*, Cambridge: Polity Press.

Asad, T. (2003), *Formations of the Secular*, Palo Alto: Stanford University Press.

Armando, S. (2016), *The Sociology of Islam: Knowledge, Power and Civility*, Chichester: Wiley Blackwell.

Ashcroft, B., G. Griffiths and H. Tiffin (2002), *The Empire Writes Back: Theory and Practice in Post-Colonial Literatures*, Abingdon: Routledge.

Asp, K. (2016), 'Mediatization: Rethinking the Question of Media Power', in K. Lundby (ed.), 349–74, *Mediatization of Communication*, Berlin: De Gruyter.

Baig, K. (2008), *Slippery Stone*, Garden Grove: Openmind Press.

Bailey, D., I. Baucom and S. Boyce (2005), *Shades of Black: Assembling the 1980s*, Durham: Duke University Press.

Baily, J. (2006) 'Music is in Our Blood': Gujarati Muslim Musicians in the UK', *Journal of Ethnic and Migration Studies*, 32 (2): 257–70.

Baily, J. and M. Collyer (2006), 'Introduction: Music and Migration', *Journal of Ethnic and Migration Studies*, 32 (2): 167–82.

Barker, C. and M. Wiatrowski, eds (2017), *The Age of Netflix: Critical Essays on Streaming Media, Digital Delivery and Instant Access*, Jefferson: McFarland.

Barry, E. (2008), 'Celebrity, Cultural Production and Public Life', *International Journal of Cultural Studies*, 11 (3): 251–8.

BBC (2016), *Diversity and Inclusion Strategy 2016–2020*, London: BBC.

Beck, U. (2012), 'Redefining the Sociological Project: The Cosmopolitan Challenge', *Sociology*, 46 (1): 7–12.

Bergson, H. (2013), *Comedy: An Essay on Comedy*, New York: Doubleday.

Bhabha, H. (1994), *The Location of Culture*, Abingdon: Routledge.

Bilici, M. (2010), 'Muslim Ethnic Comedy: Inversions of Islamophobia', in A. Shryock (ed.), *Islamophobia/Islamophilia: Beyond the Politics of Enemy and Friend*, 195–208, Bloomington: Indiana University Press.

Bluck, R. (2012), 'Buddhism', in L. Woodhead and R. Catto (eds), *Religion and Change in Modern Britain*, 131–42, Abingdon: Routledge.

Bolognani, M., et al. (2011), '101 Damnations: British Pakistanis, British Cinema and Sociological Mimicry', *South Asian Popular Culture*, 9 (2): 161–75.

Born, G. (2000), 'Inside Television: Television Studies and the Sociology of Culture', *Screen*, 41 (4): 404–24.

Bouchat, K. (2019), *Testing the Bechdel Test*, Portland: Portland State University.

Bourdieu, P. (1984), *Distinction: A Social Critique of the Judgment of Taste*, trans. R. Nice, Cambridge, MA: Harvard University Press.

Bourdieu, P. (1993), *The Field of Cultural Production: Essays on Art and Literature*, New York: Columbia University Press.

Bowen, J. R. (2004), 'Beyond Migration: Islam as a Transnational Public Space', *Journal of Ethnic and Migration Studies*, 30 (5): 879–94.

Bowman, M. and U. Valk (2014), *Vernacular Religion in Everyday Life: Expressions of Belief*, London: Routledge.

Bradford, C. (2003), 'Stronger Than Yesterday? Romance and Anti-Romance in Popular Music', in K. Mallan, S. Pearce and J. Black (eds), *Youth Cultures: Texts, Images, and Identities*, 35–47, Westport: Greenwood Publishing Group.

Brockopp, J. E. (2017), *Muhammad's Heirs: The Rise of Muslim Scholarly Communities, 622–950*, Cambridge: Cambridge University Press.

Bruce, S. (2017), 'The Demise of Christianity in Britain', in G. Davie, P. Heelas and L. Woodhead (eds), *Predicting Religion*, 53–63, London: Routledge.

Bruce, S. and D. Voas (2010), 'Vicarious Religion: An Examination and Critique', *Journal of Contemporary Religion*, 25 (2): 243–59.

Campion, M. J. (2005), *Look who's Talking: Cultural Diversity, Public Service Broadcasting and the National Conversation*, Oxford: Nuffield College Oxford.

Canclini, N. G. (2001), *Consumers and Citizens: Globalization and Multicultural Conflicts*, Minneapolis: University of Minnesota Press.

Carrette, J. and R. King (2004), *Selling Spirituality: The Silent Takeover of Religion*, Abingdon: Routledge.

Castells, M. (1997), *The Power of Identity*, Oxford: Wiley-Blackwell.

Cesari, J. (2003), 'Muslim Minorities in Europe', in J. L. Esposito and F. Burgat (eds), *Modernizing Islam*, 251–70, London: Hurst & Co.

Chalaby, J. K (2005), 'Towards an Understanding of Media Transnationalism', in J. K. Chalaby (ed.), *Transnational Television Worldwide: Towards a New Media Order*, 1–13, London: I.B. Tauris.

Chambers, C. (2011), *British Muslim Fictions: Interviews with Contemporary Writers*, Basingstoke: Palgrave Macmillan.

Citizens UK (2017), *The Missing Muslims: Unlocking British Muslim Potential for the Benefit of All*, London: Citizens UK.

Clark, L. S. and S. M. Hoover (1997), 'At the Intersection of Media, Culture and Religion', in S. M. Hoover and K. Lundby (eds), *Rethinking Media, Religion, and Culture*, 15–31, London: SAGE Publications.

Clifford, J. (1994) 'Diasporas', *Cultural Anthropology*, 9 (3): 302–38.

Cobb, K. (2008), *The Blackwell Guide to Theology and Popular Culture*, Oxford: Blackwell Publishing.

Cochrane, P. (2021), 'We Want to be the Disney of the Muslim World', *Salaam Gateway*, 18 June.

Damrel, David W. (2006), 'Aspects of the Naqshbandi-Haqqani Order in North America', in J. Malik and J. Hinnells (eds), *Sufism in the West*, 115–26, London: Routledge.

David, F. (1994), *Fashion, Culture and Identity*, Chicago: The University of Chicago Press.

Davie, G. (2007), 'Vicarious Religion: A Methodological Challenge', in N. T. Ammerman (ed.), *Everyday Religion: Observing Modern Religious Lives*, 21–36, Oxford: Oxford University Press.

Davie, G. (2014), *Religion in Britain: A Persistent Paradox*, Hoboken: John Wiley & Sons.

Davis, G. and A. Fuchs, eds (2006), *Staging New Britain: Aspects of Black and South Asian British Theatre Practice*, Brussels: Peter Lang.

de Certeau, M. (1984), *The Practice of Everyday Life*, trans. Steven Rendall, Berkeley: University of California Press.

Deacy, C. and E. Arweck, eds (2009), *Exploring Religion and the Sacred in a Media Age*, Farnham: Ashgate Publishing, Ltd.

DeHanas, D. N. and P. Mandaville (2019), *Mapping the Muslim Atlantic: US and UK Muslim Debates on Race, Gender, and Securitization*, London: British Council.

DeHanas, D. N. and P. Mandaville (2020), 'What is the Muslim Atlantic?', *Critical Muslim*, 35 (1), https://www.criticalmuslim.io/what-is-the-muslim-atlantic/ (accessed 6 June 2021).

DeHanas, D. N., R. Khan and P. Mandaville. (2020), *Living the Muslim Atlantic: Race, Gender, and the Politics of Marginality*, London: King's College London.

Delanty, G. (2009), *The Cosmopolitan Imagination: The Renewal of Critical Social Theory*, Cambridge: Cambridge University Press.

Deller, R. A. (2012), *Faith in View: Religion and Spirituality in Factual British Television 2000–2009*, Sheffield: Sheffield Hallam University.

Dessing, N., N. Jeldtoft and L. Woodhead, eds (2016), *Everyday Lived Islam in Europe*, London: Routledge.

Duderija, A. and H. Rane (2019), *Islam and Muslims in the West*, London: Palgrave Macmillan.

Dyer, R. (1987), *Heavenly Bodies: Film Stars and Society*, London: Macmillan.

Echchaibi, N. (2012), 'Mecca Cola and Burqinis: Muslim Consumption and Religious Identities', in G. Lynch, J. Mitchell and A. Strhan (eds), *Religion, Media and Culture: A Reader*, 31–9, London: Routledge.

Ellis-Petersen, H. (2015), 'True Story of Mughal Emperor who Built Taj Mahal Makes London Debut', *The Guardian*, 29 January.

El Naggar, S. (2017), 'American Muslim Televangelists as Religious Celebrities: The Changing "Face" of Religious Discourse', in A. Rosowsky (ed.), *Faith and Language Practices in Digital Spaces*, 158–82, Multilingual Matters.

Elshayyal, K. (2018), *Muslim Identity Politics: Islam, Activism and Equality in Britain*, London: Bloomsbury Publishing.

Esposito, J. (1999), *The Islamic Threat: Myth or Reality?* Oxford: Oxford University Press.

Esposito, J. L. (2016), *Islam: The Straight Path*, Oxford: Oxford University Press.

Esposito, J. L., L. Z. Rahim and N. Ghobadzadeh, eds (2017), *The Politics of Islamism: Diverging Visions and Trajectories*, London: Springer.

Fisch, S. M. (2014), *Children's Learning from Educational Television: Sesame Street and Beyond*, Abingdon: Routledge.

Flanagan, K. (2007), 'Introduction', in K. Flanagan and P. C. Jupp (eds), *A Sociology of Spirituality*, 1–22, Farnham: Ashgate.

Flood, C., et al. (2012), *Islam, Security and Television News*, London: Springer.

Flory, R. W. and D. E. Miller (2007), 'The Embodied Spirituality of the Post-Boomer Generations', in K. Flanagan and P. C. Jupp (eds), *A Sociology of Spirituality*, 201–18, Farnham: Ashgate.

Friedman, S. (2014), *Comedy and Distinction: The Cultural Currency of a 'Good' Sense of Humour*, Abingdon: Routledge.

Friedman, S. and D. O'Brien (2017), 'Resistance and Resignation: Responses to Typecasting in British Acting', *Cultural Sociology*, 11 (3): 359–76.

Frishkopf, M. (2009), 'Mediated Qur'anic Recitation and the Contestation of Islam in Contemporary Egypt', in L. Nooshin (ed.), *Music and the Play of Power in the Middle East, North Africa and Central Asia*, 93–132, Abingdon: Routledge.

Fukuyama, F. (2018), *Identity: Contemporary Identity Politics and the Struggle for Recognition*, London: Profile Books.

Fuseini, A., P. Hadley and T. Knowles (2020), 'Halal Food Marketing: An Evaluation of UK Halal Standards', *Journal of Islamic Marketing*, 12 (5): 977–91.

Geaves, R. (2000), *The Sufis of Britain: An Exploration of Muslim Identity*, Cardiff: Cardiff University Press.

Geaves, R. (2008), 'Drawing on the Past to Transform the Present: Contemporary Challenges for Training and Preparing British Imams', *Journal of Muslim Minority Affairs*, 28 (1): 99–112.

Geaves, R. (2010), *Islam in Victorian Britain: The Life and Times of Abdullah Quilliam*, Markfield: Kube Publishing Ltd.

Geaves, R. (2013), 'Transformation and Trends among British Sufis', in R. Geaves and T. Gabriel (eds), *Sufism in Britain*, 35–52, London: Bloomsbury.

Giddens, A. (1991), *Modernity and Self-Identity: Self and Society in the Late Modern Age*, Palo Alto: Stanford University Press.

Gilham, J. (2020), *The British Muslim Convert Lord Headley, 1855–1935*, London: Bloomsbury Publishing.

Gilliat-Ray, S. (2010), *Muslims in Britain*, Cambridge: Cambridge University Press.

Gilliat-Ray, S. and R. Timol (2020), 'Introduction: Leadership, Authority and Representation in British Muslim Communities', *Religions*, 11 (11): 559.

Gilroy, P. (1993), *The Black Atlantic: Modernity and Double Consciousness*, London: Verso.

Greenwood, D. (2021), 'Riz Ahmed on Spiritual Performance, Oscar Hype and Englistan', *VICE*, 2 April.

Hall, D. D., ed. (1997), *Lived Religion in America: Toward a History of Practice*, Princeton: Princeton University Press.

Hall, S. (2003), 'Encoding/Decoding', in S. Hall et al (eds), *Culture, Media, Language*, 117–27, London: Routledge.

Hall, S. (2009), 'The Rediscovery of Ideology: The Return of the Repressed in Media Studies', in J. Storey (ed.), *Cultural Theory and Popular Culture: A Reader*, 4th edn, Harlow: Pearson Education.

Hamid, S. (2016), *Sufis, Salafis and Islamists: The Contested Ground of British Islamic Activism*, London: I.B. Tauris.

Haque, Z. (2016), '#WhatMuslimsReallyThink Programme is Based on a Flawed Poll Skewed to Find a "them and us" Narrative', *Runnymede Trust*.

Hartley, J. (1996), *Popular Reality: Journalism, Modernity, Popular Culture*, London: Arnold.

Hebdige, D. (1979), *Subculture: The Meaning of Style*, London: Routledge.

Heelas, P. and L. Woodhead (2005), *The Spiritual Revolution: Why Religion is Giving Way to Spirituality*, Oxford: Wiley-Blackwell.

Held, D. (1995), *Democracy and Global Order*, Cambridge: Polity Press.

Hepp, A. (2013), *Cultures of Mediatization*, Oxford: John Wiley & Sons.

Hepp, A. and V. Krönert (2009), 'The Catholic "World Youth Day" as an Example of the Mediatization and Individualization of Religion', in N. Couldry, A. Hepp and F. Krotz (eds), *Media Events in a Global Age*, 265–82, London: Routledge.

Hepp, A., S. Hjarvard and K. Lundby (2015), 'Mediatization: Theorizing the Interplay Between Media, Culture and Society', *Media, Culture & Society*, 37 (2): 314–24.

Hjarvard, S. (2008), 'The Mediatization of Religion: A Theory of the Media as Agents of Religious Change', *Northern Lights: Film & Media Studies Yearbook*, 6 (1): 9–26.

Hjarvard, S. (2011), 'The Mediatisation of Religion: Theorising Religion, Media and Social Change', *Culture and Religion*, 12 (2): 119–35.

Hjarvard, S. (2013), *The Mediatization of Culture and Society*, Abingdon: Routledge.

Hjarvard, S. and M. Lövheim (2012), *Mediatization and Religion: Nordic Perspectives*, Nordicom: University of Gothenburg.

Hodgson, M. G. S. (1974), *The Venture of Islam, Volume 2*, Chicago: University of Chicago Press.

Hodgson, T. (2016), 'Music Festivals in Pakistan and England', in K. van Nieuwkerk, M. LeVine and M. Stokes (eds), *Islam and Popular Culture*, 347–63, Austin: University of Texas Press.

Hoover, S. M. (2006), *Religion in the Media Age*, Abingdon: Routledge.

Hoover, S. M. (2016), 'Religious Authority in the Media Age', in S. M. Hoover (ed.), *The Media and Religious Authority*, 15–36, University Park: Penn State Press.

Hoover, S. M. and K. Lundby, eds (1997), *Rethinking Media, Religion, and Culture*, London: SAGE Publications.

Hoover, S. M. and L. S. Clark, eds (2002), *Practicing Religion in the Age of the Media: Explorations in Media, Religion, and Culture*, New York: Columbia University Press.

Horsfield, P. (2015), *From Jesus to the Internet: A History of Christianity and Media*, Oxford: John Wiley & Sons.

Howell, J. D. (2008a), 'Modulations of Active Piety: Professors and Televangelists as Promoters of Indonesian "Sufisme"', in G. Fealy and S. White (eds), *Expressing Islam: Religious Life and Politics in Indonesia*, 40–62, Singapore: ISEAS Publishing.

Howell, J. D. (2008b), 'Sufism on the Silver Screen: Indonesian Innovations in Islamic Televangelism', *Journal of Indonesian Islam*, 2 (2): 225–39.

Huq, R. (2013), 'Situating Citizen Khan: Shifting Representations of Asians Onscreen and the Outrage Industry in the Social Media Age', *South Asian Popular Culture*, 11 (1): 77–83.

Ibrahiem, C. (2021), *ABX: The Abrahamix*, Keighley: Arakan Creative.

Ilyas, T. (2021), *The Secret Diary of a British Muslim Aged 13 ¾*, London: Sphere.

Ingalls, M., C. Landau and T. Wagner (eds), (2016), *Christian Congregational Music: Performance, Identity and Experience*, London: Routledge.

Inge, A. (2017), *The Making of a Salafi Muslim Woman: Paths to Conversion*, Oxford: Oxford University Press.

IQRA (2020), 'Muslim Network TV Launched in North America', *IQRA*, 19 July.

Islam, S. (2018), 'The Story of M.I.N.', *M.I.N.*, 5 February.

Janmohamed, S. (2016), *Generation M: Young Muslims Changing the World*, London: I. B. Tauris.

Janmohamed, S. and A. Miah (2018), *The Great British Ramadan*, London: Ogilvy Noor.

Jeffries, S. (2018), 'Man Like Mobeen's Guz Khan: "Citizen Khan reminds me of On the Buses"', *The Guardian*, 9 January.

Jenner, M. (2018), *Netflix and the Re-invention of Television*, London: Springer.

Jones, S. H. (2013), 'New Labour and the Re-Making of British Islam: The Case of the Radical Middle Way and the "reclamation" of the Classical Islamic Tradition', *Religions*, 4 (4): 550–66.

Kalra, V. S. (2019), *From Textile Mills to Taxi Ranks: Experiences of Migration, Labour and Social Change*, 2nd edn, London: Routledge.

Kalra, V. S., et al. (1996), 'Re-sounding (anti)racism, or Concordant Politics? Revolutionary Antecedents', in S. Sharma, J. Hutnyk and A. Sharma (eds), *Dis-orienting Rhythms: Politics of the New Asian Dance Music*, London: Zed Books.

Karim, K. H. (ed.) (2003), *Mapping Diasporic Mediascapes*, Abingdon: Routledge.

Kaya, A. (2010), 'Individualization and Institutionalization of Islam in Europe in the Age of Securitization', *Insight Turkey*, 12 (1): 47–63.

Khan, A., et al. (2021), *Missing and Maligned: The Reality of Muslims in Popular Global Movies*, Los Angeles: USC Annenberg.

Khan, U. (2009), 'BBC Receives 115 Complaints over Muslim Head of Religious Programming Aaqil Ahmed', *Daily Telegraph*, 16 May.

Khabeer, S. A. A. (2016), *Muslim Cool: Race, Religion, and Hip Hop in the United States*, New York: New York University Press.

Kim, H. (2014), *Making Diaspora in a Global City: South Asian Youth Cultures in London*, Abingdon: Routledge.

Knoblauch, H. (2014), 'Benedict in Berlin: The Mediatization of Religion', in A. Hepp and F. Krotz (eds), *Mediatized Worlds: Culture and Society in a Media Age*, 143–58, London: Palgrave Macmillan.

Knott, K., E. Poole and Taira, T. (2016), *Media Portrayals of Religion and the Secular Sacred: Representation and Change*, London: Routledge.

Korte, B. and C. Sternberg (2009), 'Asian British Cinema since the 1990s', in R. Murphy (ed.), *The British Cinema Book*, 387–94, London: British Film Institute.

Kundnani, A. (2009), *Spooked! How Not to Prevent Violent Extremism*, London: Institute of Race Relations.

Larrington, C. (2017), *Winter is Coming: The Medieval World of Game of Thrones*, London: Bloomsbury Publishing.

Larsson, G. (2011), *Muslims and the New Media: Historical and Contemporary Debates*, London: Routledge.

Laurence, J. (2011), *The Emancipation of Europe's Muslims*, Princeton: Princeton University Press.

Lawless, R. (1995), *From Ta'izz to Tyneside*, Exeter: University of Exeter Press.

Lawless, R. (1997), 'Muslim Migration to the North East of England During the Early Twentieth Century', *Local Historian London*, 27: 225–44.

LeVine, M. and J. Otterbeck (2021), 'Muslim Popular Music: An Enchanted Century', in R. Lukens-Bull and M. Woodward (eds), *Handbook of Contemporary Islam and Muslim Lives*, 1–24, Cham: Springer.

Lewis, P. (1994), *Islamic Britain: Religion, Politics, and Identity Among British Muslims: Bradford in the 1990s*, London: I.B. Tauris & Company.

Lewis, P. and S. Hamid (2018), *British Muslims: New Directions in Islamic Thought, Creativity and Activism*, Edinburgh: Edinburgh University Press.

Lewis, R. (2015), *Muslim Fashion: Contemporary Style Cultures*, London: Duke University Press.
Li, Y., A. Heath and T. Woerner-Powell (2018), 'Trapped in Poverty?: A Study of Transient and Persisting Factors for Muslim Disadvantages in the UK', *Comparative Islamic Studies*, 11 (2): 205–33.
Limov, B. (2020), 'Click It, Binge It, Get Hooked: Netflix and the Growing US Audience for Foreign Content', *International Journal of Communication*, 14: 6304–20.
Livingston, S. T. (1998), *The Ideological and Philosophical Influence of the Nation of Islam on Hip Hop Culture*, Philadelphia: Temple University.
Lövheim, M. (2014), 'Mediatization and Religion', in K. Lundby (ed.), *Mediatization of Communication*, 547–70, Berlin: De Gruyter.
Lövheim, M. and S. Hjarvard (2019), 'The Mediatized Conditions of Contemporary Religion: Critical Status and Future Directions', *Journal of Religion, Media and Digital Culture*, 8 (2): 206–25.
Ludi, Simpson (2012), 'More Segregation or More Mixing?', in *ESRC Centre on Dynamics of Ethnicity (CoDE)*, Manchester: University of Manchester.
Lundby, K., ed. (2018), *Contesting Religion*, Berlin: De Gruyter.
Lyden, J. C. (2019), *Film as Religion*, New York: New York University Press.
Lynch, G. (2005), *Understanding Theology and Popular Culture*, Oxford: Blackwell Publishing.
Lynch, G. (2011), 'What Can We Learn from the Mediatisation of Religion Debate?', *Culture and Religion*, 12 (2): 203–10.
Lynch, G., J. Mitchell and A. Strhan (2012a), 'Introduction', in G. Lynch, J. Mitchell and A. Strhan (eds), *Religion, Media and Culture: A Reader*, 1–10, Abingdon: Routledge.
Lynch, G., J. Mitchell and A. Strhan, eds (2012b), *Religion, Media and Culture: A Reader*, Abingdon: Routledge.
Malik, S. (2013), '"Creative diversity": UK Public Service Broadcasting after Multiculturalism', *Popular Communication*, 11 (3): 227–41.
Malik, S. (2019), 'Race and Ethnicity in British Cinema', in J. Hill (ed.), *A Companion to British and Irish Cinema*, 443–60, London: Wiley Blackwell.
Malik, Y. (2016) 'Islamic and Muslim Lifestyle Programming Gaining Market Share in $42 bln US TV Industry', *Salaam Gateway*, 11 July.
Mandaville, P. (2007), 'Globalization and the Politics of Religious Knowledge: Pluralizing Authority in the Muslim World', *Theory, Culture & Society*, 24 (2): 101–15.
Mandaville, P. (2009), 'Islam and International Relations in the Middle East: From Umma To Nation State', in L. Fawcett (ed.), *International Relations of the Middle East*, 170–87, Oxford: Oxford University Press.
Mansfield, K. (2017), 'BBC Puts Muslim in Charge of Religious Television Shows', *Daily Express*, 25 February.
Martin, R. A. and T. Ford (2018), *The Psychology of Humor: An Integrative Approach*, Cambridge: Academic Press.

Martino, L. M. S. (2016) *The Mediatization of Religion: When Faith Rocks*, Abingdon: Routledge.

Matar, N. (1998) *Islam in Britain, 1558–1685*, Cambridge: Cambridge University Press.

McCutcheon, R. T., ed. (1999), *The Insider/Outsider Problem in the Study of Religion: A Reader*, London: A&C Black.

McGuire, M. B. (2008), *Lived Religion: Faith and Practice in Everyday Life*, Oxford: Oxford University Press.

McLane, B. A. (2013), *A New History of Documentary Film*, London: Bloomsbury Publishing USA.

McLoughlin, S. (2010), 'Religion and Diaspora', in J. Hinnells (ed.), *The Routledge Companion to the Study of Religion*, 2nd edn, 572–94, Abingdon: Routledge.

McLoughlin, S. (2019), 'Mapping the UK's Hajj Sector: Moving Towards Communication and Consensus: An Independent Report, 2019', Centre for Religion and Public Life: University of Leeds.

McRae, S. (ed.) (1999), *Changing Britain: Families and Households in the 1990s*, Oxford: Oxford University Press.

Meer, N. (2010), *Citizenship, Identity and the Politics of Multiculturalism: The Rise of Muslim Consciousness*, Basingstoke: Palgrave Macmillan.

Meer, N. and T. Modood (2009) 'The Multicultural State we're in: Muslims, "multiculture" and the "civic re-balancing" of British Multiculturalism', *Political Studies*, 57 (3): 473–97.

Mellor, J. and S. Gilliat-Ray (2015), 'The Early History of Migration and Settlement of Yemenis in Cardiff, 1939–1970: Religion and Ethnicity as Social Capital', *Ethnic and Racial Studies*, 38 (1): 176–91.

Meyer, B. and A. Moors, eds (2005), *Religion, Media, and the Public Sphere*, Bloomington: Indiana University Press.

Miles, T. (2015), 'Halal? Ha! LOL: An Examination of Muslim Online Comedy as Counter-Narrative', *Comedy Studies*, 6 (2): 167–78.

Mills, B. and E. Horton (2016), *Creativity in the British Television Comedy Industry*, London: Routledge.

Moberg, M. (2018), 'Mediatization and the Technologization Of Discourse: Exploring Official Discourse on the Internet and Information and Communications Technology within the Evangelical Lutheran Church of Finland', *New Media & Society*, 20 (2): 515–31.

Moore, K., P. Mason and J. M. W. Lewis (2008), *Images of Islam in the UK: The Representation of British Muslims in the National Print News Media 2000–2008*, Cardiff: Cardiff University.

Morey, P. and A. Yaqin (2011), *Framing Muslims*, Cambridge, MA: Harvard University Press.

Morris, C. (2016), 'Music and Materialism: The Emergence of Alternative Muslim Lifestyle Cultures in Britain', in T. Hutchings and J. McKenzie (eds), *Materiality and the Study of Religion: The Stuff of the Sacred*, 67–84, London: Routledge.

Morris, C. (2018), 'Re-Placing the Term "British Muslim": Discourse, Difference and the Frontiers of Muslim Agency in Britain', *Journal of Muslim Minority Affairs*, 38 (3): 409–27.

Morris, C. (2019a), 'The Rise of a Muslim Middle Class in Britain: Ethnicity, Music and the Performance of Muslimness', *Ethnicities*, 20 (3): 628–48.

Morris, C. (2019b), 'Islamic Cosmopolitanism: Muslim Minorities and Religious Pluralism in North America and Europe', in Jan-Jonathan Bock, John Fahy and Samuel Everett (eds), *Emergent Religious Pluralisms*, 21–48, London: Palgrave Macmillan.

Murthy, D. (2010), 'Muslim Punks Online: A Diasporic Pakistani Music Subculture on the Internet', *South Asian Popular Culture*, 8 (2): 181–94.

Muslim Council of Britain (2015), *British Muslims in Numbers: A Demographic, Socio-Economic and Health Profile of Muslims in Britain Drawing on the 2011 Census*, London: Muslim Council of Britain.

Mutman, M. (2013), *The Politics of Writing Islam: Voicing Difference*, London: A&C Black.

Nelson, K. (2001), *The Art of Reciting the Qur'an*, Cairo: The American University in Cairo Press.

Nielsen, J. (1987), 'Muslims in Britain: Searching for an Identity?', *New Community*, 13 (3): 384–94.

Nieuwkerk, K. van (2008), 'Creating an Islamic Cultural Sphere: Contested Notions of Art, Leisure and Entertainment. An Introduction', *Contemporary Islam*, 2 (3): 169–76.

Nwonka, C. J. and S. Malik (2018), 'Cultural Discourses and Practices of Institutionalised Diversity in the UK Film Sector: "Just get Something Black Made"', *The Sociological Review*, 66 (6): 1111–27.

O'Brien, D. and K. Oakley (2015), *Cultural Value and Inequality: A Critical Literature Review*, London: Arts and Humanities Research Council.

O'Connor, J. (2000), 'The Definition of the "cultural industries"', *The European Journal of Arts Education*, 2 (3): 15–27.

Ofcom (2018) 'TV Streaming Services Overtake Pay TV for First Time', *Ofcom*, 17 July.

Ogunnaike, O. (2018), 'Performing Realization: The Sufi Music Videos of the Taalibe Baye of Dakar', *African Arts*, 51 (3): 26–39.

Orsi, R. A. (2010), *The Madonna of 115th Street: Faith and Community in Italian Harlem, 1880–1950*, New Haven: Yale University Press.

Otterbeck, J. (2004), 'Music as a Useless Activity: Conservative Interpretations of Music in Islam', in M. Korpe (ed.), *Shoot the Singer!: Music Censorship Today*, 11–16, London: Zed Books.

Otterbeck, J. (2008), 'Battling over the Public Sphere: Islamic Reactions to the Music of Today', *Contemporary Islam*, 2: 211–28.

Palmer, J. (1987), *The Logic of the Absurd: On Film and Television Comedy*, London: British Film Institute.

Peitz, M. and T. M. Valletti (2008), 'Content and Advertising in the Media: Pay-tv versus Free-to-Air', *International Journal of Industrial Organization*, 26 (4): 949–65.

Perkins, C. and M. Schreiber (2019), 'Independent Women: From Film to Television', *Feminist Media Studies*, 19 (7): 919–27.

Peter, F. (2006), 'Individualization and Religious Authority in Western European Islam', *Islam and Christian–Muslim Relations*, 17 (1): 105–18.

Petley, J. and R. Richardson, eds (2013), *Pointing the Finger: Islam and Muslims in the British Media*, London: Simon and Schuster.

Poole, E. (2002), *Reporting Islam: Media Representations of British Muslims*, London: I.B. Tauris.

Poole, E. and J. E. Richardson, eds (2010), *Muslims and the News Media*, London: Bloomsbury Publishing.

Potter, S. J. (2012), *Broadcasting Empire: The BBC and the British World, 1922–1970*, Oxford: Oxford University Press.

Power, D. and A. J. Scott (2004), *Cultural Industries and the Production of Culture*, Abingdon: Routledge.

Qasim, D. (2020), 'The Commodification of Worship: How Automation Dilutes the Meaning of Seeking Laylat Al-Qadr', *Shaykhs Clothing*, 18 May.

Ramadan, T. (2004), *Western Muslims and the Future of Islam*, Oxford: Oxford University Press.

Rasmussen, A. K. (2010), *Women, the Recited Qur'an, and Islamic Music in Indonesia*, Berkeley: University of California Press.

Reddie, R. S. (2009), *Black Muslims in Britain*, London: Lion.

Robbins, K. (2006), *The Challenge of Transcultural Diversities: Cultural Policy and Cultural Diversity*, Strasbourg: Council of Europe.

Robinson, F. (2009), 'Crisis of Authority: Crisis of Islam?', *Journal of the Royal Asiatic Society*, 19 (3): 339–54.

Roof, W. C. (2001), *Spiritual Marketplace*, Princeton: Princeton University Press.

Rose, T. (1994), *Black Noise: Rap Music and Black Culture in Contemporary America*, Middletown: Wesleyan University Press.

Rovisco, M. and M. Nowicka, eds (2011), *The Ashgate Research Companion to Cosmopolitanism*, London: Routledge.

Roy, A. G. (2017), *Bhangra Moves: From Ludhiana to London and Beyond*, London: Routledge.

Rozehnal, R. (2016), *Islamic Sufism Unbound: Politics and Piety in Twenty-First Century Pakistan*, New York: Palgrave Macmillan.

Saha, A. (2012), '"Beards, scarves, halal meat, terrorists, forced marriage": Television Industries and the Production of "race"', *Media, Culture & Society*, 34 (4): 424–38.

Saha, A. (2015), 'The Marketing of Race in Cultural Production', in K. Oakley and J. O'Connor (eds), *The Routledge Companion to the Cultural Industries*, 528–37, Abingdon: Routledge.

Said, E. (1994), *Culture and Imperialism*, London: Vintage Books.

Saleh, I. (2012), 'Islamic Televangelism: The Salafi Window to Their Paradise', in T. Pradip and Philip Lee (eds), *Global and Local Televangelism*, 64–83, London: Palgrave Macmillan.

Sarrazin, N. (2013), 'Devotion or Pleasure? Music and Meaning in the Celluloid Performances of Qawwali in South Asia and the Diaspora', in K. Salhi (ed.), *Music, Culture and Identity in the Muslim World: Performance, Politics and Piety*, 194–215, Abingdon: Routledge.

Saunders, G. (2015), *British Theatre Companies: 1980-1994: Joint Stock, Gay Sweatshop, Complicite, Forced Entertainment, Women's Theatre Group, Talawa*, London: Bloomsbury Publishing.

Sayyid, S. (1997), *A Fundamental Fear: Eurocentrism and the Emergence of Islam*, London: Zed Books.

Sayyid, S. (2005), 'Introduction: BrAsians: Postcolonial People, Ironic Citizens', in N. Ali, V. S. Kalra and S. Sayyid (eds), *A Postcolonial People: South Asians in Britain*, 1–10, London: C Hurst & Co (Publishers) Ltd.

Scourfield, J., et al. (2013), *Muslim Childhood: Religious Nurture in a European Context*, Oxford: Oxford University Press.

Shaw, A. (2014), *Kinship and Continuity: Pakistani Families in Britain*, Abingdon: Routledge.

Shiloah, A. (1995), *Music in the World of Islam*, Detroit: Wayne State University Press.

Shiloah, A. (1997), 'Music and Religion in Islam', *Acta Musicologica*, 69 (2): 143–55.

Sian, K., I. Law and S. Sayyid (2012), 'The Media and Muslims in the UK', *Consultado*, 15.

Smethurst, J. (2006), 'The Black Arts Movement and Historically Black Colleges and Universities', in A. Nelson et al (eds), *New Thoughts on the Black Arts Movement*, 75–91, New Brunswick: Rutgers University Press.

Spickard, J. V. (2017), *Alternative Sociologies of Religion*, New York: New York University Press.

Spivak, G. (1988), 'Can the Subaltern Speak?', in C. Nelson and L. Grossberg (eds), *Marxism and the Interpretation of Culture*, 66–111, London: Macmillan.

Spivak, G. (2013), *The Spivak Reader: Selected Works of Gayati Chakravorty Spivak*, Abingdon: Routledge.

Stabile, C. A. (2000), 'Nike, Social Responsibility, and the Hidden Abode of Production', *Critical Studies in Media Communication*, 17 (2): 186–204.

Storey, J. (2018), *Cultural Theory and Popular Culture: An Introduction*, London: Routledge.

Surooprajally, Z. B. (2018), '5 Inspirational Pieces of Wisdom we Learnt from the 2nd ever Muslim Influencer Meet Up!', *M.I.N*, 27 February.

Swedenburg, T. (2001), 'Islamic Hip Hop versus Islamophobia', in T. Mitchell (ed.), *Global Noise: Rap and Hip hop Outside the USA*, 57–85, Middletown: Wesleyan University Press.

Taha-Cisse, H. A. (2007), *The Future of the Tariqa Tijaniyya in America*, Forum for the Followers of the Tijaniyya Order, Fes, Morocco, 28 June.

Tanner, K. (1997), *Theories of Culture: A New Agenda for Theology*, Minneapolis: Fortress Press.

Tate, G. (2019), 'Guz Khan Interview: 'When I Was Growing Up, Either you Made People Laugh or you Got Beaten Up', *Evening Standard*, 23 January.

Tezcan, L. (2005), 'The Problems of Religious Modernity', *Asian Journal of Social Science*, 33 (3): 506–28.

Tomlin, L. (2015), *British Theatre Companies: 1995-2014: Mind the Gap, Kneehigh Theatre, Suspect Culture, Stan's Cafe, Blast Theory, Punchdrunk*, London: Bloomsbury Publishing.

Toynbee, J. (2000), *Making Popular Music: Musicians, Creativity and Institutions*, London: Arnold.

Tsagarousianou, R. (2001), '"A space where one feels at home": Media Consumption Practices among London's South Asian and Greek Cypriot Communities', in R. King and N. Wood (eds), *Media and Migration: Constructions of Mobility and Difference*, 158–72 Abingdon: Routledge.

Turner, B. S. (2002), 'Cosmopolitan Virtue: Globalization and Patriotism', *Theory, Culture and Society*, 19 (1): 45–63.

Turner, G. (2003), *British Cultural Studies: An Introduction*, Hove: Psychology Press.

Tusing, D. (2010), 'Sami Yusuf Talks about Spiritique, his New Sound', *Gulf News*, 11 August.

Um, H (2012), 'The Politics of Performance and the Creation of South Asian Music in Britain: Identities, Transnational Cosmopolitanism and the Public Sphere', *Performing Islam*, 1 (1): 57–72.

Varga, I. (2007), 'Georg Simmel: Religion and Spirituality', in K. Flanagan and P. C. Jupp (eds), *A Sociology of Spirituality*, 145–60, Farnham: Ashgate.

Visram, R. (2002), *Asians in Britain: 400 Years of History*, London: Pluto.

Weber, M. (2004) 'Politics as a Vocation', in D. Owen and T. B Strong (eds), *Max Weber: The Vocation Lectures*, trans. R Livingstone, 32–94, Indianapolis: Hackett Publishing Company.

Werbner, P. (1990), 'Manchester Pakistanis: Division and Unity', in S. Vertovec, C. Peach and C. Clarke (eds), *South Asians Overseas: Migration and Ethnicity*, 331–47, Cambridge: Cambridge University Press.

Werbner, P. (2002), *Imagined Diasporas Among Manchester Muslims: The Public Performance of Pakistani Transnational Identity Politics*, London: James Currey Publishers.

Werbner, P. (2004), 'Theorising Complex Diasporas: Purity and Hybridity in the South Asian Public Sphere in Britain', *Journal of Ethnic and Migration Studies*, 30 (5): 895–911.

Werbner, P. (2006), 'Seekers on the Path: Different Ways of Being a Sufi in Britain', in J. Malik and J. Hinnells (eds), *Sufism in the West*, 137–51, London: Routledge.

Williams, R. (1983), *Keywords: A Vocabulary of Culture and Society*, Oxford: Oxford University Press.
Wise, L. (2006), 'Meet Islam's Biggest Rock Star', *TIME*, 31 July.
Woodhead, L. (2013), 'Tactical and Strategic Religion', in N. Dessing, N. Jeldtoft and L. Woodhead (eds), *Everyday Lived Islam in Europe*, 9–22, London: Routledge.
Yaqin, A. (2007), 'Islamic Barbie: The Politics of Gender and Performativity', *Fashion Theory*, 11 (2–3): 173–88.
Yusuf, S. (2009), 'Sami Yusuf's Response to the Release of the CD "Without You"', https://samiyusufofficial.com/boycott-the-fake-new-album/ (accessed 11 May 2020).
Yusuf, S. (2016), 'Sufism Represents the Inner Spiritual Dimension of the Faith. Without it, the Faith is Incomplete', [Twitter], 31 December, https://twitter.com/samiyusuf/status/815250454917554176?lang=en-GB (accessed 8 July 2019).
Yusuf, H, cited in S. Hamid, (2016), *Sufis, Salafis and Islamists: The Contested Ground of British Islamic Activism*, London: I.B. Tauris.
Zimbardo, Z. (2014), 'Cultural Politics of Humor in (de) Normalizing Islamophobic Stereotypes', *Islamophobia Studies Journal*, 2 (1): 59–81.

Selected Film and Television References

A Beginner's Guide to Andalusi Calligraphy (2017), [Film] Dir Zakariyya Whiteman, Spain: Barzakh.
A Mosque in the Park (1973), [Film] Dir Yavar Abbas, UK: Thames Television Production.
A Vicar's Life (2018), [TV programme], BBC, 12 January.
Ackley Bridge (2016), [TV programme], Channel 4, 7 June.
Aga Khan's Platinum Jubilee (1954), [Film], UK: Pathé, 11 February.
Alif and Sofia (2019), [TV programme], Blindspot Studios, 10 May.
An Oriental Atmosphere (1928), [Film], UK: Topical Budget, 4 June.
Andrew Marr's History of Modern Britain (2007), [TV programme], BBC, 22 May.
Ask the Alim (2014), [TV programme], British Muslim TV, 10 June.
Blessed Are The Strangers (2017), [Film], Dir Ahmed Peerbux and Sean Hanif Whyte, UK: C Media.
Bodyguard (2018), [TV programme], BBC, 26 August.
Bond's Greatest Moments (2013), [TV programme], Sky Movies, 1 January.
Britz (2007), [Film], Dir Peter Kosminsky, UK: Channel 4.
Christianity: A History (2009), [TV programme], Channel 4, 11 January.
Citizen Khan (2012), [TV programme], BBC, 27 August.
Diriliş: Ertuğrul (2014), [TV programme], Tekden Film, 10 December.
Egypt: Ramadan Fast Begins (1956), [Film], UK: Reuters.
Extremely British Muslims (2017), [TV programme], Channel 4, 2 March.
Faces of Islam (1999), [TV programme], BBC, 10 December.

Fall in Love with the Qur'an (2020), [TV programme], Islam Channel.
Finding Fatimah (2017), [Film], Dir Oz Arshad, UK: Icon Films.
Four Lions (2010), [Film], Dir Christopher Morris, UK: Film4.
Freesia (2017), [Film], Dir Conor Ibrahiem, UK: Arakan Creative.
Game of Thrones (2011), [TV programme], HBO, 18 April.
Gay Muslims (2006), [TV programme], Channel 4, 23 January.
Great British Islam (2005), [TV programme], BBC.
Islam in London (1926), [Film], UK: Topical Budget, 7 October.
Islam Q and A (2020), [TV programme], Islam Channel.
Islam Year Zero (1996), [TV programme], BBC.
Islam's Militant Tendency (1995), [TV programme], BBC.
Leaving Neverland: Michael Jackson and Me (2019), [TV programme], HBO, 6 March.
Line of Duty (2012), [TV programme], BBC, 26 June.
Man Like Mobeen (2017), [TV programme], BBC, 17 December.
Me, Myself and Allah (2020), [TV programme], Islam Channel.
Mowgul Mowgli (2020), [Film], Dir Bassam Tariq, UK: Pulse Films.
Muslamic (2019), [TV programme], BBC, 22 July.
Muslim Protest March in London (1938), [Film], UK: Reuters, 22 August.
Muslims Like Us (2016), [TV programme], BBC, 12 December.
My Jihad (2014), [TV programme], BBC, 10 March.
New Muslim Cool (2009), [Film], Dir Jennifer Taylor, USA: Specific Pictures.
Pilgrimage to Mecca (1946), [Film], UK: Pathé, 6 November.
Posh People: Inside Tatler (2014), [TV programme], BBC, 24 November.
Ramadan Reminders (2020), [TV programme], Islam Channel.
Rapping for Islam (1997), [TV programme], Roger Bolton Productions.
Roadman Ramadan (2015), [TV programme], BBC, 18 June.
Rogue One: A Star Was Story (2016), [Film], Dir Gareth Edwards, USA: Lucasfilm Ltd.
Salaam Dunk (2011), [Film], Dir David Fine, USA: Seedwell Digital Media.
Saladin (2010), [TV programme], Young Jump Animation Studio, September.
Schools for Moslems (1980), [TV programme], London Weekend Television.
Small Deeds Massive Rewards (2020), [TV programme], Islam Channel.
Sound of Metal (2019), [Film], Dir Darius Marder, USA: Amazon Studios.
South Park (1997), [TV programme], Comedy Central, 28 March.
South Shields (1937), [Film], UK: Pathé, 25 February.
Spooks (2002), [TV programme], BBC, 13 May.
The Fast and the Fool (2015), [TV programme], BBC, 18 June.
The Feast of Sacrifice (1919), [Film], UK: Pathé, 11 September.
The Greatness of Allah (2020), [TV programme], Islam Channel.
The Office (2001), [TV programme], BBC, 9 July.
The Path to 9/11 (2006), [TV programme], ABC, 10 September.
The Qur'an (2008), [TV programme], Channel 4, 14 July.
The Reluctant Fundamentalist (2012), [Film], Dir Mira Nair, USA: Cine Mosaic.

The Road to Guantanamo (2006), [TV programme], Film 4, 9 March.
The Spirit of Islam (1995), [TV programme], BBC.
The Tez O'Clock Show (2019), [TV programme], Channel 4, 25 July.
Things I Have Been Asked as a British Muslim (2015), [TV programme], BBC, 18 June.
Trouble Up North (2001), [TV programme], BBC, 17 December.
Venom (2018), [Film], Dir Ruben Fleischer, USA: Marvel Entertainment.
Voting for the Veil (1991), [TV programme], BBC.
What Muslims Want (2006), [TV programme], Channel 4, December.
What British Muslims Really Think (2016), [TV programme], Channel 4, April.
Who Speaks for Muslims? (2006), [TV programme], Channel 4.
Wisdom and Tea (2020), [TV programme], British Muslim TV.

Selected discography

Aashiq al-Rasul. *The Essence of al-Mustafa* (2010) Dervish Promotions Ltd.
Amir Awan. *What Will We Say* (2009).
Blakstone. *Darkdayz* (2005).
Celt Islam. *Dervish* (2009) Urban Sedated Records.
Labbayk. *Rhymes of Praise* (2008) Safar Media.
Mohammed Yahya. *Beyond Conflict* (2008).
Nazeel Azami. *Dunya* (2006) Swansea: Awakening Records.
Pearls of Islam. 'Love is My Foundation' (2012).
Poetic Pilgrimage. *Freedom Times* (2009).
Poetic Pilgrimage. *Star Women: The Mixtape* (2010) London: Downtown Soul Records.
Quest Rah. *Ancient Tapes Vol.1* (2008).
Quest Rah. *Ancient Tapes Vol.2 – The Lost Art* (2011).
Rakin Niass. *The Road Less Travelled* (2010).
Sami Yusuf. *al-mu'allim* (2003) Swansea: Awakening Records.
Sami Yusuf. *My Ummah* (2005) Swansea: Awakening Records.
Sami Yusuf. *Wherever You Are* (2010) ETM International.
Shaam. *Spring Has Come* (2003) Meem Music.
Shaam. *Mercy Like the Rain* (2002) Meem Music.
Silk Road. 'Ask My Heart' (2011).
Various. *Eternity: Music for the Soul* (2012) The Rabbani Project.
Yusuf Islam. *Footsteps in the Light* (2006) Mountain of Light Productions Ltd.

Index

Aashiq al Rasul   53, 84, 124, 142, 180, 203
Abbas, Yavar   40
Ahmadiyya Muslim community   35, 67
Ahmed, Aaqil   60
Ahmed, Babikir   69, 110, 199
Ahmed, Munir   69, 199
Ahmed, Riz   6, 20, 26, 48, 60, 72, 73, 151, 171–2, 176, 180, 186, 207
Ahmed, Sarah   61
Ahmed, Shakeel   135, 166–7
Akhtar, Adeel   1
Akhtar, Navid   25, 76, 91, 96–8, 137, 144, 184, 202
Alchemiya   2, 25, 76, 91, 162, 165, 184–7, 201–2, 208
Al-Dunya, Ibn Abi   120
Ali, Baba   76, 113, 114
Ali, Luqman   57, 168
Ali Huda   16, 77
Ali Official   18, 63, 140, 177, 180
Allah Made Me Funny   62–4
Allen, Shane   64, 165–6, 168
Amla, Taiba   62, 128, 130, 166–7, 170
Arakan Creative   2, 74, 168
Arshad, Oz   73, 135, 164
Asim, Qari   128
Awakening Music   2, 91, 139, 159–60, 187, 208
Awan, Amir   54, 125, 203
Azhar, Mobeen   1
Azmat, Sadia   65–6, 135, 168, 176–7

Belal, Muslim   199
Bhangra   19, 39
Bhikka, Zain   199
Black Arts Movement   3, 46, 57, 210–11
Blakstone   55
Bourdieu, Pierre   8, 138
British Muslim Awards   70
British Muslim TV   2, 19–20, 69, 71, 93, 110, 112–19, 123–4, 162–5, 183, 199

Church of England   44, 61
Common Wealth   58
cosmopolitanism   11, 25, 95–9
Creedo   40

Da'wah   6, 69, 76, 106, 113, 164, 197
Deobandis   69, 146
Deventi Group   139–40, 144
Din, Ishy   58, 60, 88, 131–2, 148, 150, 167, 170, 200
Diriliş: Ertuğrul   21, 202–3
Du Bois, W. E. B.   157–8, 177

Edge Theatre, the   58
El-Khairy, Omar   59
Ellahi, Amran   53, 85, 103–4, 126
Eman Channel   20, 70–1, 110, 112, 196, 198–9
Emel Magazine   69, 109
everyday religion   129–30

Freedom Studios   58
Fun-Da-Mental   47

Global Urban Muslims   25, 76, 95–9, 137, 144, 202
Green, Abdur Rahmeen   70, 198

Harrath, Mohammed Ali   69
Harris J   140, 145, 159, 161, 208
Hizb ut-Tahrir   45, 195
Hussain, Abrar   93

'I Am Malcolm X' tour   55
Ibrahiem, Conor   2, 6, 18, 74, 86, 108–9, 147, 154, 168
Ilyas, Tez   2, 4, 8, 62, 65, 68, 87, 130–1, 135, 145, 168, 176–7, 205, 208
intersectionality   5, 19, 209
Islam, Saiful   5
Islam, Yusuf   42, 47, 141
Islam Channel   2, 67–8, 110, 112, 114–19, 162–5, 183, 187

Islamic Society of Britain 13, 195, 199
Islam of the Global West 21–2, 27, 63, 77, 98, 120, 130, 180–1, 185, 187, 193, 206
Islamophobia 2, 7, 14, 18, 57, 74, 87, 128, 132, 156, 168, 170–4, 181, 193, 207–8, 211

Jamaat-e-Islami 13
Jamiat-ul-Muslimin 36
Joseph, Sarah 69

Kelwick, Adam 140
Kempson, Wasim 71, 198
Khan, Afi 60
Khan, Asif 58, 61
Khan, Fozia 61
Khan, Guz 18, 61–2, 65, 87–8, 135–6, 152, 168, 180
Khan, Sadiq 128
Khayaal Theatre Company 57, 91, 168
Kureishi, Hanif 5
Kurtis, Mesut 159, 187

Labbayk Nasheeds 203
Latif, Nadia 59

Malcolm X 47, 55
Mecca2Medina 55, 197
Mediatization 12, 15, 25, 88–95, 105
  of political and cultural identities 94–5
  of religious authority 90–2
  of religious practice 92–4
Menk, Ismail 71, 110
Mirza, Shazia 62–4
Mogra, Ibrahim 69, 199
Mohammed, Zara 128
Mosque and Imam Advisory Board 128
mosques in Britain 9–10, 12–13, 16, 20, 26, 38–9, 46, 83, 89, 150, 170
Muhammad, Boona 199
Mumisa, Michael 110
Murad, Abdul Hakim 110, 193
music, religious injunctions against 120–7
Muslim Brotherhood 45
Muslim Council of Britain 10–11, 13, 44, 128, 212

Muslim Influencer Network 140–1
Muslim Kids TV 2, 16, 68, 77, 183–7
Muslim Popular Culture, typology of
  Islamic 15, 25, 80, 83–5, 106
  Islamically conscious 15, 25, 80, 83, 85–6, 106
  secular-civic 15, 25, 80, 83, 87–8, 106

na'at 41, 46, 53, 111–12
Naik, Zakir 70
nasheeds 8, 12–15, 25, 46, 51–5, 84, 86, 121, 154, 161, 186, 198–9, 203
National Youth Theatre 59
newsreels 24, 31, 33, 35–6, 40, 50
Niass, Rakin 55, 123, 197–9
Noor, Sukina 56, 111, 152–3, 161, 192
Northern Writers Award 62, 166

Ofcom 61, 75
Orientalism 24, 31–3, 35, 45–6, 49–50, 98, 136, 207, 212

Peace TV 70, 183
Pearls of Islam 55, 198
Peerbux, Ahmed 1, 61, 74, 146, 154, 165, 170, 191
Penny Appeal 59, 70, 74, 93, 164
Philips, Bilal 70, 76
Philips, Trevor 170
piety 14–15, 18, 71, 106, 112, 114, 119, 194, 202
Planets, the 55, 126, 161
Platform Magazine 160
Poetic Pilgrimage 7, 55, 56, 88, 111, 134, 149, 152–4, 161, 179, 189, 191–2, 197, 205
Prevent programme 59

Qawwali 19, 39, 41, 46, 51, 54, 180
Q-News 47
Quest Rah 55–6, 161
Quick, Abdullah Hakim 70, 110
Quilliam, Abdullah 35
Quranic recitation 46, 53–4
Qureshi, Faisal 60, 72, 156, 167–8, 170

Radical Middle Way 55, 160
Ray, Adil 64
Raze, Ayman 55, 126–7, 144, 161, 200

Regan, Omar 76
Rehman, Usman 147
Rich Mix 58
Riz Test, the 171–2
Rushdie, Salman 33
Rushdie Affair 13, 43–4, 51

Said, Edward 4, 32, 50
Salafism 17, 46, 69–71, 76, 110, 113, 120, 122–3, 194–200
Salaria, Fatima 1, 61, 133, 174
securitization 14, 18–19, 95, 181, 204
Shaam 53, 203
Silk Road 6, 123, 133–4, 148–9, 151–3
Spirituality 7, 14–15, 26, 42, 55, 85–7, 93, 113, 146, 150–4
Sufism 17, 41–2, 53–4, 68–9, 71, 107, 113, 118, 121–3, 151, 181–2, 193–9
   Naqshbandi-Haqqani, Sufi order 124, 196–8
   Neotraditional Sufism 110, 193
   Tijaniyyah, Sufi order 182, 196–8

Teledawah 6, 15–16, 18, 90–1, 103–5, 112–19, 210
Thames Television 40

Thompson, Danny 42
Thompson, Linda 42
Thompson, Richard 42
Time magazine 2, 72

Ulfah Arts 58
Umma 20, 44, 56, 126, 146, 180–2, 200–1, 204–5
Ummah Channel 67, 71

Warsi, Sayeda 128
Weber, Max 114
Wharnsby, Dawhud 186, 199
Whiteman, Ian 42
William, Muneera 56, 88, 134, 149
Woking Mosque 34, 37

Yahya, Mohammed 55, 108, 153, 161, 179, 181, 197, 205
Younis, Adeem 69–70, 74, 164
Yousufzai, Faraz 123, 133–4, 148–9
Yusuf, Hamza 70, 110, 186, 193
Yusuf, Sami 2, 8, 54, 86, 109–10, 126, 142, 152, 159–61, 198, 199, 203–5, 208

Zain, Maher 143, 159
Zia, Aisha 58

www.ingramcontent.com/pod-product-compliance
Lightning Source LLC
Chambersburg PA
CBHW062216300426
44115CB00012BA/2080